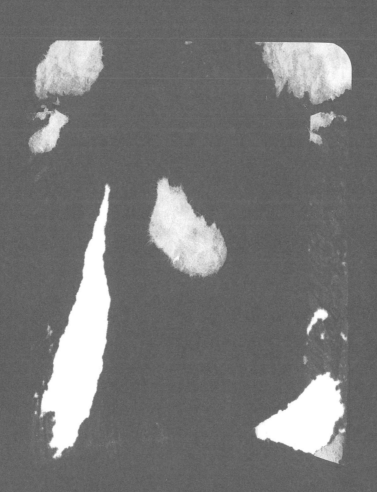

BOEING
PLANEMAKER TO THE WORLD

BOEING
PLANEMAKER TO THE WORLD

ROBERT REDDING & BILL YENNE

THUNDER BAY
P·R·E·S·S

Published by
Thunder Bay Press
5880 Oberlin Drive, Suite 400
San Diego, California 92121

Produced by
Brompton Books Corporation
15 Sherwood Place
Greenwich, CT 06830

ISBN 1-57145-045-9

Printed in China

Revised and updated in 1997

Page one: The P-26 **Peashooter**, which made its appearance in 1932, was the US Army Air Corps' first all-metal monoplane fighter and probably Boeing's most famous fighter. In its day it was the fastest fighter in service and though outclassed by the time of World War II, it gave a good account of itself in the war's first week.

Previous pages: A stunning view of a **747-400** jetliner climbing into the sky after its take-off from Boeing Field. Introduced in 1988, the 747-400 was characterized by its extended upper deck and by its fuel-saving winglets which are clearly in evidence here.

Below: A billboard on Seattle's Airport Way, circa 1941. In the 1930s, an aircraft with two or three engines was considered large. Boeing president Claire Egtvedt passionately believed that his company could—and should—take the next step. The results were the Model 314 Clipper, the Model 307 Stratoliner and the Model 299 (B-17) Flying Fortress seen on the sign. Both the Clipper and Flying Fortress went on to become truly legendary aircraft.

CONTENTS

Charts and Production Closeups

TER OF 4-ENGINE AIRPLANE DEVELOPMENT
S FLYING FORTRESSES

BOEING AND THE NORTHWEST

The Boeing Company, together with its subsidiaries, is one of America's major aerospace firms, the largest manufacturer of transport aircraft in the Western world and the largest non-agricultural employer in the Northwestern United States. Boeing exerts a powerful and unique influence on that area of the Northwest around the city of Seattle, providing fully ten percent of the jobs in the area. There is a saying in the Northwest that sums up Boeing's importance: 'As goes Boeing, so go I.' It is significant that this notion permeates the thinking of an entire region.

Boeing's principal business is conducted through four divisional 'Companies,' Boeing Commercial Airplane Company, Boeing Aerospace Company, Boeing Military Airplane Company and Boeing Vertol Company. Of Boeing's roughly one hundred thousand employees, half (49.5 percent) are employed by the Boeing Commercial Airplane Company, 17.8 percent are employed by the Boeing Military Airplane Company, 17.2 percent are employed by Boeing Aerospace, 4.6 percent are employed by Boeing Vertol while 6.4 percent are employed in Boeing's Computer Service Company.

Boeing was born in Seattle, and continues to maintain its corporate headquarters there, with many of its important activities in or very near to Seattle. Three quarters (74.9 percent) of Boeing's employees work in the Seattle area, compared to 15.4

Below: **Boeing Field** circa 1983, looking south toward Mount Rainier, with examples of all of Boeing's 707 through 767 airframes visible in the foreground.

percent in Wichita, headquarters of Boeing Military Airplane Company, and 4.6 percent near Philadelphia, the headquarters of Boeing Vertol.

William E Boeing began building aircraft in 1915 on the shores of Lake Union in the center of Seattle, and on 15 July 1916 Pacific Aero Products was incorporated. In April 1917 the company name was changed to The Boeing Airplane Company and the company moved to the present headquarters site in the southern part of the city adjacent to the Seattle/King County Airport (Boeing Field). The headquarters site centers on Plant 2, the famous factory complex which has presided over the construction of many of Boeing's most famous aircraft from the *Monomail* through the B-17 to the B-52. Today the Plant 2 complex houses the corporate headquarters, the wind tunnel, the E-3A (Airborne Warning and Control System, or AWACS) Program, the E-4A & B Advanced Airborne Command Post Program, the Minuteman Missile Modification Program, sheet metal and line gear operations for the Fabrication Division as well as the Roland Missile Program. Adjacent to Plant 2 are the Customer Training Center and the Thompson Tract, which is the site of new program engine buildup. Down the road a short distance is the Boeing Developmental Center, site of Military Airplane Development Management, the Minuteman Program, the Army Systems Division, the Short Range Attack Missile (SRAM) Program and the MX Missile Program. Across the street (East Marginal Way South) at Boeing Field is the Boeing

Flight Center and the final delivery point for all commercial aircraft, except the 747 and 767.

In the course of the expansion of the Company during World War II a new plant was built in Renton at the southern tip of Lake Washington. Today Renton is the headquarters site of the Boeing Commercial Airplane Company and the manufacturing site for 707, 727, 737, 757 and E-3A (AWACS) aircraft. Renton is also the headquarters of Boeing Marine Systems and, because of the close proximity to Lake Washington, the manufacturing site for Marine Systems' military hydrofoils and commercial Jetfoils.

In 1966, with the go-ahead for the 747 Program, Boeing acquired 780 acres adjacent to Paine Field in Everett, 30 miles north of Seattle, on which to construct the 747 manufacturing complex. Included in the complex is the world's largest building in volume. Originally containing 200 million cubic feet, the building was enlarged in the early 1980s to 285 million to accommodate production of the 767 jetliner. As a result, major portions of manufacturing, sub-assembly and final assembly for both aircraft are housed under one roof. As the 767 Program evolves into the 777 Program, this development may take place at the huge Everett site. About another 30 miles north from Everett at Tulalip, Boeing has located its Hazardous Testing Site.

South of the Seattle/Renton area at Kent are the Boeing Space Center and the Spares Support Center. The Boeing Space Center houses the headquarters of the Boeing Aerospace Company, engineering and high technology aspects of Boeing Computer

Below: An open house at **Boeing Field** circa 1955, with all of Boeing's major military aircraft of the previous two decades: a B-17, a B-29, a B-47, a KC-97, the then brand-new B-52A and the XB-52 in the background.

BOEING COMPANY CORPORATE ORGANIZATION

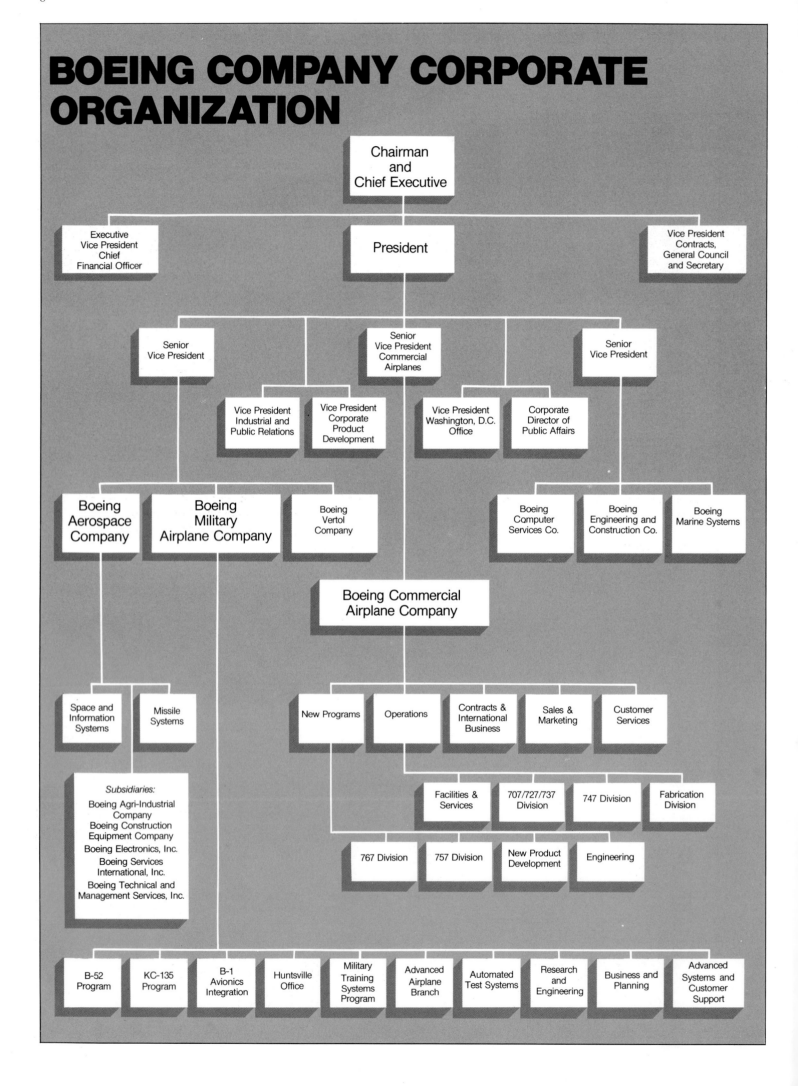

Chairman and Chief Executive

Executive Vice President Chief Financial Officer

President

Vice President Contracts, General Council and Secretary

Senior Vice President

Senior Vice President Commercial Airplanes

Senior Vice President

Vice President Industrial and Public Relations

Vice President Corporate Product Development

Vice President Washington, D.C. Office

Corporate Director of Public Affairs

Boeing Aerospace Company

Boeing Military Airplane Company

Boeing Vertol Company

Boeing Computer Services Co.

Boeing Engineering and Construction Co.

Boeing Marine Systems

Boeing Commercial Airplane Company

Space and Information Systems

Missile Systems

New Programs

Operations

Contracts & International Business

Sales & Marketing

Customer Services

Subsidiaries:

Boeing Agri-Industrial Company
Boeing Construction Equipment Company
Boeing Electronics, Inc.
Boeing Services International, Inc.
Boeing Technical and Management Services, Inc.

Facilities & Services

707/727/737 Division

747 Division

Fabrication Division

767 Division

757 Division

New Product Development

Engineering

B-52 Program

KC-135 Program

B-1 Avionics Integration

Huntsville Office

Military Training Systems Program

Advanced Airplane Branch

Automated Test Systems

Research and Engineering

Business and Planning

Advanced Systems and Customer Support

Services, Missile and Space programs management, Product Development and the Air Launched Cruise Missile (ALCM) Program. The Spares Support Center houses the Boeing Computer Services Company, Boeing Surplus Sales and a warehouse complex. The Boeing Employment Center, and the Boeing Engineering and Construction Company are based at Southcenter, while the Fabrication and Spares divisions of the Boeing Commercial Airplane Company are located still farther south at Auburn.

Boeing's principal locations outside the Seattle area at Wichita and Philadelphia were acquired in 1934 and 1960 respectively. In 1934 Boeing bought the Stearman Aircraft Company of Wichita which became the Wichita Division of Boeing in 1939. After

Above: Boeing's **Renton** facility at the foot of Lake Washington is the site of the Boeing Commercial Airplane Company headquarters as well as the Boeing Marine Systems headquarters. The jetliner models 707, 727, 737 and 757 are all produced here.

World War II Boeing's military operations were gradually concentrated in Wichita. Boeing acquired the Vertol Aircraft Company (formerly Piasecki Aircraft Corporation) in 1960 as the Boeing Vertol Division. In 1972 the Division became the Boeing Vertol Company.

Boeing is today the largest manufacturer of commercial jetliners in the Western world, outdistancing McDonnell Douglas and Lockheed combined. While Boeing was rolling out its quiet

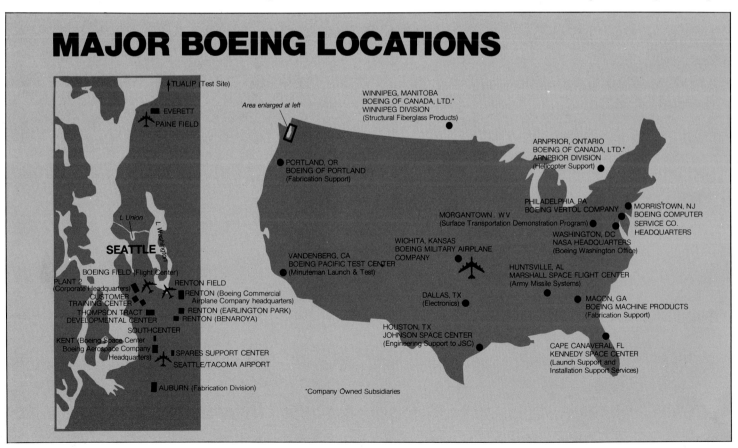

and fuel efficient 757 and 767 in the early 1980s, McDonnell Douglas had nothing on the horizon to succeed or complement its DC-9 and DC-10, and Lockheed was announcing the closing of its L-1011 assembly line. Boeing's principal competition in the 1980s and 1990s is seen to be Airbus Industries, a European consortium based in Toulouse, France. While in the early 1980s Airbus moved ahead of McDonnell Douglas and Lockheed in worldwide sales volume with its popular A300, it has yet even to approach Boeing. Of the jetliners presently in service with the world's airlines (excluding Aeroflot of the USSR), Boeing enjoys a comfortable market share in excess of 60 percent.

Boeing's family tree reads like a Who's Who of American aircraft history. The Model 314 Clipper was a household word on the transpacific and transatlantic airways in the years before the war, while during World War II the B-17 and B-29 were certainly among the dozen or even half dozen most important and famous of the thousands of aircraft types that served. Today planes like the 707, 727 and certainly the 747 are household words among the millions who fly on business and pleasure.

Many other companies and regions have profited from Boeing's success. In the 757 Program, for example, Boeing has awarded sub-contracts to the value of some $2,000,000,000 to 1400 companies for the production of major and minor components. US companies have received the largest share but not all. Manufacturers in Australia, Canada, England, Northern Ireland, Japan and Spain are also involved.

When the giant superjet, the 747, was in production, about 50 percent of the work (by value) was subcontracted to other firms. Approximately 1500 primary suppliers and 15,000 secondary suppliers, located in 47 states of the USA and six foreign countries, could thank Boeing for at least a portion of their income.

The airplane business fluctuates. Some years are better than others, and knowing this, Boeing has diversified even beyond the areas already mentioned. Among other projects the company has undertaken recently is a study of backaches. Much of the company's work comes through competitive bidding. Recently a $200,000 NASA contract to see how supersonic transport technology could be applied to combat aircraft was won. For Boeing this is not a large contract but the point was not so much the money involved as the contact with a new opportunity. Eventually jobs may be the fruit of the contract, jobs not only for Seattle and the Northwest, but for the United States as a whole and for other countries.

While Boeing owes its success to a variety of factors, what it all seems to boil down to is the Company's reputation for building sound, dependable, thoroughly thought out, high quality products. Each member of the Boeing Jetliner family, for example, is thoughtfully designed for a specific market. The 737 is designed to serve short feeder routes, the 727 and now the 757 for intermediate distances, and the 747 and 767 for long distance intercontinental flights. As one airline executive put it, Boeing is always coming up with the right plane, at the right price, and at the right time.

William Boeing once wrote, 'Our task is to keep everlastingly at research and experiment, to adapt our laboratories to production as soon as practicable, to let no new improvement in flying and flying equipment pass us by.'

They are words for any company to live by.

Facing page: A 1989 photograph of Boeing Field with 737s, 757s and 747s being prepped for delivery. *Above*: The 737 production line at Renton, Washington.

THE EARLY YEARS

On 4 July 1914, a barnstormer named Terah Maroney was hired to put on a flying exhibition as part of the Independence Day festivities in Seattle, Washington. Having put on a display of acrobatics in his Curtiss seaplane, Maroney landed and offered to take up passengers. A lumber company owner named William Edward Boeing stepped up and allowed as how he would like to take a ride. What happened in the next 30 minutes changed the course of aviation history and the history of the Northwest as well. William E Boeing had caught the flying bug. He was never to recover. During the ensuing two decades Bill Boeing built one of the most successful aircraft manufacturing companies in the country as well as being a founding partner in the air passenger service that would become United Airlines, today the largest airline in the world.

Right: The **B & W**, the first Boeing plane, is launched from Boeing's factory on the shores of Lake Union. The plane, whose profile resembled that of the seaplane Bill Boeing had purchased earlier from Glenn Martin, was supposed to make its maiden flight on 29 June 1916 with Herb Munter at the controls. For some reason Munter was late in arriving for the event, so Boeing himself climbed into the rear cockpit and took his Model 1 aloft. When he brought the plane back down, Munter was the first to greet him. When asked how the flight had gone, Boeing responded by telling the small group of workers assembled at the Lake Union plant that they were at last in the airplane business.

Bill Boeing had a tenacious mind, one that viewed the world as a place full of opportunities. In addition to his timber interests, he owned a furniture factory and a boat yard. They were successful, and aircraft, he reasoned, had potential. Public opinion would not have agreed with Boeing's optimism. Flying was considered a dangerous game, a plaything for stuntmen and thrill seekers. During the years since Orville and Wilbur Wright first took a heavier-than-air craft aloft at Kitty Hawk, in 1903, flying had not advanced far into the public consciousness as a means of transportation. Though Louis Bleriot had flown across the English Channel on 25 July 1909, aircraft were not taken seriously. Even when so serious a man as Alexander Graham Bell, inventor of the telephone, experimented with flight, public opinion still catered to the flamboyant. When another American,

PRODUCTION CLOSE-UP:
BOEING AIRCRAFT 1916-1935

	100	200	400

Model 1: *"B&W":* Twin-pontoon biplane. (1916)
2

Model 2-5: *"C"* and *"EA":* Twin-pontoon biplane (except *"EA"/Model 4,* which were 2 experimental landplane versions). (1917-18)
58

Model 6: *B-1:* Pontoon-hulled biplane, first Boeing aircraft of completely original design. (1919-28)
9

Model 7-8: *BB-1* and *BB-L6:* The former was a smaller development of the *B-1,* while the latter was a landplane version of the *BB-1.* (1919-20)
2

Model 10: *GA-1* and *GA-2:* Two dissimilar Army ground-attack aircraft given the same model number. (1920)
12

Model 15: *PW-9* (Army Designation) and *FB-1* (Navy Designation): Biplane fighter with a watercooled engine. (1923-28)
123

Model 16: *DH-4B:* In 1920 Boeing received an Army contract to modernize surplus deHavilland DH-4 World War I aircraft. (1920-25)
111 (Rebuilt wooden fuselage)
187 (Boeing-designed tube-steel fuselage)

Model 21: *NB-1* and *NB-2:* Biplane trainers designed to operate as either a landplane or a single-pontoon seaplane. (1923-27)
76

Model 40: *Model 40:* A commercial transport originally designed as a mail plane, the *40* became Boeing's first multi-passenger airliner. (1925-32)
86

Model 42: *XCO-7:* An experiment in designing and building new wings for aging DH-4's. (1925)
3

Model 50: *PB-1* (Renamed *PB-2* when re-engined): Built to satisfy a Navy requirement for a patrol seaplane with a 2400-mile (California-Hawaii) range. (1925)
1

Models 53, 54, 55, 67: *FB-2* through *FB-5:* Re-engined and modified fighter variations on the *Model 15* in Navy service. (1925-26)
33

Models 58, 66, 68, 93: *XP-4, XP-8, AT-3* and *XP-7:* Re-engined and modified fighter and trainer variations on the *Model 15* in Army service. (1926-28)
4

Model 63: *TB-1:* A large all-metal Navy biplane torpedo bomber which could also be converted to a landplane for aircraft-carrier operations. (1927)
3

Models 64 and 81: *Model 64* was designed as a possible successor to the *Model 21. Model 81* was a landplane development of the same idea. (1926-28)
3

Model 69: *F2B-1:* Another development of the *Model 15* series. (1926-28)
35

Model 70, 75, 76 *(Stearman Kaydet): Model 70, 75, 76.* Army Designation *PT-13, PT-17* and *PT-27:* (1935-45)
10,346

Models 74 and 77: *XF3B* and *F3B:* An improvement of the *F2B* design. The latter was the production version with new, larger wings. (1927-28)
74

Models 80 and 226: *Model 80* and *Model 226:* A trimotor biplane carrying 12 passengers, the *Model 80* was the last word in luxury. The 11th production *Model 80* was completed as a deluxe oil-company executive aircraft designated *Model 226.* (1928-30)
16

Model 95: *Model 95:* An open-cockpit mail plane similar to, but slightly smaller than, the *Model 40.* (1928-29)
25

Model 96: *XP-9:* An unsuccessful experimental fighter design. Boeing's first monoplane.
1

Model 100 Series: *XF4B-1 (Models 83 & 89), F4B-1 (Model 99), Model 100, XP-12A (Model 101), P-12B (Model 102), Model 218, P-12C (Model 222), F4B-2 (Model 102), Model 218, P-12C (Model 222), F4B-2 (Model 223), P-12D (Model 227), P-12E (Model 234), F4B-3 & -4 (Model 235), F-12F (Model 251), F4B-4 (Model 256):* A series of single-engine biplane fighters of advanced design. (1928-33)
189: US Navy (F4B)
366: US Army (P-12)
23: Demonstrators, export models, etc.

Models 103-199: Model numbers assigned to Boeing-designed airfoil sections.

Model 200 & 221: *Monomail:* A monoplane of revolutionary design with a powerful engine, clean lines and retractable landing gear. (1930)
2

Model 202 and 205: *XP-15* and *XF5B-1:* All-metal monoplane versions of the *P-12* and *F4B* respectively. (1930)
2

Model 203: *Model 203:* A commercial biplane trainer built for the Boeing School of Aeronautics, 2 of which were built by students. (1926-36)
7

Model 204: *Model 204:* Further development of the *Model 6.* (1929)
8

Model 214, 215 and 246: *Y1B-9, Y1B-9A* and *YB-9:* A twin-engined open-cockpit monoplane heavy bomber in Army service. (1930-33)
7

Model 236: *XF6B-1:* An all-metal biplane Navy fighter. The last improvement of the *F4B* design, it came when it was clear that the era of biplane fighters was past. (1933)
1

Models 238 and 239: *Models 238 and 239:* A trimotor monoplane development study for a 12-passenger commercial airliner. (1933)
0

Model 247: *Model 247:* A twin-engine, 10-passenger airliner. Boeing's first really modern airliner. (1933-35)
75

Models 248, 266 and 281: *P-26:* A fixed-gear, open-cockpit Army fighter. *Model 281* was the export version. (1934-35)
151

Models 264 and 273: *XP-29* and *XF7B:* An experimental retractable-gear monoplane intended to update *P-26* techonology. (1933-34)
4

Biplanes
Monoplanes
Triplanes

Above: The twin-pontooned **B & W** during taxiing trials on Lake Union.

Glenn Curtiss, remained aloft for two hours and fifty-one minutes in 1910, flying was still a curiosity.

However, Boeing had met Navy Commander Conrad Westervelt in Seattle. Westervelt was stationed at the Naval shipyards in Bremerton, across Puget Sound. The two men hit it off from the start. They went boating together on Boeing's yacht, and among the many topics discussed was that of aviation, in which both were deeply interested. Prompted by this interest, Boeing finally took his first airplane ride. He and Westervelt both went aloft with Terah Maroney in a Curtiss seaplane with a pusher type engine. The excursions convinced Boeing that he should build his own plane, and he had the means to do so. To Westervelt's astonishment, Boeing asked him to design the aircraft, which was to be a seaplane. Westervelt had had no experience in aircraft design. Few people did. Testing facilities were just as scarce. There was only one wind tunnel in existence capable of such a large job, and that was at the Massachusetts Institute of Technology, some 3000 miles away. Nor were aircraft engineers plentiful. Aeronautics was not exactly a hot item in the university curriculum. But Westervelt accepted the challenge. He contacted the right people, learned from them what he could, and designed what came to be named the B & W, after the initials of the two originators.

The B & W was a utility aircraft, accommodating two, seated in tandem. It was powered by a Hall-Scott A-5, water-cooled, 125 horsepower (hp) engine, and the wingspan was 52 feet. The length, overall, was 27 feet 6 inches. The aircraft was designated, simply Model 1. The B & W was built in two different locations. The fuselage was put together in a hangar on Seattle's Lake Union. The wings and floats were assembled at the Heath Shipyard, on Puget Sound's Elliot Bay. Boeing had purchased the shipyard primarily as a repair shop for his yacht, but he quickly changed it into a factory. There were few aircraft technicians, so carpenters, shipwrights and cabinet makers from Boeing's furniture factory were employed. Ed Heath, a man familiar with boats, supervised the construction of the pontoons.

In the meantime, Boeing had taken flying lessons at Glenn Martin's school in Los Angeles. He returned to Seattle in October 1915, after purchasing a ten thousand dollar seaplane

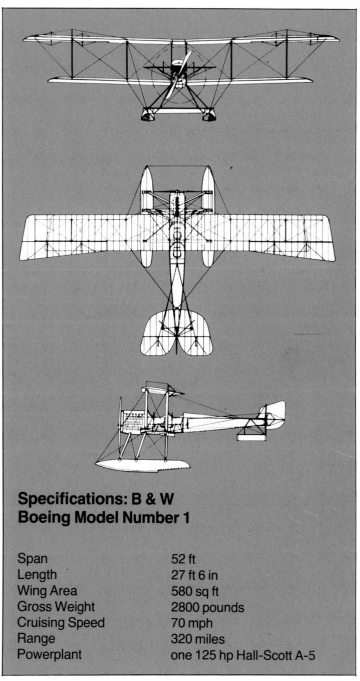

Specifications: B & W
Boeing Model Number 1

Span	52 ft
Length	27 ft 6 in
Wing Area	580 sq ft
Gross Weight	2800 pounds
Cruising Speed	70 mph
Range	320 miles
Powerplant	one 125 hp Hall-Scott A-5

Below: The **EA**, Boeing Model 4, was the landplane version of the Model C (model numbers 2, 3 and 5). The US Army ordered a pair of EAs as trainers with side-by-side seating and a 90hp Curtiss OX-5 engine.

Specifications: Model C/EA
Boeing Model Numbers 2-5

Span	43 ft 10 in
Length	27 ft
Wing Area	495 sq ft
Gross Weight	2395 pounds
Cruising Speed	65 mph
Service Ceiling	6500 ft
Range	200 miles
Powerplant	one 100 hp Hall-Scott A-7A
Capacity	1 passenger

from Martin. Floyd Smith, his instructor, went to Seattle to uncrate and assemble the plane. Aircraft were shipped in crates, hence the expression 'crate,' meaning aircraft, which came into popular use during World War I.

Herb Munter, a 22-year-old mechanic, who had built and flown his own planes, was hired to fly the Martin. Munter, an expert at improvization, shaped his own aircraft from wood and home-sewn fabrics. The engines usually sat just behind the cockpit, and would, said Munter laconically, replace the pilot in case of a head-on crash. Munter was the first of Boeing's employees in the aircraft business, the first of thousands, though the 34-year-old timberman had not thought that far ahead yet.

Work on the B & Ws had progressed to a point, where in June 1916, the first of the pair was ready. It was named *Bluebill*, and

Boeing himself tested it. This was a crucial moment. Though Westervelt had designed it, the plane was Boeing's baby.

The engine sputtered into action and as Bill Boeing floated down Lake Union, the eyes of his factory workers followed his progress. He revved the engine, and zipped over the lake's placid surface. In moments, he was airborne, and a feeling of relief brought a smile. Bill Boeing had a good airplane, and he knew it. Munter tried the B & W next, and gave an affirmative report. That was all Boeing needed to hear. He contacted the Navy, asking for a chance to show his plane. Once more, much was on the line. If the Navy liked the B & Ws, there might be a contract for more, meaning that he was in the airplane business to stay.

The Navy liked the plane, but it had a tendency to tilt while airborne. Though the matter was corrected in a couple of hours, the final decision was no. That was a disappointment to Boeing, but, by then, he was hooked. He was able to make good airplanes, and he knew it and he was determined to prove it to others as well.

Prior to the Navy tests, Boeing lost his partner Commander Westervelt to World War I. Although America had not yet joined the war, Westervelt had been ordered to the east coast and Boeing was on his own. On 15 July 1916, the Pacific Aero Products Company was incorporated with Boeing as president, and his cousin, E N Gott, vice president.

After the failure of the B & W to bring contracts, Boeing hired T Wong, a brilliant Chinese designer. Wong developed the Model C, a twin-float ship. Boeing was proud of his product, calling it the first 'all-Boeing' design, because his B & W had borrowed some wing data from Martin. Herb Munter, however, didn't like the plane. He felt the rudder was too small, and there was no horizontal stabilizer. Against his better judgment, he took the

William Edward Boeing was born in Detroit on 1 October 1881, the son of a wealthy lumberman. He was educated in the United States and in Switzerland and entered Yale Sheffield School of Science in the class of 1904. He then spent five years learning the timber business and indulging in his hobby of aeronautics and flying.

On 15 July 1916 Boeing incorporated his small biplane-manufacturing operation as Pacific Aero Products, and a few months later he changed the name to Boeing Airplane Company. By 1928 his company had become one of the nation's largest aircraft builders, the success of which can be attributed to Boeing's belief in the importance of research and experimentation. In his desire to strengthen the aircraft industry, he effected the formation of the United Aircraft and Transport Corporation and became the firm's first chairman. The new company included the Boeing Airplane Company, Pratt & Whitney, Chance Vought, Hamilton Propeller Co and Boeing Air Transport. In 1934 the government ordered the corporation split up on the grounds it was a monopoly.

Boeing retired as chairman of the company in 1934. His only association thereafter was during World War II, when he returned in an advisory capacity.

When William Boeing died on 28 September 1956 his company was a world leader in the production of multi-engine aircraft, and had entered the field of commercial jet transportation. Boeing was active in the aviation industry for only 18 years, but few men in United States' history have contributed so greatly to the development of a single industry.

Below: The famous '**Red Barn**,' seen here on 8 June 1917, was the first Boeing company headquarters building on the present site south of downtown Seattle. Because Boeing was manufacturing aircraft for the war effort, military guards were stationed outside.

plane up, and nearly crashed. The plane proved unstable, and only skilful piloting landed it safely. He refused to fly it again until a larger rudder had been installed. On 9 April 1917 Munter again lofted the Model C into the sky. This time, he brought better news to Boeing. The plane was airworthy, and the twin pontoons felt good in rough water.

Boeing immediately headed east to drum up Navy interest. Two Model Cs were crated and shipped to the Naval Air Station, Pensacola, Florida. Herb Munter and another pilot, Claude Berlin, were handed the responsible task of impressing the critical eyes of the inspectors. The importance of their mission was not lost on them. Success could mean an order for more. However, the Navy was no pushover. The B & W, a good plane, had been turned down, and so could the C. It was a chancy business!

The two pilots came through with more than just flying colors. Boeing received an order for 50 Model Cs, to be used as trainers. Things were falling into place, and the president of Pacific Aero Products Company was satisfied. But in the midst of success came another setback. T Wong, the Chinese designer, resigned.

Unable to find good engineers in the east, Boeing returned to Seattle, and now his genius came to the fore. He knew how to pick good men, and once he had them, he knew how to delegate authority. He wanted ideas men, but the ideas had to be practical enough to turn into reality. It was good to dream, but the dream had to be based on firm foundations.

At the University of Washington, he consulted with Professor C C Moore, and on his recommendation hired two engineering seniors. One was Clairmont Egtvedt, who had failed his military fitness requirements and was out of the running for wartime service. Boeing put him in charge of calculating stresses, something that appealed to Egtvedt. He was to remain with the Boeing company for nearly 50 years. He was its president on two different occasions, and during World War II, he became known as the 'father of the four-engined bomber.' The other student was Philip G Johnson, who turned out to be an organizational expert. He was ambitious and capable, and by 1920 he was a superintendent. In 1921 he was made vice-president, and in 1926, president. He was just 31 years old. Bill Boeing had chosen his men well.

In those early days of the aircraft industry, airplanes designed by one company were often built by rivals on government contract. With America's entry into World War I Boeing accepted a contract from the Navy to build 50 Curtiss HS-2L flying boats. Business, at this point, was firm.

During the war, the orders came in, but the men of the Boeing Airplane Company, as the organization was renamed in April 1917, were not necessarily happy about the cause. Nobody liked

Clairmont L Egtvedt was born on a farm near Stoughton, Wisconsin, on 18 October 1892. He received his degree in mechanical engineering from the University of Washington and joined the Boeing Company as a draftsman in 1917, following his graduation. Within a year 'Claire' Egtvedt was chief experimental engineer and soon after, chief engineer. America was then in World War I and Boeing was building trainers for the air force. These were aviation's early days and Egtvedt's time was consumed by testing glues, woods and varnishes as well as metals.

In 1926 Egtvedt was named general manager and vice-president, and in 1933 he became president. During this period he guided Boeing to the forefront of the revolution that produced large bombers, the Model 314 flying boats and Stratoliners with the first pressurized cabins used in civilian flights. Egtvedt also developed the B-17, and it was this plane that earned him his reputation as 'father' of the four-engined bomber.

Egtvedt was elected chairman of the company in 1939. When company president Phil Johnson died in 1944, Egtvedt resumed the presidency for a year until William Allen took over. Egtvedt retired in 1966. He died on 25 April 1975, closing a career which had helped to change the face of aviation across the world, to bring a company to leadership in an industry, to win wars and to shrink distances on the globe.

Below: On the banks of the **Duwamish River**. In 1917 Boeing moved the Pacific Aero Company south to its present site and changed the company name to the Boeing Airplane Company. The Red Barn can be seen directly below.

Left: **Edward Hubbard** was an army pilot instructor at Rockwell Field, San Diego, California, during World War I, and from 1917 to 1920 he worked for the Boeing Company as an experimental pilot. Following the first-ever international mail flight to Vancouver in 1919, Hubbard began an airmail service between Seattle and Victoria, BC, operating by private contract. For the next five years he worked under the name Seattle-Victoria Air Mail Line, flying between 25,000 and 50,000 pounds of mail annually.

He did not live to see the growth of another of his ideas, United Airlines, the largest airline in the western world. The day after its formation, on 18 December 1928, he died in Salt Lake City, where he was vice-president in charge of operations of the Boeing company and, unknown to the many who flew with him, a millionaire.

Below: Dateline Seattle, 2 March 1919, Eddie Hubbard (left) and Bill Boeing (center) climb aboard a **Model C** mailplane for what would become the first international airmail flight to take off from the United States. The two aviators began with a pouch of US mail under dark overcast skies, and ran into a heavy snowstorm en route. With visibility down to nearly zero, they made a landing at Anacortes, Washington, where they spent the night. The next day, the storm past, they continued on their way, landing at the Royal Vancouver Yacht Club Basin. They picked up a pouch of Canadian mail and three hours later were parked on Lake Union in Seattle.

Above: The **B-1** used by Eddie Hubbard for most of his mail flights.

war. Egtvedt, for one, looked forward to the time when Boeing could design a commercial aircraft. He believed the real future lay in commercial endeavors, rather than with the military.

After the Armistice was signed in November 1918, there were cuts in military spending, and hundreds of surplus military aircraft flooded the civilian market. The Navy canceled half its order for the Curtiss HS-2Ls, and the Boeing Airplane Company, along with the aircraft industry as a whole, went into a slump.

Bill Boeing fought back. He was still very much a timberman, and he was involved in related industries. He returned to making furniture and cabinets. He also experimented with Sea-Sleds, in vogue then. He took on any job that would keep his employees working. Nevertheless, in 1920, the company lost $300,000.

While the company concentrated on non-aircraft activities such as furniture making, the airplane side was not dormant. Having made a moderate success of its Model C (Boeing Models 2 through 5), the company in 1919 began development of its next series of aircraft. With the myriad of lakes and rivers of the Northwest in mind, the Boeing engineers began work on a small commercial flying boat that could serve the area carrying passengers and mail. The plane was the B-1 (Model 6), powered by a 200hp Hall-Scott L-6 pusher type engine. Two variations on the B-1 followed. First there was the BB-1 (Model 7), essentially a smaller (45 feet 6 inches versus 50 feet 3 inches span), shorter (27 feet 8 inches versus 31 feet 3 inches) B-1 with a 130hp Hall-Scott L-4. Finally, there was the BB-L6 (Model 8), a still smaller land plane with a front mounted 214hp Hall-Scott L-6.

Neither variation on the B-1 went past the single prototype stage and it was not until the resurgence of interest in aviation generated by Lindbergh's 1927 Paris flight that the B-1 itself

Specifications: B-1
Boeing Model Number 7

Span	50 ft 3 in
Length	31 ft 3 in
Wing Area	492 sq ft
Gross Weight	3850 pounds
Cruising Speed	80 mph
Service Ceiling	13,000 ft
Range	400 miles
Powerplant	one 200 hp Hall-Scott L-6
Capacity	1 passenger

began to sell. Nonetheless, pilot Eddie Hubbard was to use his re-engined B-1 (it had a war surplus 400hp Liberty) with great success for over eight years on his Seattle to Victoria international air mail run.

Despite these successes in design, the Boeing Airplane Company was not doing well. The furniture department was not bringing in the hoped-for revenue, and experiments with Sea-Sleds were scrapped. Boeing was digging into his own pocket to meet payrolls, but he told his executives that unless something positive happened, the company would fold. It was a roller-coaster situation, one that was common to the airplane industry of the time. Chicken on Sunday, feathers on Monday. This, said the chief, has to stop. Men were laid off. J W Miller, head of engineering, departed, leaving only two engineers on the staff, Claire Egtvedt and Louis Marsh. The horizon was not exactly golden.

Then the company received a military contract to rebuild a number of Liberty-engined wartime De Havilland DH-4 aircraft. Though the contract was happily received, there was, also, a feeling that the Boeing Airplane Company should be designing and building its own planes. Claire Egtvedt felt so strongly about this that, along with Louis Marsh, he went to see the company's president to stress his point. Bill Boeing kept on top of his many interests from an office in the Hoge Building in downtown Seattle.

'We are in the business to build airplanes, not sidewalks,' he told his boss. 'If you want planes you'll have to hire designers.' Bill Boeing agreed, and gave Egtvedt the go-ahead. The young engineer had already decided that what was needed was a plane to interest the Army. Military contracts were the largest contracts, and it paid to favor their interest. He began plans on a Boeing pursuit plane that would become the PW-9, but the work was kept secret. When the time was right, he would let the right people know.

The DH-4 modernization contract in hand, Boeing next received a direct boost from the Army Air Service. General Billy Mitchell, then assistant to the chief, believed that a large air force was necessary for future security. Boeing was awarded a contract to build 20 Army designed planes called the GAX, for Ground Attack, Experimental. They were to be triplanes, with a pair of Liberty engines, a 20mm cannon, and eight machine guns. The cockpits were to be heavily armored to provide protection from ground fire.

This was all to the good, and Boeing's skilled production staff went to work with a will. The men were no longer the uninitiated craftsmen who had worked on the B & W. These were men who had built hundreds of aircraft for military use and knew their way around an airplane.

However, the military changed its mind about the GAX, and altered the order from 20 to 10. Yet, even as the order was halved, another order came through to build three GA-2s, which the Army redesigned from a twin-engine triplane GAX into a single-engined biplane.

The GAX, in all its phases, proved too clumsy for an attack plane. The armored cockpits were difficult to see from, and met with general disfavor among the Army pilots. It was such a chore to fly the planes that commanding officers threatened their men with a tour of duty on the GAX if they stepped out of line.

Eventually, the GAX was phased out, and once again the chicken and feathers pattern loomed on the Boeing Airplane Company's economic horizon. Plenty of work one month, little of it the next. Ed Gott, still vice-president, grumbled that he didn't like what was going on. The military was the largest customer, and you had to build to their designs. If you submitted your own design, you did not necessarily get to build the plane. Another company, such as Curtiss, might underbid and get the

Left: The Boeing 26-foot **Standard Sea-sled** was fitted with two 6-cylinder Model C-6 Van Blerck engines. Moments after this picture was taken, in Boston at 4:30 am on 9 July 1914, the boat left on a run for Bar Harbor, Maine. The total running time was 8 hours 20 minutes for 230 miles in open water, or an average speed at sea of over 25mph. Pictured in the foreground are John A Murray, C B Page and C F Chapman, with Holly MacRae aft at the steering wheel. The picture shows the position of extra seats in the forward cockpit.

Below: The **BB-1** (Model 7), a smaller three-seat version of the B-1 (Model 6), made its first flight on 7 January 1920, only 11 days after the first flight of the B-1. It was powered by a 130hp Hall-Scott L-4 engine. The BB-L6 (Model 8), a three-seat landplane version, made its first flight on 24 May.

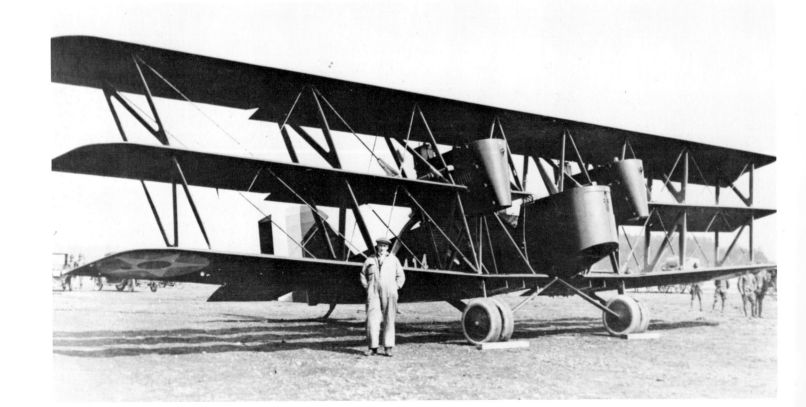

Below left: Boeing's only triplane was built to satisfy an Army requirement for an armored ground-attack aircraft under the designation GAX (Ground Attack Experimental). Ten of the planes, redesignated **GA-1** when delivered, were built under an early post-war policy whereby the Army designed its own aircraft and contracted for their manufacture. Boeing employee Charlie Thompson is seen here at Camp Lewis with one of the first GA-1s.

Below: The heavily armed and armored **GA-2** was the result of a redesign of the cumbersome GA-1. Despite the redesign, the aircraft proved itself in flight testing to be impractical and the program was abandoned.

Specifications: GA-1 **Boeing Model Number 10**	
Span	65 ft 6 in
Length	33 ft 8 in
Wing Area	1016 sq ft
Gross Weight	10,426 pounds
Bomb Capacity	250 pounds
Top Speed	105 mph
Cruising Speed	95 mph
Range	350 miles
Service Ceiling	9600 ft
Powerplant	two 435 hp Liberty 12A
Armament	eight 0.3 in Lewis machine guns and one 37 mm Baldwin cannon

Specifications: GA-2 **Boeing Model Number 10**	
Span	54 ft
Length	36 ft 9 in
Wing Area	851 sq ft
Gross Weight	8691 pounds
Top Speed	113 mph
Cruising Speed	100 mph
Range	200 miles
Service Ceiling	12,000 ft
Powerplant	one 750 hp Army Engineering Division W-18
Armament	six 0.3 in Lewis machine guns and one 37 mm Baldwin cannon

Top: The crackup of an **MB-3** at Camp Lewis in June 1922 went a long way toward convincing Bill Boeing (standing, far right) that the idea of the much superior PW-9, then under consideration within the company, was worth exploring.

Above: **Edgar N Gott** was born in Detroit, Michigan, in 1887 and received a BS in chemical engineering from the University of Michigan in 1909. Eventually migrating to Tacoma, he entered the lumber business, where he met Bill Boeing. He became general manager of the Boeing Company in 1917 and served as president from 1923-25. He went on to become a vice-president of Fokker Aircraft Corporation from 1925-26. After leaving Fokker, he served as president of Keystone Aircraft and later as vice-president of Consolidated Aircraft.

work. This was one of the reasons Claire Egtvedt was keeping his pursuit design under wraps. Airplane construction was a new and highly competitive field, and ideas were 'borrowed' without conscience. It was a case of survival of the fittest.

Despite Gott's feelings about government methods of awarding contracts, it worked in favor of Boeing. The company was awarded a contract to build 200 MB-3 pursuit planes, designed by the Thomas Morse Company. Their bid for the job was $1,448,000, which was lower even than the bid submitted by Thomas Morse, the designer. Gott was alarmed by this. How could Boeing bid so low and come out ahead? The answer was simple: Bill Boeing, always the timberman, had large holdings of spruce in the state of Washington. Spruce was essential in the construction of aircraft, and who could get it more cheaply than the man who owned the rights to vast forests?

The MB-3 contract proved a financial success, and Boeing Airplane Company ended the year 1922 in the black. The employees received a Christmas bonus, and feelings were high. It looked as if the plant would remain in business.

On 23 April 1923, the Boeing Model 15, Claire Egtvedt's new pursuit plane, Army designation PW-9 (Pursuit, Water cooled), was tested by Frank Tyndall. He liked it, but cautioned that the stability could be better. Stability was the bugbear haunting manufacturers of the time. It was a trial and error matter, because aircraft construction was still new in the world. Nobody knew very much yet.

The day after Tyndall's trial, he ground looped the PW-9, damaging the propeller. Because tests were due to take place at McCook Field in a couple of weeks, there was no time for detailed repairs. The propeller was repaired, and the plane shipped. The results for the Boeing Airplane Company were not good.

General Mason Patrick, procurement officer for the Air Service, told Egtvedt the PW-9 didn't match the performance of the Curtiss PW-8. Another propeller was substituted, and the PW-9 performed better, but still not well enough for General Patrick. In addition, the General told Egtvedt that Boeing's plant was not large enough to handle big orders. Egtvedt held his tongue diplomatically, but he would have liked to remind the General that the Boeing plant was turning out hundreds of

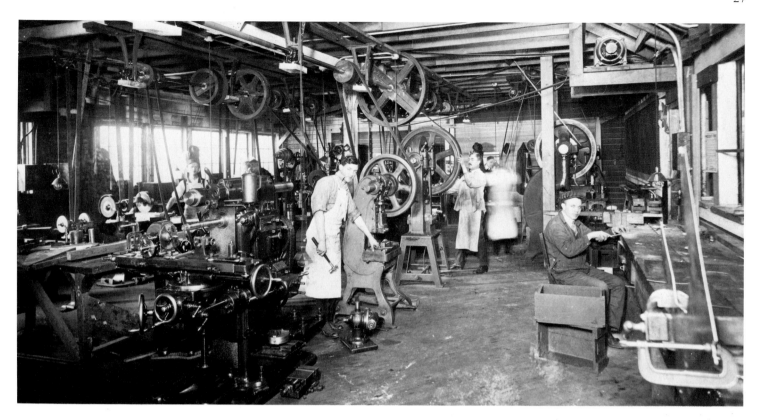

Above: The **Boeing machine shop** as seen in January 1918.

Below: The **NB-1**, like its successor the NB-2, was a Navy trainer designed to function as either a landplane or a seaplane.

MB-3s and DH-4s. The upshot of the McCook tests was an order for the PW-9 being tested, and two more. No great shakes, but it was something.

During the course of his dealings with the Army, Egtvedt was invited to watch an aerial bombing. Two obsolete battleships, the *New Jersey* and the *Virginia*, were to undergo the test. The young executive witnessed an eye-opening drama from the deck of the *St Mihiel*, a transport standing off from the field of action. Both battleships were sunk with direct hits from bombing aircraft. This result would have far-reaching effects on military thinking. It also started Egtvedt down a long trail of experimentation. Bombers? What about them? Egtvedt was impressed by what had seen, and he began what was to be a life-long relationship with an aircraft which would be called, in full development, the Flying Fortress.

While Egtvedt was tending to business in the east, another trainer was being readied back at the plant in Seattle. It was the NB-1 (Model 21), and was aimed at the Navy. Eddie Hubbard tested it, and declared the plane the best ever. However, in the competition for contracts at the Naval Air Station, Pensacola, the Navy could not make up its mind. Other entries by Martin and Huff Deland were also good. No conclusion was drawn, and the matter was left dangling, like a stranded kite. The winter of 1923–24 proved to be a slow one. Again the specter of closing loomed on the horizon. But in the spring of 1924, the Navy finally declared Boeing the winner of the competition. The company was awarded a contract to build 49 NB-1s, together with its companion the NB-2. The planes would be used as trainers.

On top of this success, the Post Office authorized an experimental design for an air mail plane. It was to be constructed with a plywood body, and a Liberty engine. Success breeds success, and next the Air Service sent word that it approved Egtvedt's PW-9. 'Drives as easy as a car,' declared the approving pilots. The Army was impressed with the welded steel tube fuselage, a major improvement over the MB-3, and accordingly ordered an additional series of rebuilt DH-4s that incorporated a steel tube fuselage.

Things were once more on the upswing. Then, bad news: the Navy NB-1 was having problems. Planes were crashing. Engi-

Specifications: NB-1 and NB-2
Boeing Model Number 21

Span	36 ft 10 in
Length	28 ft 9 in
Wing Area	344 sq ft
Gross Weight	2837 pounds (NB-1)
Bomb Capacity	3037 pounds (NB-2)
Top Speed	99.5 mph
Range	300 miles
Service Ceiling	10,200 ft
Powerplant	one 200 hp Wright J-4 (NB-1)
Armament	one 0.3 in Browning machine gun in rear cockpit of gunnery trainers

Below: A **PW-9 (Model 15)** in Boeing markings prior to being transferred to the Army.

neers decided the plane needed a different kind of wing, and another was developed. Again, Eddie Hubbard took the plane up. It crashed, but Hubbard escaped uninjured. The Navy complained loudly, and Phil Johnson explained that Boeing would have to keep experimenting. Nobody knew all the answers. Finally, the body of the NB was lengthened, and the plane flew nicely. No crashes. However, it proved *too* stable. It could not be made to spin. It would have to spin, said Navy inspectors, because the trainees have to know about spinning. An adjustment was made to the elevators, and the Navy accepted it in January 1926. The NB was considered suitable for training purposes – but no stunting was allowed.

Some big changes were taking place in the Boeing Airplane Company at this time. Ed Gott resigned after a dispute with Bill Boeing. Phil Johnson was named president, and Claire Egtvedt became vice president and chief engineer. Boeing himself assumed the chairmanship.

There was a big change in government supervision of the airways as well. President Calvin Coolidge had created the Morrow Board to study the growing aviation industry. Its report moved Congress into passing the Aviation Five-Year Program, and the Army Air Service was re-named the Army Air Corps. The Board also gave industry proprietary rights to the planes it designed, a matter that should have pleased Ed Gott, now an executive for Fokker in the US. The Air Commerce Act was passed to encourage civil aeronautics, and the Post Office turned the air mail service over to private operators. The Boeing Airplane Company now had 500 employees, and 50 engineers. They were kept busy with another order for 40 PW-9C pursuits, with a 435hp Curtiss engine.

Meanwhile the Navy began to order PW-9s. They began with ten Model 15s which were designated FB-1 in Navy nomenclature, followed by a pair of FB-2s for aircraft carrier use. Because of design changes, the Boeing model number for the FB-2 was 53. Three FB-3s (Model 55) with Packard engines and an FB-4 (Model 54) followed. In October 1926 a Navy FB-3 set world speed records for pursuit planes at the National Air Races in Philadelphia. Such triumphs brought the attention that the

company would need to survive. Publicity was an important ingredient in the survival mixture.

Between 1923 and 1928 Boeing built 113 Model 15s (as PW-9) for the Army and 10 Model 15s (as FB-1) for the Navy. In 1926 an Army PW-9A was built as an advanced trainer and designated by the Army as AT-3, being given the Boeing model number 68. For the AT-3, the 435hp Curtiss was replaced by a 180hp Wright E engine.

In addition to the six variations in the Model 53–55 series, the Navy ordered 27 Packard-powered Model 67s, which were designated FB-5. Subsequent to its order of FB-5s, the Navy decided to discontinue use of aircraft with liquid-cooled engines aboard carriers, so they experimentally re-engined their FB-5s with a Pratt & Whitney 425hp air-cooled Wasp engine. This plane was then redesignated FB-6.

In May of 1924 the Army's complicated 1919 nomenclature for aircraft was scrapped in favor of a more simplified system. Under the old system a pursuit plane might have had one of five different prefix designations. PA stood for Pursuit, Air-cooled engine; PG for Pursuit, Ground attack; PN for Pursuit, Night; OS for Pursuit, Special alert and of course PW for Pursuit, Water-cooled engine. One is uncertain what horrible grief might have come to the Army's official giver of numbers should an aircraft with a PN prefix be found flying in the daytime with an air-cooled engine. After 1924, all pursuit planes, except those already in production like the PW-9 (which would retain their old nomenclature), were simply given the prefix P. Initial experimental prototypes of any series would continue also to be given an X for experimental, however.

Boeing's first Army contract under the new nomenclature was its Model 58 in 1926. The plane, designated XP-4 by the Army, was actually an outgrowth of the PW-9. It had a basic PW-9 airframe with longer wings and, for high altitude operations, the engine was fitted with a turbo-supercharger. The last PW-9, a PW-9D, was experimentally equipped with a 600hp Curtiss V-1570 as Boeing Model 93, and redesignated XP-7. Another stepchild of the PW-9 was Boeing's Model 66 which had an experimental inverted Packard engine and which was purchased by

Below: A Navy **FB-5 (Model 67)** designed for aircraft-carrier operation is seen here in September 1926 at the time of the first test flights.

Above: The **FB-4 (Model 54)**, seen here at the time of its delivery in January 1926, was equipped with a 400hp Wright P-1 radial engine. It was the lightest of the FB series and was redesignated FB-6 when retrofitted with a 425hp Pratt & Whitney R-1340B Wasp radial engine.

Specifications: PW-9C
Boeing Model Number 15

Span	32 ft
Length	23 ft 5 in
Wing Area	252 sq ft
Gross Weight	3170 pounds
Bomb Capacity	244 pounds
Top Speed	163 mph
Cruising Speed	142 mph
Range	390 miles
Service Ceiling	21,000 ft
Powerplant	one 435 hp Curtiss D-12C
Armament	two 0.3 in Browning machine guns, or one 0.3 in Browning plus one 0.5 in Browning

Specifications: FB-5
Boeing Model Number 67

Span	32 ft
Length	23 ft 9 in
Wing Area	241 sq ft
Gross Weight	3249 pounds (landplane)
	3593 pounds (seaplane)
Top Speed	176 mph
Range	420 miles
Service Ceiling	22,000 ft (landplane)
	17,800 ft (seaplane)
Powerplant	one 520 hp Packard 2A-1500
Armament	two 0.3 in Browning machine guns, or one 0.3 in Browning plus one 0.5 in Browning

Above: The **PB-1**, nicknamed the 'Flying Dreadnought,' is seen here during trials in August 1925. The PB-1 was the largest aircraft Boeing had built up to that time. To reduce weight the hull was constructed of aluminum below the water line and wood above.

Specifications: PB-1
Boeing Model Number 50

Span	87 ft 6 in
Length	59 ft 4 in
Wing Area	1801 sq ft
Gross Weight	23,500 lb
Bomb Capacity	2000 lb
Top Speed	112 mph
Cruising Speed	94 mph
Range	2450 miles
Service Ceiling	9000 ft
Powerplant	two 800 hp Packard 2A-2500
Armament	three 0.3 in Browning machine guns

The single prototype became the PB-2 when re-engined with the 800 hp Pratt & Whitney Hornet radials.

Specifications: F2B-1
Boeing Model Number 69

Span	30 ft 1 in
Length	23 ft
Wing Area	242 sq ft
Gross Weight	2804 pounds
Bomb Capacity	125 pounds
Top Speed	160 mph
Cruising Speed	132 mph
Range	358 miles
Service Ceiling	21,200 ft
Powerplant	one 425 hp Pratt & Whitney Wasp
Armament	one 0.3 in and one 0.5 in Browning machine gun

Specifications: XP-9
Boeing Model Number 96

Span	36 ft 6 in
Length	25 ft 2 in
Wing Area	210 sq ft
Gross Weight	3623 pounds
Bomb Capacity	125 pounds
Top Speed	213 mph
Cruising Speed	180 mph
Range	425 miles
Service Ceiling	26,800 ft
Powerplant	one 600 hp Curtiss Conqueror SV-1570-15 with F2A superchargers
Armament	two 0.3 in Browning machine guns

Above: The Army-designed **XP-9** was Boeing's first monoplane. With its unorthodox wing structure, dreaded by test pilots, it was probably the worst plane ever built by Boeing.

Below: The Navy **F2B-1**, seen here in September 1927 prior to its first delivery, was an outgrowth of the FB-4 and FB-6 experiments as well as Boeing's experience with the Army XP-8.

the Army as XP-8. Only a single prototype of each of these three models was built.

The XP-9 (Model 96), Boeing's first monoplane, was designed at Army request and built with the single wing fixed to the fuselage directly ahead of the cockpit. On the single prototype, this configuration was shown to restrict the pilot's vision so severely (the test pilot called it a menace) that the whole design concept was swiftly scrapped.

While it was building the various derivatives of the Model 15 pursuit plane for both services, Boeing was also undertaking a couple of quite different projects for the Navy. In 1925 the Navy requested a flying boat capable of flying the 2400 miles from the US mainland to Hawaii non-stop. The result was Boeing's Model 50, Navy designation PB-1 (Patrol, Bomber). The PB-1, with an 87 feet 6 inches wingspan, was the largest aircraft yet built by Boeing. The Navy later redesignated the single PB-1 as PB-2 when they replaced the two liquid-cooled 800hp Packard engines with a pair of Pratt & Whitney Hornet air-cooled radials. In 1927 the Navy ordered three Boeing Model 63s, which were designated TB-1 for Torpedo, Bomber. The TB-1 was a twin pontoon seaplane designed to be used as either a reconnaissance aircraft or as a torpedo bomber with the torpedo slung under the fuselage between the pontoons. The versatile TB-1 was also designed to operate with wheels from the deck of an aircraft carrier.

While the PW-9s evolved into the P-4, P-7 and P-8 in Army service, their twin brothers, the Navy FBs, were spawning further developments. The F2B-1 (in Navy nomenclature FB was the equivalent of F1B), Boeing's Model 69, was a carrier-based fighter incorporating the use of the 425hp Pratt & Whitney Wasp that had been tested in the FB-6. The Navy bought the XF2B-1 prototype and 32 production F2B-1s between 1926 and 1928. Boeing exported two of the planes as Model 69B. In 1927 Model 74, a further improved F2B, was presented under the designation XF3B-1. After initial flight tests, the plane was sent back to Boeing for redesigning. The result was the Model 77 (F3B-1) with larger wings and greatly enhanced high altitude performance. In 1928 the Navy received 73 F3Bs.

A lesson learned was a lesson never forgotten. Mistakes flushed out in designs were not slipped into a lower drawer. They marched side by side with successes, and this mating of information was to serve well in the coming years. This policy was one of the great strengths of the company.

Left: **F3B-1** fighters prepare to take off from the flight deck of the USS *Saratoga* (CV-3) circa 1929. In addition to its service as a carrier-based fighter, the F3B could also operate as a seaplane and be catapulted from the decks of battleships or cruisers.

Above: The **TB-1** torpedo bomber was designed as a replacement for the Martin T3M. A large aircraft, its wings could be folded for storage aboard aircraft carriers. The bombardier's position can be seen on the bottom of the plane below the cockpit.

Specifications: F3B-1
Boeing Model Number 77

Span	33 ft
Length	24 ft 10 in
Wing Area	275 sq ft
Gross Weight	2945 pounds
Bomb Capacity	125 pounds
Top Speed	156 mph
Cruising Speed	131 mph
Range	340 miles
Service Ceiling	21,500 ft
Powerplant	one 450 hp Pratt & Whitney Wasp
Armament	one 0.3 in and one 0.5 in Browning machine gun

Specifications: TB-1
Boeing Model Number 63

Span	55 ft
Length	40 ft 10 in
Wing Area	868 sq ft
Gross Weight	9786 pounds
Bomb Capacity	one 1740 pound torpedo
Top Speed	115 mph
Cruising Speed	100 mph
Range	878 miles
Service Ceiling	12,500 ft
Powerplant	one 730 hp Packard 3A-2500
Armament	two 0.3 in Browning machine guns

In 1928 eight improved versions of the B-1 flying boat (Model 6), Boeing's first flying boat, that had made its initial lift off from the waters of Lake Union nine years before were built. Improved structural innovations and more power were built into the B-1, and the resulting plane was called the Model 204. One of these was a dual-control ship, the 204A, especially engineered for Bill Boeing himself. Four of the eight constructed were built by Boeing-Canada, and were called Model C-204 *Thunderbirds*.

While Boeing was being blessed with continued success in designing and building military aircraft, Claire Egtvedt had been toying with the idea of starting a passenger service in the Northwest. A route connecting Seattle, Vancouver and Victoria might be expected to pay off. It might have paid handsomely had there not come a knock on the door from Eddie Hubbard. Hubbard, who had earlier operated an air mail route through the same airspace, appeared in Egtvedt's office. He was excited about a new proposal. The Post Office department was about to let its air mail run from Chicago to San Francisco go into private hands. The stipulation was that the successful bidder would have to furnish 25 planes by 1 July 1927. Hubbard was certain that the Boeing Airplane Company could compete successfully.

Egtvedt was doubtful. He pointed out the hazards of the night flying which would be necessary. Hubbard countered with a proposal for setting up searchlights every 25 miles. For every doubt Hubbard had a solution, and as he argued for his idea, Egtvedt's doubts diminished. After all, Eddie was an experienced airman, and Egtvedt listened with respect. It was decided to present the idea to Bill Boeing, and they went to the Hoge Building together. To their dismay, Boeing was not for the idea. He had the same doubts as Claire Egtvedt, and remained adamant – at first. After the men left his office, he mulled the plan over. That night he talked to his wife about it, and she suggested that Hubbard was right.

The next morning he called Egtvedt, and gave the green light. Twenty-five Model 40 airplanes quickly went into production. The Model 40 had been designed, and a prototype built, for a Post Office competition two years earlier. The Post Office had bought the prototype and nothing more, so the Model 40 program sat on the shelf for two years. The 40s were powered with a 420hp Pratt & Whitney air-cooled engine, and had an all-steel frame. They were capable of carrying two passengers, and a thousand pounds of mail.

Specifications: Model 204
Boeing Model Number 204

Span	39 ft 8 in
Length	32 ft 7 in
Wing Area	470 sq ft
Gross Weight	4940 pounds
Cruising Speed	95 mph
Service Ceiling	9000 ft
Range	350 miles
Powerplant	one 410 hp Pratt & Whitney Wasp
Capacity	4 passengers

Specifications: Model 203A
Boeing Model Number 203A

Span	34 ft
Length	24 ft 4 in
Gross Weight	2625 pounds
Cruising Speed	92 mph
Range	400 miles
Powerplant	one 165 hp Wright Whirlwind

Below: The **Model 203** was built exclusively for use by the Boeing School of Aeronautics, the flying-school division of Boeing Air Transport established at the Oakland, California, Municipal Airport on 16 September 1929 to provide training for BAT personnel. The school was acquired as part of BAT by United Airlines in 1934 and its activities were suspended 1 August 1942, by which time 2801 students from around the world had graduated.

Above: The **Model 204** was the ultimate fisherman's plane. The dedicated fisherman could climb into a 204 after a busy week at the office, be whisked to a remote and unspoiled lake in the far reaches of British Columbia or the Cascades and catch a creelfull of rainbow trout, literally a few steps from the flying boat.

LIEUT.
BERNARD
THOMPSON

CAPT.
CLAIR
STREETT

CLAIR
VANCE

HAROLD
LEWIS

LIEUT.
NEWTON
LONGFELLOW

CAPTAIN
IRA
EAKER

BOEING HORNET
SHUTTLE

Above: In 1929 Boeing carried out its earliest air-to-air refueling experiments using a Boeing **Model 95** mail plane known as the *Hornet Shuttle* as a receiver and a Boeing **Model 40B** as tanker. In these tests a trailing hose was extended from the tanker and the two airplanes were flown into position so a receiver crew member could grasp the nozzle and fit it into the fuel-tank filler pipe. The men pictured were company and Army fliers who accomplished a transcontinental flight from Oakland to New York with aerial refueling over Elko, Nevada, Cheyenne, Wyoming, Omaha and Cleveland, Ohio.

Far right: Three view of a Boeing **Model 40**.

Below: A **40B-4** in Pacific Air Transport (the Boeing System) markings parked in front of the company administration building on Boeing Field in May 1930.

BOEING
C
5390
DIABLO

US
MAIL
C.A.M. 8

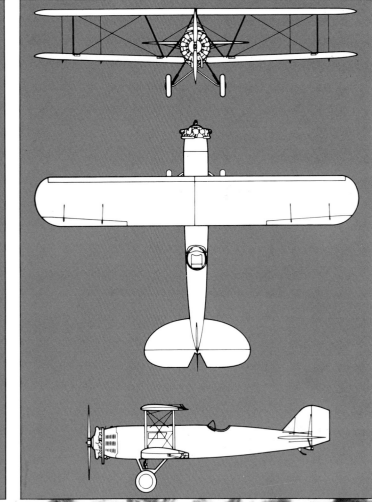

Specifications: Model 40
Boeing Model Number 40

Span	44 ft 2 in
Length	33 ft 2 in
Wing Area	547 sq ft
Gross Weight	5495 pounds
Cruising Speed	135 mph
Service Ceiling	15,800 ft
Range	700 miles
Powerplant	one 400 hp Liberty
Capacity	2 passengers (but principally a mail plane)

Specifications: Model 40B-4
Boeing Model Number 40B-4

Span	44 ft 2 in
Length	33 ft 3 in
Wing Area	545 sq ft
Gross Weight	6075 pounds
Cruising Speed	125 mph
Service Ceiling	16,100 ft
Range	535 miles
Powerplant	one 525 hp Pratt & Whitney Hornet
Capacity	2 passengers

On 1 July 1927, they were lined up, ready to go. The mail contract, bid under the name of Edward Hubbard and Boeing Airplane Company, was won easily – so easily, in fact, that the Post Office officials frowned. The bid, they felt, was too low – an opinion shared by others. But the new operators were successful. The lighter Wasp engine enabled them to carry the two paying passengers, and that made the difference. During the first year of operation 1863 passengers paid $400 each to fly the route.

This was a time of great expansion among airline companies. The Ford Motor Company developed an all-metal trimotor airplane, which carried 15 passengers. Pilots affectionately called it the 'tin goose,' and it was widely used by both the military and civilians. Commander Richard Byrd was to fly a Ford Trimotor in his triumphant flight over the South Pole in November 1929. The Curtiss Condor appeared in 1929, carrying 18 passengers. It was soundproofed, and the cabin was heated, something new in passenger comfort. European air companies had also been moving ahead for some time in the civilian transportation market. The German Junkers F-13, an all-metal, low-wing monoplane produced early in 1919, was called the 'father of world civil aviation.' The Fokker F-3, another development, carried five passengers, and was popular in Europe in the 1920s. A Farman Goliath had the distinction of carrying the first international civilian passengers on a flight from Paris to London on 8 February 1919. The Europeans were ahead in the passenger business, but that did not deter Bill Boeing. With the success of the Model 40, he thought a larger plane should be created. The result was the Model 80, which was delivered to Boeing Air Transport in August 1928. BAT was the wholly-owned subsidiary set up by Boeing to carry passengers and mail.

The Model 80 had room for 12 passengers in a heated cabin with hot and cold running water. There was forced air ventilation, individual reading lamps, and leather upholstery. The pilot and co-pilot sat in a forward cabin, closed off from passengers. They kept on top of weather conditions by using a two-way radio system, developed in part by Western Electric.

The 80 was so successful that the 80A was a natural successor. This large trimotored craft was powered by larger Pratt & Whitney Hornet engines. The same luxury appeared in the cabin, but there was more. It had been noticed that occasionally passengers needed attention, especially in rough skies, so registered nurses were employed as flight attendants and box lunches were also served.

The Boeing Airplane Company was now on firm financial ground, an established business, a force to be reckoned with in the fiercely competitive world of airplane manufacture. This was only the beginning. Officials of the company, including Bill Boeing, Claire Egtvedt and Phil Johnson, knew that air travel

Below: The **Model 80B**, seen here in July 1930, was a variation on the 80A designed with an open cockpit because pilots liked the feel of wind in their faces.

Right: The **Model 80s** operated by the Boeing system were the last word in luxury. There were leather upholstered seats, reading lamps and the first-ever airline stewardesses.

had only started. A door had been opened, and through it interested observers saw vast skies of promise. Flying in the 1920s and 1930s was not, however, fully integrated into the American consciousness. The rich could afford to fly, the adventurous took wing and business people saw the advantage of swift travel. The man in the street, meanwhile, still preferred train and boat, and, increasingly, private automobile.

Questions lay unsolved in the public's mind. Was air travel safe? Could it not cost a bit less? A passenger paid up to $900 for passage across the States. Was flying not still more of a plaything than a serious mode of travel? There was another problem, too. Once an airplane reached its final destination, that did not necessarily mean the passenger's journey was over. It was often necessary to transfer to a train or a car. That was a nuisance. Airports had not yet been established in sufficient numbers to accommodate trunk lines and air taxi services. There was one more problem, and this was admitted by the air industry as serious. Airplanes were noisy, and made the skeptical nervous. Soundproofing was still more idea than fact. Noise kept passengers away, so something would have to be done about noise! With commercial airplane sales an on-and-off matter, manufacturers suffered. In order to survive, Boeing and other companies continued to go after military orders. Uncle Sam was a valuable customer.

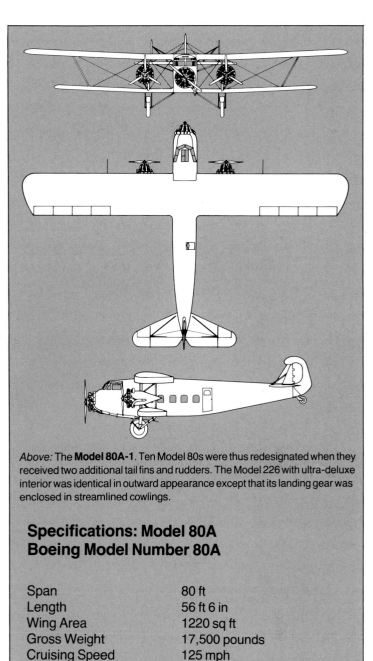

Above: The **Model 80A-1**. Ten Model 80s were thus redesignated when they received two additional tail fins and rudders. The Model 226 with ultra-deluxe interior was identical in outward appearance except that its landing gear was enclosed in streamlined cowlings.

Specifications: Model 80A
Boeing Model Number 80A

Span	80 ft
Length	56 ft 6 in
Wing Area	1220 sq ft
Gross Weight	17,500 pounds
Cruising Speed	125 mph
Service Ceiling	14,000 ft
Range	460 miles
Powerplant	three 525 hp Pratt & Whitney Hornets
Capacity	18 passengers

Specifications: Model 80
Boeing Model Number 80

Span	80 ft
Length	54 ft 11 in
Wing Area	1220 sq ft
Gross Weight	15,276 pounds
Cruising Speed	115 mph
Service Ceiling	14,000 ft
Range	545 miles
Powerplant	three 425 hp Pratt & Whitney Wasps
Capacity	12 pasengers

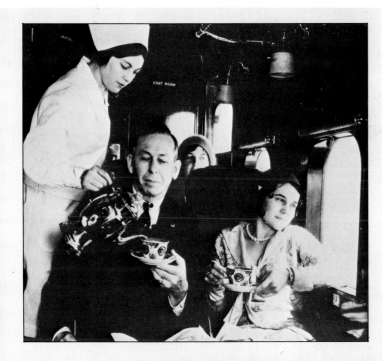

Above: A **Model 80A** parked on the east side of Boeing Field in August 1929.

Above: The colors depicted in this restoration are typical of the Army color scheme of the early 1930s (the kicking-mule emblem was the insignia of the 95th Pursuit Squadron). The **P-12B** and the export Model 100 generally did not have their engines enclosed with the bulky cowling typical of most later aircraft in the P-12/F4B series.

Right: A restored Stearman **Kaydet Model 75** biplane. The Kaydet was Lloyd Stearman's most successful design and became a Boeing plane when Bill Boeing bought him out in 1934.

Above: The ubiquitous Stearman **Kaydet** was a sound and durable little plane. It can be found to this day parked at small airports, dusting crops or pulling banners from California to the Carolinas.

Below: The **P-26A 'Peashooter'** was probably Boeing's most famous Army pursuit plane. The example shown here is painted in the colors of the 34th Pursuit Squadron (17th Pursuit Group), which was based at March Field, California, in 1934.

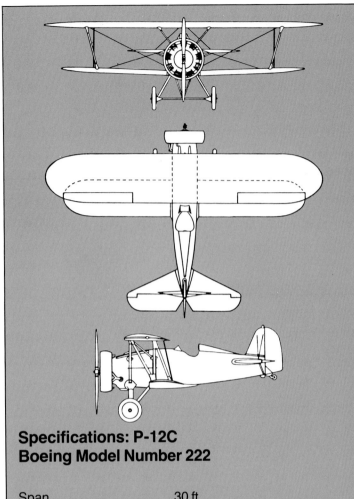

Specifications: P-12C
Boeing Model Number 222

Span	30 ft
Length	20 ft 1 in
Wing Area	228 sq ft
Gross Weight	2629 pounds
Top Speed	178 mph
Cruising Speed	150 mph
Range	675 miles
Service Ceiling	26,200 ft
Powerplant	one 450 hp Pratt & Whitney R-1340-9 Wasp
Armament	two 0.3 in Browning machine guns

Specifications: Model P-12F
Boeing Model Number 251

Span	30 ft
Length	20 ft 3 in
Wing Area	227.5 sq ft
Gross Weight	2726 pounds
Bomb Capacity	232 pounds
Top Speed	194 mph
Cruising Speed	180 mph
Range	300 miles
Service Ceiling	31,400 ft
Powerplant	one 600 hp Pratt & Whitney R-1340-19 Wasp
Armament	two 0.3 in Browning machine guns

Early in 1928, Boeing presented two prototype pursuit planes to the Navy for consideration. They were Models 83 and 89, and the company had built them at its own expense. Executives were confident that prior experience in constructing this type of aircraft would be a favorable factor. Hopes were justified, and the gamble bore fruit in a series of pursuit planes that were to become Boeing's most successful aircraft design of the period between World War I and World War II. The use of bolted aluminum in the fuselage structure, instead of the standard welded steel tubing, which Boeing had earlier promoted as being superior to wood, was a selling feature. Aluminum meant less weight. Less weight meant more speed, and speed was always important in a pursuit design.

Following tests of both the Model 83 and 89, as the XF4B-1, the Navy ordered 27 to be used as carrier-based fighter-bombers. An improved Boeing Model 99 became the Navy's F4B-1. The Army, on the basis of the tests, ordered 10 of the airplanes; the first, Boeing Model 101, was designated XP-12A, the other nine would be the P-12, which was Boeing's Model 102.

While initial production got underway, four commercial and export derivatives were developed as the Model 100. A special two-seater, the 100A, was also built. Two 100s were kept by Boeing, and used extensively in developing improved features to be used in manufacturing 90 P-12Bs (Model 102B), 96 P-12Cs (Model 222), 46 F4B-2s (Model 223), and 35 P-12Ds (Model 227).

In 1930, a major structural development was tested in the Model 218, which utilized a semi-monocoque duraluminum fuselage. Both the Army and Navy tested the 218, and placed large orders. The single prototype was sold to China in 1932.

In March 1931 the Army ordered 135 P-12Es, Boeing's Model 234, as a result of the 218 tests. This was the largest order the company had received since 1921, when it was contracted with to build the 200 Thomas-Morse MB-3As. The Navy followed with an order for 113 similar airplanes (Model 235) as 21 F4B-3s, and 92 F4B-4s. The latter had larger vertical tail surfaces for tighter control. Fourteen F4B-4s were exported to Brazil and nine additional aircraft combining features of both the P-12E and the

Above: The **F4B-4 (Model 235)** was the most popular Navy fighter that Boeing was ever to produce. Seventy-one served the Navy as carrier fighters until 1938 and another 21 went to the Marines.

Below: Captain Ira Eaker beside an early Army Air Corps **P-12 (Model 102)** on 26 February 1929. Captain Eaker, who was to be a participant in the first aerial refueling experiments (see p 36), was closely associated with Boeing's B-17 Flying Fortress during World War II when, as General Eaker, he commanded the Eighth Air Force in England.

Below: The Stearman **Kaydet** served as a trainer with the US Navy and the US Army Air Force as well as the air forces of a number of foreign countries, including China, Great Britain, Brazil, Argentina, Canada and the Philippines. This Kaydet, now based at the Sonoma County Airport in California, has been restored with British Royal Air Force markings.

F4B-3 were sold to Brazil as Model 267s. The last variants for the Army were 25 P-12Es completed as P-12Fs (Model 251), although modifications by the Army resulted in model designations through P-12L.

Counting all models in the overall series, 586 airplanes were sold. The last one was an F4B-4, delivered to the Navy on 28 February 1933, although it may be said that the last plane in the series was a single prototype biplane, the XF6B-1 (Model 236) which was also delivered in 1933. The all-metal XF6B-1 sought to include the best of everything from the whole P-12/F4B program.

By the early 30s, however, the era of the biplane pursuit aircraft was clearly drawing to a close. Boeing was looking to develop a monoplane successor to the P-12/F4B. A pair of nearly identical all-metal monoplane prototypes, Model 202 and Model 205, were produced. One went to the Army as XP-15 and one to the Navy as XF5B-1. Though neither was put into production, the monoplane design experience was to prove invaluable to the Boeing engineers as the monoplane era dawned.

Specifications: F4B-4
Boeing Model Number 235

Span	30 ft
Length	20 ft 5 in
Wing Area	228 sq ft
Gross Weight	2898 pounds
Bomb Capacity	232 pounds
Top Speed	187 mph
Cruising Speed	160 mph
Range	585 miles
Service Ceiling	27,500 ft
Powerplant	one 550 hp Pratt & Whitney R-1340-16 Wasp
Armament	two 0.3 in Browning machine guns

Below: The **XF6B-1 (Model 236)** compared to its predecessor, the highly successful F4B-4 (*inset, left*). The XF6B was really the ultimate F4B, incorporating and refining all of the best features of that classic. Only one F6B was built, however, since the type became a victim of the trend toward monoplanes.

Specifications: XF6B-1
Boeing Model Number 236

Span	28 ft 6 in
Length	22 ft 2 in
Wing Area	252 sq ft
Gross Weight	3704 pounds
Bomb Capacity	700 pounds
Top Speed	200 mph
Cruising Speed	170 mph
Range	525 miles
Service Ceiling	24,400 ft
Powerplant	one 625 hp Pratt & Whitney R-1535-44 Twin Wasp Jr
Armament	two 0.3 in Browning machine guns

Specifications: XP-15
Boeing Model Number 202

Span	30 ft 6 in
Length	21 ft
Wing Area	157 sq ft
Gross Weight	2746 pounds
Top Speed	190 mph
Cruising Speed	160 mph
Range	420 miles
Service Ceiling	26,550 ft
Powerplant	one 525 hp Pratt & Whitney Wasp SR-1340D
Armament	two 0.3 in Browning machine guns

Below: The Army Air Corps **XP-15 (Model 202)** and its Navy sister ship XF5B-1 (Model 205) were submitted to the respective services in 1930 as possible monoplane successors to the P-12/F4B series.

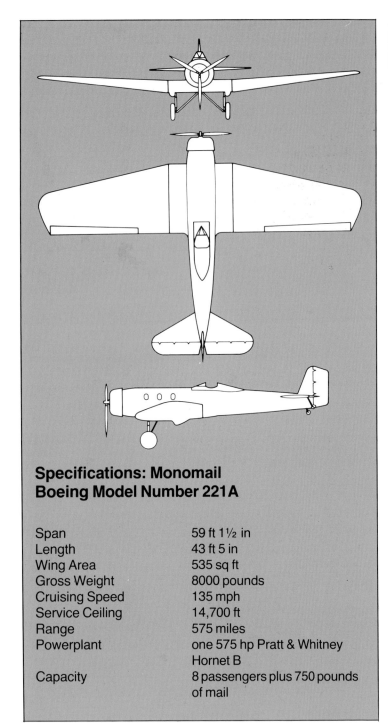

Specifications: Monomail
Boeing Model Number 221A

Span	59 ft 1½ in
Length	43 ft 5 in
Wing Area	535 sq ft
Gross Weight	8000 pounds
Cruising Speed	135 mph
Service Ceiling	14,700 ft
Range	575 miles
Powerplant	one 575 hp Pratt & Whitney Hornet B
Capacity	8 passengers plus 750 pounds of mail

It was Eddie Hubbard again who first advanced the notion of an all-metal monoplane transport. Even though he was not working for Boeing, it was still natural for him to bring his ideas to the people he knew at Boeing. He was a Boeing man at heart and both Claire Egtvedt and Bill Boeing himself were usually receptive to Eddie's ideas. Hubbard, in fact, rejoined the Company as vice-president in charge of operations, but before he could witness the fruits of his efforts, he died suddenly and unexpectedly on 18 December 1928. Nevertheless, the Boeing engineers were already at work. The new airplane, Boeing Model 200, would become the *Monomail*, and the work was kept secret. 'Borrowing' by designers working for rival plane makers was always possible, and secrecy was necessary. When the *Monomail* was first flown by test pilot Eddie Allen on 22 May 1930, Seattle people witnessed a plane unlike anything they had ever seen before.

It was a sleek, dark ship, truly streamlined, and has been called the first modern air transport. The combination of an all-metal, semi-monocoque construction, together with a single, low wing of cantilever design, and retractable landing gear, put the *Monomail* ahead of its time in aerodynamic design. The drag of the engine was reduced by enclosing it in a newly developed 'anti-drag' cowling. Advanced design, rather than brute strength, achieved major performance increases. The pilot, however, still flew the plane from an open cockpit.

The first *Monomail*, (the first airplane of Boeing design to carry a proper name), was fitted to haul only mail and cargo. A second airplane was built that featured a six-passenger cabin, based on that of Boeing's well-known Model 40. The second *Monomail* (Boeing Model 221) also took up to 750 pounds of cargo and mail, but the pilot still sat in the lone glory of an open cockpit. Many pilots of the time preferred the style, claiming an inside cabin made it difficult to see what they were doing. They wanted the feel of the weather, and a clear, unobstructed look at both the sky and ground, the better to fly their craft.

The *Monomail* did not catch on as Boeing hoped. A major drawback was its design, which was too advanced for current development in propellers and powerplants. The efficient use of the *Monomail*'s capabilities required a coarse-pitch propeller for takeoff and climb, and a fine-pitch for cruising. By the time a variable pitch prop was ready the Boeing 247 had superseded the *Monomail*.

A direct offspring of the *Monomail* was the B-9 bomber. There were two versions, Boeing Models 214 and 215 which became the Army's Y1B-9 and YB-9 respectively. The Y prefix indicated that

Below: The **Model 200 Monomail** was 8 inches shorter but cruised 23mph faster than the Model 221 Monomail.

Right: Mail sacks are loaded into the forward cargo compartments of the single **Model 200**.

Below: Two planes ahead of their time. In the foreground is the original **Y1B-9A (Model 246)** with original tail. Behind it is Boeing's prototype for the P-26 series originally designated by Boeing **XP-936 (Model 248)**.

the Army considered the prototypes to be service test rather than experimental aircraft. The Y prefix generally denotes the intermediate step between experimental (X prefix) and production aircraft (no prefix). The intervening 1 was used in designations between 1931 and 1936 to indicate that the specific aircraft was purchased with supplementary (F-1) funds rather than regular fiscal year funding.

The B-9 was an outstanding airplane. First flying on 29 April 1931 with a pair of 600hp Pratt & Whitney Hornets, it cruised at nearly 160mph, faster than most contemporary pursuit planes! An Army purchase order was issued in August 1931 for the two prototypes and an additional five more advanced Model 246s which were designated Y1B-9A. The B-9, while never ordered in quantity, was a tremendous technological leap from the biplane bombers that dominated the Army bomber squadrons at the time. It was a true turning point, and pointed the way to the B-17s and B-29s that were to follow.

The most famous of Boeing's between-the-wars pursuit planes was the P-26. Here, once more, Bill Boeing and his key executives, Claire Egtvedt and Phil Johnson, took the matter into their own

Specifications: Y1B-9A
Boeing Model Number 246

Span	76 ft
Length	51 ft 5 in
Wing Area	960 sq ft
Tail Height	12 ft 9 in
Gross Weight	13,919 pounds
Bomb Capacity	2400 pounds
Top Speed	186 mph
Cruising Speed	158 mph
Range	1150 miles
Service Ceiling	20,150 ft
Powerplant	two 600 hp Pratt & Whitney R-1860-11 Hornets
Armament	two 0.3 in Browning machine guns in nose and rear cockpit

Above: These Army **P-26As** carry the insignia of the 20th Pursuit Group which was based at Barksdale Field, Louisiana, in 1936.

Below: Three view of the **P-26A.**

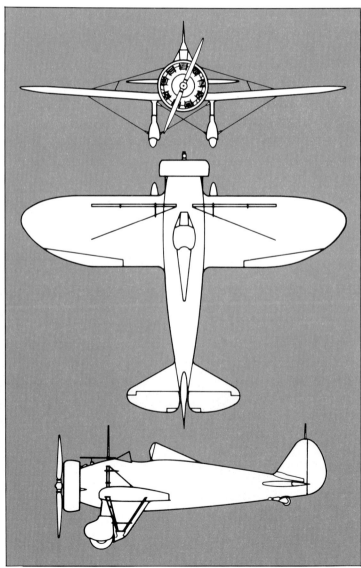

Specifications: P-26A
Boeing Model Number 266

Span	28 ft
Length	23 ft 7 in
Wing Area	149 sq ft
Gross Weight	2995 pounds
Bomb Capacity	200 pounds
Top Speed	234 mph
Cruising Speed	200 mph
Range	635 miles
Service Ceiling	27,400 ft
Powerplant	one 600 hp Pratt & Whitney R-1340-27 Wasp
Armament	two 0.3 in Browning or one 0.5 in plus one 0.3 in Browning machine gun

hands. Feeling that a better fighter could be built than even their own P-12, by using new techniques learned on the *Monomail* and B-9 programs, the latest brain-child went on the drafting boards as the Boeing Model 248.

Three of these monoplane aircraft were assembled, at Boeing expense, between January and March 1932. The design was closely coordinated with the Army, to assure that military requirements were met. Though Boeing was willing to gamble his own money, smart business sense led the company to cover as many bases as possible. The powerplants, instruments, and military equipment were lent to the company by the Army.

After testing the XP-936, the Army bought the three proto-types, changing the designation to XP-26. These became the Y1P-26 for service testing, and, finally, P-26.

One hundred and thirty-six production Model 266s were ordered, 111 of these as the P-26A, two as the P-26B, and 23 as the P-26C. All P-26s were later modified by the addition of wing flaps to reduce their high landing speed to that of contemporary biplanes. Twelve export versions of the P-26 were manufactured, 11 for China, and one for Spain.

US Army pilots liked the sleek P-26, referring to it, affectionately, as the 'little pea shooter.' A squadron of P-26As was turned over to the Philippine Army in late 1941. One of these became one of the first Allied fighters to down a Japanese airplane, when Philippine installations were attacked in December 1941, at the beginning of the Pacific War. Though quickly replaced by better armed and armored fighters in the technological boom that accompanied the war, the P-26 was a fine plane, and holds an honored place in the history of aircraft.

I n 1934 the Boeing Airplane Company acquired the Stearman Aircraft Company of Wichita, Kansas which became first a Boeing subsidiary and then in 1939, the Wichita Division of Boeing. In purchasing the Stearman Company, Boeing inherited an outstanding little biplane trainer called the Kaydet. Designed by Lloyd Stearman as the Model 70, it was used as a training airplane for both the US Army and Navy, and many foreign air forces. When World War II called for more trainers, the Boeing Wichita plant moved into full production. Several variations of

Specifications: Stearman Kaydet (PT-13/N2S-5) Boeing Model Number 75

Span	32 ft
Length	25 ft 0¼ in
Wing Area	298 sq ft
Gross Weight	2810 pounds
Top Speed	122 mph
Cruising Speed	107 mph
Ferry Range	440 miles
Service Ceiling	11,700 ft
Powerplant	one 220 hp Lycoming R-680

When most of the existing Kaydets were converted to agricultural aircraft after World War II they were re-engined with 450 hp Pratt & Whitney Wasp Jrs.

the Model 70 appeared as the Boeing Model 75, Army designation PT-13, PT-17 and PT-18; Navy designation N2S. Though the Kaydet was not an original Boeing design, it brought pride and honor to the parent company by training more than 60,000 cadets to fly.

After the war, over 4000 Kaydets were converted to crop-dusting planes. More than 30 years after hostilities, nearly 1600 are still in service someplace. It was a plane built to last.

Counting all models of the Kaydet, from the 70 through Model 76, 10,346 were built between 1934 and 1945. This, in itself, was a fine achievement.

Military sales were important to the aircraft industry. The government's pocketbook, if not always bountiful, was available when other pocketbooks were not.

The Boeing Airplane Company was to remain involved in the manufacture of military aircraft, but company eyes studied other markets, too. Executives felt that more attention should be paid to civilian markets if their firm was to remain healthy. With that in mind, it was decided to make a deeper thrust into civilian skies.

Below: The US Army Air Corps primary trainer version of the Stearman Kaydet was originally designated **PT-13 (Boeing Model 75)**, however, later versions such as this A75N1 were redesignated PT-17 and PT-17A.

THE FLYING PULLMANS

Along with the building of the B-9 bomber, other plans had advanced for a new concept in commercial aircraft. If the *Monomail* had been revolutionary, the Boeing Model 247 would push that concept to the limits of technological experience – and a little beyond. With every Boeing design, something new had been added.

Bill Boeing believed in using lessons of the past, mistakes and successes, but he also believed in men. He was a shrewd judge of character. Even so, he could not have seen how acute his own judgement was the day he picked Claire L Egtvedt and Philip Johnson to work for him in 1917. They loved airplanes and they were leaders. They were dreamers with their dreams based on the possible, not the impossible, and their eyes were on the future. They took chances when it came to be their turn to lead the company, and they lost some, gained some, just as Bill Boeing had done. The airplane business in the 1930s was still a chancy business, and air travel had yet to win hearty public support. But this did not deter Boeing, Egtvedt or Johnson. They made plans.

The Boeing Airplane Company had acquired the Hamilton Aero Manufacturing Company in 1929. This was to become the Hamilton Standard Propeller Corporation, and it developed the variable pitch propeller. The *Monomail* lacked this innovation

Below: A **Model 247D** in the markings adopted by UAL after it ceased to be a part of Boeing, across Boeing Field from Plant 2.

and died young. The Model 247 acquired it, and that made a difference.

The Model 247's design had actually been on the drafting boards before the B-9 was completed. It was a remarkable ship in that it was the first streamlined, all-metal transport in America. Taking lessons from the B-9, the 247's engines were mounted in nacelles that flowed into the wing. This was an anti-drag advantage that helped the airplane to fly up to 70 miles an hour faster than its competitors. And, as with the *Monomail*, the landing gear folded neatly into the wings. With such attention paid to the problem of drag, the 247 was the first twin-engined monoplane able to climb on one engine with a full load. Details of the new aircraft were circulated among the several airlines that comprised the Boeing Air Transport System (soon to become United Air Lines). Boeing Air Transport placed an order for 60, even while the plane was still in mockup stage.

Although smaller than the Boeing Model 80, the speedy 247 supplied most of the 'Flying Pullman's' comforts to its ten passengers. There were no berths, but the seating was spaced with plenty of leg room, and there was no rackety engine noise. Lessons from the noisy Model 40 and 80 had been carried forward to the 247, and sound-proofing was born. The crew was made up of two pilots and a stewardess.

The 247 was a twin-engined monoplane, leaving the nose space vacant. The empty area was occupied by additional radio equip-ment and 400 pounds of mail. A new feature for airliners was the installation of supercharged engines, and pneumatically operated de-icer 'boots' on the leading edges of the wings and tail surfaces. Ice was a major handicap, sheeting the wings in such a way as to change aerodynamic configuration. This caused a loss in efficiency and control.

The first 247 flew in February 1933, and all 60 were delivered to United Air Lines within a year. Further sales brought the total to 75. These included a special 247A with newly developed 625hp twin-row P&W engines for both domestic and foreign customers. A special militarized 247Y was sold to a private owner in China.

In 1934 a 247 was modified for Roscoe Turner and Clyde Pangborn, as the 247D. They were to fly it as an American entry in the McRobertson race from England to Australia. The airline furnishings were removed, and extra fuel tanks added. The 247D placed third in the overall race, second in the transport category. In order to attain this victory, the major change was from fixed propeller to the Hamilton Standard hydraulically controlled variable-pitch propeller. This change enabled the 247D to cruise seven miles an hour faster than the original. After that, most of the 247s were equipped with the new Hamilton Standard, and were designated 247D.

Boeing designers also added another invention, 'trim tab control,' on the 247. These were small, tab-like, movable surfaces on the ailerons, rudder and elevators, which used the airstream

Above: **Libby Wurgaft**, a stewardess with UAL while it was still part of Boeing, playfully dons her skates prior to going to work on a scheduled flight aboard a 247.

Below: His office in the sky. A Phillips Petroleum executive confers with the office from the company-owned **247D**.

itself to help control large surfaces. Pilots no longer had to have the muscles of Hercules to steer a large airplane. Though a small thing in itself, servo trim tabs were a key contribution to future big plane designs.

The Boeing 247, along with Douglas DC-2s and DC-3s, ushered in a new era of civil aviation. The 247 design won Bill Boeing the 1934 Guggenheim Medal for 'Successful pioneering and advancement in aircraft manufacturing and transport.'

It was a versatile airplane and pioneered the skies far from established routes. It became acquainted with make-do landing fields in Mexico, northern Canada and Alaska, hauling everything from passengers to dynamite. One of the strangest cargoes recorded was one of 26 babies. This event took place in December 1944. The infants, packed three to a crib, were loaded on a 247 and flown from Quebec to Chicoutimi. The babies were from LaCreche Saint Vincent-de-Paul Orphanage, and were traveling to new homes. The flight lasted for an hour, but was so smooth the children awoke only after landing.

Because of its quick acceptance of conditions, (one was nicknamed 'Adaptable Annie'), the 247 was supreme on American airways for two years. In addition to its ease in meeting unusual circumstances, the 247 could fly across the United States in $19\frac{1}{2}$ hours, cutting $7\frac{1}{2}$ hours off previous airliner time.

After the United States entered World War II, a number of the 247s were drafted into the US Army Air Force. Given the designation of C-73, they were used for both transport and training duties. At the end of the war, the planes were released and acquired by small airlines in the US and abroad. Though she performed well in the war, the 247 also made another contribution that was important long after hostilities. The idea of coupling an autopilot to an Instrument Landing System, ILS, enabling an airplane to fly itself down to land was tried first at Delford, England, in 1944. The aircraft used in this experiment was the famous Adaptable Annie, and it was a success. All modern automatic landing systems in use around the world evolved from these first flights.

Below: **Amelia Earhart**, the world famous aviatrix, waves from the cockpit of a Boeing 247.

Inset: **Ms Earhart** is joined by Erik Nelson and Mrs W E Boeing, during a visit to Seattle, and Boeing's Plant 2 during the early 1930s.

Although the 247 was a great airplane, only 75 were sold. Along with its success came that of the Douglas models, the DC-2 and the DST, for Douglas Sleeper Transport, Model DC-3. United Airlines and other large companies switched to the speedier 190mph Douglas transports. The DST was fitted with berths for 14 people, and was equipped with separate dressing rooms for men and women. As a day plane, when berths were not used, the DC-3 carried 21 passengers, 11 more than Boeing's 247. In 1940, 80 percent of airplanes on scheduled routes in the United States were DC-3s. It was a tough competitor. With the failure of 247 sales, the Boeing Airplane Company experienced a financial slump. Lean times had come again.

In 1934, even as Bill Boeing was being awarded his Guggenheim Medal, the Federal Government belatedly accused Boeing and other airlines of collusion in acquiring mail contracts. This went back to a time when, in the late 1920s, the Postmaster General had summoned the leaders of airline companies to his Washington office. The purpose was to talk about those contracts. That, declared the government in 1934, was favoritism, and unfair practice. Something would have to be done to make it right.

In February 1934 President Franklin Roosevelt signed White House Order No. 6591. It cancelled private mail contracts, and directed that Army fliers take over air routes. The results were chaotic. The Army pilots were good, but were not prepared for this kind of duty. They were unaccustomed to night flying, fighting storms or long hours, and the experiment ended badly. In one month, 12 Army pilots were killed. The Army, it was discovered, was a national defense mechanism, not a public service organization. On 10 March Roosevelt rescinded his order, and indicated the mail would be returned to private carriers.

On 12 June 1934 the Black-McKeller Bill passed. This was the Air Mail Act, and its repercussions were disastrous for large airlines. It was decreed that no airline company could be associated with a company that built planes. The huge United Aircraft and Air Transport Corporation, chaired by William E Boeing, was ordered to split up in three ways. United Air Lines was given the airways, the United Aircraft Corporation would handle the manufacture of industry related materials and the Boeing Airplane Company, including the Stearman Aircraft Company of

Wichita, could continue to build airplanes. It was the smallest of the three pieces.

William E Boeing was bitter over what he considered an injustice, and he resigned, leaving the airplane business altogether. In the years since 1916, he had done much for the young industry. His designs were true pioneering endeavors, reaching into present times. He was never afraid to tackle new ideas and put his own money on the line.

Although he declared himself out of the industry, Bill Boeing kept in touch. In May 1954 he was guest of honor at the Renton plant when the first commercial jet built in the United States, the Boeing 707 prototype, was rolled out. It was a great moment in his life. Witnesses to the event record that his eyes, unsentimental in matters of business, were, on this occasion, misty. Two years later, at the age of 74, this man of facts died aboard his yacht *Taconite*. His name lives on.

The government-ordered split affected another Boeing man, Philip Johnson. Johnson had risen steadily within the organization. When the smoke of litigation cleared, he was appointed president of the newly formed United Air Lines. He was very well qualified for the job, but he felt that his presence was not in the company's best interest. As a top Boeing executive, he had come under considerable fire during the investigation, so he, too, resigned. Those in the airplane industry knew that Johnson had committed no wrong, but was the victim of high-handed tactics. The minister of transport in Canada, C D Howe, apparently paid little attention to the affair. All he knew was that an organizational genius was at liberty, and he invited Johnson to Canada. He wanted the ex-Boeing man to organize Trans-Canada Airways. Johnson had the airline going in 18 months.

When Hitler threatened world stability, Phil Johnson was invited back to the United States and made president of the Boeing Airplane Company. The government had by then reversed its decisions of 1934, admitting that the mail contracts of the 1920s had been legally granted, through open competitive bidding rather than collusion. (What effect this all had on Johnson goes unrecorded. It is possible that he entertained some choice thoughts).

Johnson achieved miracles at wartime Boeing, but his efforts cost him his life. He died of a stroke in 1944, a victim of overwork,

Right: The Luft-Hansa **247** after receiving German markings. In addition to the German sale, Boeing exported a single 247Y armed with three machine guns to Chinese warlord Chang Hsuech-liang.

Below: One of the pair of **247As** sold to Deutsch Luft-Hansa in 1934, upon its arrival in Germany. The 247A was powered with new 625hp twin-row Pratt & Whitney engines and, like the 247 before it, was 3 inches shorter and a thousand pounds lighter than the 247D.

Philip G Johnson was born on 5 November 1894 in Seattle, Washington, and he joined Boeing in 1917 while a senior in mechanical engineering at the University of Washington. By 1920 he was superintendent, in 1921 he was named vice-president and in 1926, at age 31, he became president of the Boeing Airplane Company.

In 1931 Boeing Air Transport, National Air Transport, Pacific Air Transport and Varney Air Lines, the four airlines of the United Aircraft and Transport Corporation, combined to become United Air Lines. Johnson became president, retaining the presidency of the Boeing organization. In 1933 he moved to New York as president of the industrial giant and relinquished his presidency of the Boeing Airplane Company. He was forced to resign in 1934, however, to enable United to regain its government airmail contracts. Johnson and several associates went to Canada in 1937 to organize Trans-Canada Airways. He returned to Boeing as president in 1939, a day after President Roosevelt declared a state of national emergency, and set the pace for the company's war-production effort.

On 14 September 1944, while visiting Boeing's B-29 plant in Wichita, Kansas, Johnson collapsed and died of a stroke. He had been a true pioneer of aviation and one of the outstanding executives in the country. He built one of the great airline systems in the world and helped direct Boeing to its world-renowned position. It was his genius for production that geared the Boeing Company for its unmatched output in World War II.

and a real casualty of the war. By then, he had company production going so smoothly, that literally hundreds of Flying Fortresses, as well as other kinds of aircraft, were rolling out the doors every month.

After the corporate breakup in 1934, Claire Egtvedt became president of the Boeing Airplane Company. He had problems. Without sales for the 247 transport, there was nothing in the way of commercial airplane prospects on the horizon. Only $600,000 remained in the treasury, not much when large payrolls were to be met. Workers were laid off, and the employee total dropped from 1700 to 600.

To help out in this tight situation, an idea was advanced by employees. Why not let one group work two weeks, while another laid off? After two weeks the second group worked, while the first one was furloughed, a sort of alternating payroll. The plan was put into effect, but many appeared during their off periods and worked without pay. In addition to Boeing's corporate troubles, the country was in the middle of the Great Depression of the thirties.

Then an event occurred that spelled freedom from immediate financial straits, if it would not exactly bring riches. In 1934 the

Army awarded Boeing a contract to develop the XB-15 bomber. This was to be a big, long-range airplane, and became Boeing's Model 294.

Engineers and designers put their best into the project, and the XB-15 eventually flew in October 1937, the largest aircraft ever built in the United States up to then. One important benefit was the XB-15's design which influenced the successful Boeing flying boats known as Clippers, developed a couple of years later.

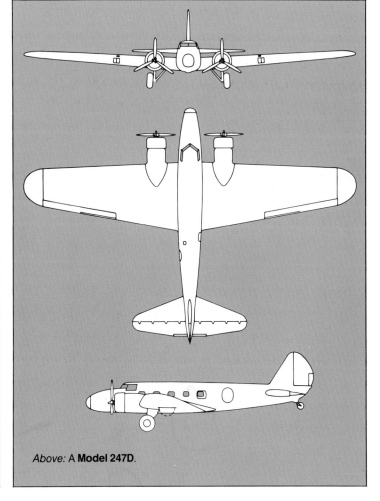

Above: A **Model 247D**.

Specifications: Model 247D
Boeing Model Number 247D

Span	74 ft
Length	51 ft 7 in
Wing Area	836 sq ft
Gross Weight	13,650 pounds
Cruising Speed	189 mph
Service Ceiling	25,400 ft
Range	745 miles
Powerplant	two 550 hp Pratt & Whitney R-1340-S1H1G Wasps
Capacity	10 passengers plus 125 cu ft of baggage and cargo, and 400 pounds of mail

The man who dreamed up the Boeing Clippers was Wellwood Beall. He had been an engineering instructor at the Boeing School of Aeronautics in Oakland. Because of his dynamic personality and practical knowledge, he was moved to Seattle, and put in charge of sales.

In 1934, Beall was in China selling Boeing pursuit planes, and word came to him that Pan American Airways had landed a Sikorsky flying boat at Midway Island. It was rumored that this was only the first part of a plan to connect China to the United States by air. 'Poppycock!' declared Wellwood Beall. He felt that aeronautical technology had not yet come to terms with the great distances across the Pacific. Someday, perhaps, but not yet. His wife, Jeannie, was with him, and knew his sentiments. She chided him, asking how a man who knew airplanes so well could downgrade their potential.

Beall thought it over. When he returned to the United States, he drew up some rough plans for a flying boat. The more he worked on the idea of an airplane that could cross oceans, the more excited he grew. Glenn Martin had built the *China Clipper* for Pan Am, and in 1935, it did cross the Pacific. Sikorsky's flying boat, the S-42, was successfully piloted by Pan Am crews from California to New Zealand, also in 1935. This was the longest over-ocean route in the world.

If the Boeing Airplane Company wanted a successful career in commercial sales, it would have to give customers what they wanted. Flying boats were the solution to long-distance flights. They handled heavy loads and accommodated passengers at the same time – and they could land wherever there was water. It was

a safety factor to be considered. Wellwood Beall presented his ideas to Egtvedt, and they talked the problem over. Egtvedt gave the green light, and Beall's great airplane was underway.

Designated the Boeing Model 314, Beall's design was to be a four-engined flying boat. It incorporated the wing and horizontal tail surfaces of the XB-15, then under construction. And as in the XB-15, the 314 was designed with a control cabin, which displayed the instruments used by the flight engineer, navigator, and radio operator. The pilots were stationed on the 'flight deck,' forward of the wings. It was decided to go all out on the 314, to make it a luxury plane, a true Pullman of the Sky, that would give stiff competition to the Martin and Sikorsky boats.

In February 1936 Pan Am invited Boeing to submit its designs for consideration, and on 21 June Boeing was granted a three million dollar contract. It called for six 314s, with an option for six more. The 314 went into immediate production, and all of the first six were delivered between January and June, 1939. The second six encountered a different fate. When they were ready, World War II had begun, and aircraft were in demand. Three of the Clippers, with Pan Am approval, went to the British Overseas Airways Corporation, better known as BOAC. The remaining three went into service with Pan American.

The Clippers, known by such romantic names as *Honolulu Clipper*, *California Clipper*, *American Clipper*, *Dixie Clipper* and others, went on to earn a reputation as safe, reliable ships. At first, though, the 314 had problems. The first six Model 314s, were powered by 1500hp Wright Double Cyclone engines which did not deliver the power hoped for, so the second six were

Above: The first **Model 314 Clipper** during evaluation on Puget Sound.

equipped with engines delivering 100 more horsepower each. This earned them the designation Model 314A, and, eventually, the first six were also converted.

In all examples the huge semi-monocoque hull was 19 feet in depth, and divided into two decks. The lower deck was for passengers, and was fitted with large windows for viewing, lounge chairs, a private bridal suite, separate dressing rooms and lavatories for men and women. A dining salon featured tables and cutlery, and could be turned into a recreational area after meals. The meals were catered, and the first passenger flight to Europe, on 28 June 1939, was catered by the Lord Baltimore Hotel. The *Dixie Clipper* treated her passengers to a dinner of breast of chicken, with strawberry shortcake Sullivan for dessert. Later meals were prepared by chefs of the New Yorker Hotel, New York, in special kitchens at La Guardia Field. The decks of this luxury flying boat were carpeted, and the davenport lounge chairs could be converted into berths at night. It was considered one of the most comfortable airliners crossing either the Atlantic or Pacific Oceans.

The upper deck belonged to the crew. It was here they worked and were quartered. The huge, single wing had been built in five sections, the same as the XB-15, and was an all-metal, truss-type structure. There were companionways inside the wings, allowing access to each engine. The nacelles were so large a mechanic could stand in them to make minor repairs en route. Fuel was stored in the wing tanks and sponsons. The sponsons provided stability on the water and helped in lift when the boat was taking off. The hull below decks was divided into a series of watertight

Top: The **Clipper**'s spacious lounge provided more than ample space for a variety of passenger activities. The lounge was situated toward the center under the large wing. The door in the background here is clearly shown in the picture on p 64.

Above: The mysterious lady dines alone. The lounge of a Lisbon-bound **Clipper** during the elegant evening meal.

compartments. They carried 34 passengers on transoceanic flights, and on shorter, over-water trips, they carried 74 passengers, a crew of ten, and could be fitted with as many as 40 berths.

Fifty thousand parts went into this giant, and it was so bulky it had to be constructed in two steps. The hull assembly was completed inside the factory, where the frames were mounted in 'docks' more than 100 feet long. They were 30 feet wide and 35 feet high. There were two of these docks, so that work could go ahead on two airplanes at the same time. For the final assembly, Boeing engineers developed an 'outdoor dock,' of comparable proportions. At the outdoor dock, the wings were mounted on the hull, and the engines were placed in the leading edge of the wing. For this heavy work, a special crane was stationed by the outdoor dock.

The finished 314 was a thing of beauty. Though it was remarked that she had the 'body of a whale,' she nevertheless struck the eye pleasantly. Though the Martin and Sikorsky boats were important competitors, Boeing's design was brought to the attention of Juan Trippe, president of Pan American. He liked the fact the Model 314 was not only larger, but promised a 600 mile increase in range.

On 31 May 1938 the first model was floated down the Duwamish River to Puget Sound. Test pilot Eddie Allen was at the controls. Allen revved the engines with their 14-foot propellers. There would be no flight that day. The engines rumbled, and Allen brought the ship back. All 56 spark plugs were fouled and had to be changed.

Below: Clad in their crisp dress whites, the captain and crew of a New Zealand-bound **Clipper** are the last to disembark at an exotic South Pacific stopover.

On Friday 3 June, Allen eased the whale-bodied Clipper out on the Sound once more. A sudden gust of wind tipped the plane, and the starboard wing nearly went under. Allen managed to level his ship before there was any damage, but he brought her back to shore again. The plane was too light, and more sandbag ballast was added. Again the 314 ventured forth, and again the wing nearly caught. This time it was pilot error. The co-pilot, unaccustomed to such large aircraft, misjudged power on a turn, and the plane tipped dangerously. Another factor contributing to these problems was a powerful new 100 octane fuel. Few had used it before, and its power was not well known.

On 7 June Eddie Allen finally took off to make a successful flight of 38 minutes, before coming down on Lake Washington. However, Allen still was not pleased. 'It's like herding a reluctant buffalo,' he said to an anxious Wellwood Beall. 'I had to steer with the engines. There isn't enough surface control.'

The engineers went to work, and the tail assembly was altered so that there were three vertical tail fins instead of one. The dihedral angle of the short seawings was changed to help stabilize the plane on the water. These alterations were kept quiet, and proved to be the final ones before the Boeing *Clipper* was granted approval by the Civil Aeronautics Authority in January 1939. The big boats were ready for customers.

Pan American pilots approved the 314s from the start. They found them superior in performance, and liked the way they flew. Captain Joseph Chase skippered the first 314 released, the *Honolulu Clipper*, flying it to Hawaii successfully. This was followed by Captain Harold Gray's flight across the Atlantic Ocean in the *Yankee Clipper*. There were no paying passengers, only Pan Am officials and newsmen. Captain R O D Sullivan made the first Atlantic crossing with paying passengers on 28 June 1939, in the *Dixie Clipper*, with the delicious catered menu.

Not just anybody could slip into the pilot's seat of a Pan American Clipper. Before that, each skipper was given intense training. If the Boeing Airplane Company was a stickler for testing its aircraft, Pan American Airways placed itself on the same high level in training its captains. Extensive schooling was given in mechanics (license required), radio (commercial license a necessity), navigation and meteorology. When a Pan American

pilot took the controls of a Clipper, he was designated a 'master of ocean flying boats.' Because of this training, Pan Am Clipper pilots could fly anyplace in the world without getting nervous. If anything went wrong, as it sometimes did, they could fix it themselves.

After World War II came to the United States with the Japanese attack on Pearl Harbor, the commercial flying picture changed. Those Clippers in the Pacific at that time were more or less on their own.

The *Pacific Clipper*, under Robert Ford, had just completed a San Francisco to Auckland, New Zealand run. Rather than risk the loss of ship and crew by returning to the US over what was now considered a combat zone, Ford took the long way home. He set a western course to Australia, India, Arabia, central Africa, and across the Atlantic to South America. He then flew to New York, landing there on 6 January 1942. The *Pacific Clipper* had flown 34,500 miles. Except for the breadth of the US, the big flying boat had circumnavigated the world.

After America entered the conflict, three of the Clippers were taken by the Navy, but they were operated by Pan Am crews. Others were pressed into Army service as C-98s, but were later given to the Navy.

There was only one serious Clipper accident during the war. On 22 February 1942, the *Yankee Clipper* crashed in the Tagus River near Lisbon. There were 39 people aboard, and 24 were killed. Singer Jane Froman was among the passengers, and, though injured, she was saved by the efforts of Fourth Officer John Burns. Romance blossomed after the tragedy and the two were later married. The *Yankee Clipper* had by then made 240 safe Atlantic crossings, and had logged over 1,000,000 miles. The tragedy was blamed on pilot error.

There were famous names aboard the Clippers during the war. President Franklin Roosevelt, the first American president to fly, traveled to the Casablanca Conference on the *Dixie* in 1943. Winston Churchill, Prime Minister of Britain, rode the *Atlantic Clipper* to the States on urgent business. In what was nearly a tragic accident, Churchill was returning to England from Bermuda when his Clipper, the *Berwick*, was almost shot down by Royal Air Force pilots as an 'unidentified aircraft.' Fortunately,

the *Berwick*, one of the three Clippers which had been taken by BOAC established its identity and reached home safely.

Nor were the *Clippers* without heroics. They flew spare parts for P-40 fighters to General Chennault's China command. Clippers also rushed emergency supplies to General Montgomery's British troops in North Africa, and hauled special equipment to England two weeks before the D-Day invasion of France.

After the war, the gallant Boeing Clippers were no longer in such demand as they had been four years earlier. Civilian airlines were discovering the Douglas DC series, and even Boeing was competing with its own Stratocruisers.

Several of the 314s were dry-docked, and two were purchased from the War Assets Administration by new airlines. The *Honolulu Clipper*, first of the series to test its wings, developed engine trouble and had to set down at sea. The USN aircraft carrier *Manila Bay* went to the rescue, but alas for the noble effort. Though all passengers and crew were saved, the *Honolulu Clipper* bashed into its large benefactor and was so badly mangled that it had to be sunk. Over 1000 rounds of heavy caliber machine-gun ammunition were fired into the stricken hulk before it sank. In another accident, the *Pacific Clipper* was left useless, and sold for parts by her owners, Universal Airlines. The *Capetown*, one of the BOAC planes, was being returned to the States in October 1947. She was forced down because of a fuel shortage, and the Coast Guard ship *Bibb* went to the rescue. Plane and ship collided, and the *Capetown* emerged the loser. She, too, had to be sunk.

By 1951, all of the Model 314s and 314As had been scrapped, except for the *Bristol*, another returned BOAC craft. The *Bristol* had been sold to a clergyman who called himself Master X. It was his purpose to fly to Russia and talk peace with Stalin. The USA and Russia were then in the grip of the Cold War, and it was feared another shooting war might develop. Master X's aims were high, but not those of the *Bristol*. She was anchored in Baltimore Harbor when a fierce storm sent her to the bottom. She was eventually raised out of the mud and scrapped, the last of the Boeing Clippers.

In aggregate, the three BOAC Clippers flew 4,258,876 miles. They made 596 Atlantic crossings, and carried 40,042 passengers. The nine other Clippers flew, as of 1946, 8,300,000 miles on 3650 ocean flights, Atlantic and Pacific. Each Clipper averaged 18,000 hours of flying time.

Early models of the B-17, the Flying Fortress, had already been in production when Claire Egtvedt consulted Ed Wells about pressurizing airplane cabins. Wells, chief engineer, had been working on that idea for the B-17s, but his conclusions pointed to a different design than that of the bomber.

He handed Egtvedt a drawing of a fuselage that was a perfect circle. The circular form would make it easier to maintain pressurization. The completed airplane would have the same four engines, wings, and tail as the B-17. The fuselage, however, would be its own, and it would be capable of high altitude flying. This would increase speed significantly, and Boeing executives, with an eye on the competition, would have to beat the fast and powerful Douglas DC-4 if they chose to remain in the commercial field.

Juan Trippe, the president of Pan American Airways, was always open to new ideas. He wanted his airline to become, and remain, the best in the world, and he looked at all new developments with that in mind. He saw the possibilities for high-altitude pressurized flight, and underwrote the expense for three aircraft to try out the new concept. These became the Boeing Model 307 and were given the name Stratoliner.

There were, in all, ten Stratoliners produced. The prototype was tested by Eddie Allen, and proved airworthy. It quickly attracted the interest of both domestic and foreign airlines. Transcontinental & Western Air (now TWA, Trans-World Airlines) ordered five more. Howard Hughes ordered another so he could beat his own around-the-world record of 91 hours. High altitude flying practically guaranteed it. With orders for nine on the books, Boeing executives were optimistic. The Stratoliner was as far ahead of its time as the Model 247 or Model 80 had been, and it seemed like good times were ahead. At the crest of triumph, however, lurked tragedy.

In March 1939 two representatives from the Dutch airline KLM were at Boeing's Seattle plant. They expressed interest in the Stratoliner, and asked for a test flight. With pilot Julius Barr at the controls, the airliner took off. Jack Kylstra, project engineer, was on board, as well as seven others and the two KLM men. The takeoff was smooth, then came disaster. The plane was close to Mount Ranier in the Cascade Mountains, flying at about 5000 feet, when it went into a sudden spin. Witnesses said the plane whirled almost to the earth before it was abruptly brought out of its fierce descent. The pressure was too great, and the wings and

Above: The British Airways **Clipper** *Bristol* was one of the Clippers transferred from Pan Am during the 1940s. The *Bristol* was painted in camouflage colors, a contrast to the natural metal finish of the Pan Am Clippers.

tail broke off. The plane crashed, and all aboard were killed. For a while Pan American Airways and TWA hesitated to buy the plane but a new tail design convinced them to go ahead and production continued.

Though Stratoliner sales were not big, its advanced design provided the initial thrust to air supremacy that Boeing hoped for. It was a luxury ship designed for passenger comfort. Sound-proofing was so efficient that the four engines sounded like a distant hum. There was air conditioning in addition to the super-charger pressurization. Individual seat lights, ash trays and separate restrooms all offered creature comforts. As a Pullman, the Stratoliner provided 16 berths, and nine reclining easy chairs. There was plenty of room because the circular body, the first of the wide transports, was nearly 12 feet in diameter.

Passengers were attracted to this sleek aircraft, and traveling at high altitudes caught on. Orders came in, but World War II came along with its bomber priorities, and production of the Stratoliner was shelved. Yet, along with the XB-15 and the Clippers, Boeing was gaining experience in making big airplanes that was to give an edge over competition in the years to come.

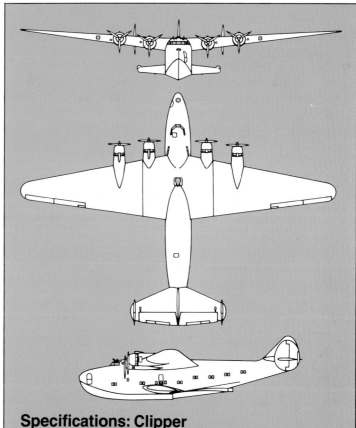

Specifications: Clipper Boeing Model Number 314

Span	152 ft
Length	106 ft
Wing Area	2867 sq ft
Tail Height	20 ft 4½ in
Gross Weight	82,500 pounds
Cruising Speed	193 mph
Service Ceiling	16,000 ft
Range	4900 miles
Powerplant	four 1500 hp Wright GR-2600 Twin Cyclones
Capacity	74 passengers

Specifications: Clipper Boeing Model Number 314A

Span	152 ft
Length	106 ft
Wing Area	2867 sq ft
Tail Height	20 ft 4½ in
Gross Weight	84,000 pounds
Cruising Speed	199 mph
Service Ceiling	19,600 ft
Range	5200 miles
Powerplant	four 1600 hp Wright GR-2600 Twin Cyclones
Capacity	77 passengers

Above: A Pan Am **Model 307** makes an over-water approach.

The Stratoliners did not escape the war. Five were taken by the Army as C-75s. They were used to train pilots in long-range four engine operations. They also carried passengers and cargo and were the ships that pioneered the Air Transport Command's transatlantic routes.

In the spring of 1942 one Stratoliner had a passenger list which included Generals George C Marshall, H H 'Hap' Arnold, and Dwight D Eisenhower, plus Admirals Ernest J King and J H Towers. It was a great vote of confidence for the big airplane, because these men were America's top military leaders and crucial to the war effort. Had something happened to them, it is possible the war could have taken a different course.

Before the C-75s were returned to civilian use after the war, they experienced some exciting moments. On one occasion an Allied destroyer, mistook a C-75 for a German bomber and fired a 20mm cannon shell into its tail. The Stratoliner managed to escape more damage and made it home safely. In another incident near Natal, Brazil, the pilot brought his plane in too low, and damaged the landing gear skimming a dike. The plane set down under emergency conditions and passengers and crew walked away unharmed.

During the course of military service, the C-75s logged more than 45,000 hours flying time, and made 3000 ocean crossings. In 1944 they were returned to the factory, and reworked to include a redesigned landing gear, a modified wing and new horizontal tail surfaces. An improved electrical system was also installed as were four 1200hp Wright engines. The exchange of engines provided an increase of 100hp over the earlier Wright Cyclones. With these changes, passenger capacity was increased from 33 to 38, and for the first time the flight engineer became a crew member on domestic service.

The Stratoliners continued in airline operation in the United States until 1952. Then a group of them were sold to a French company. Thirty years after the first ship cut through the thin upper reaches of earth's atmosphere, five Stratoliners were still in service. Boeing's engineering had once more designed a product meant to last.

Specifications:
Pan American Airlines Stratoliner
Boeing Model Number 307

Span	107 ft 3 in
Length	74 ft 4 in
Wing Area	1486 sq ft
Tail Height	20 ft 9½ in
Gross Weight	42,000 pounds
Cruising Speed	215 mph
Service Ceiling	23,300 ft
Range	1750 miles
Powerplant	four 1100 hp Wright GR-1820-G102
Capacity	33 passengers

Left: The perfectly circular fuselage of the **307** is evident in this photograph taken during assembly in Plant 2. Note the throttle levers (center).

Below: A lady travelling aboard a 307 could avail herself of the 307's **'Charm Room'** (circa 1940).

Above and below: The **Model 307B** served Transcontinental and Western Air (TWA), later Trans World Airlines (TWA). It cruised 5mph faster, 2900 feet higher and ranged 640 miles farther than the Model 307. The 307B-1 could accommodate 38 passengers.

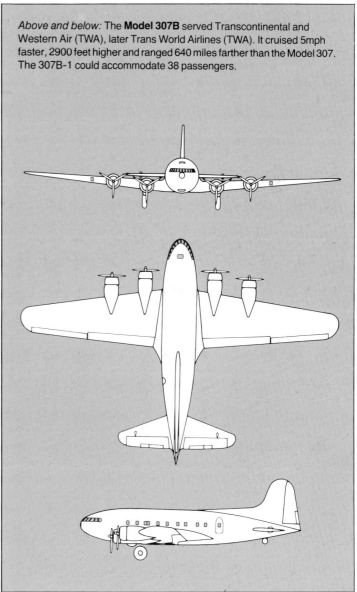

PRODUCTION CLOSE-UP
BOEING AIRLINERS 1933-1950

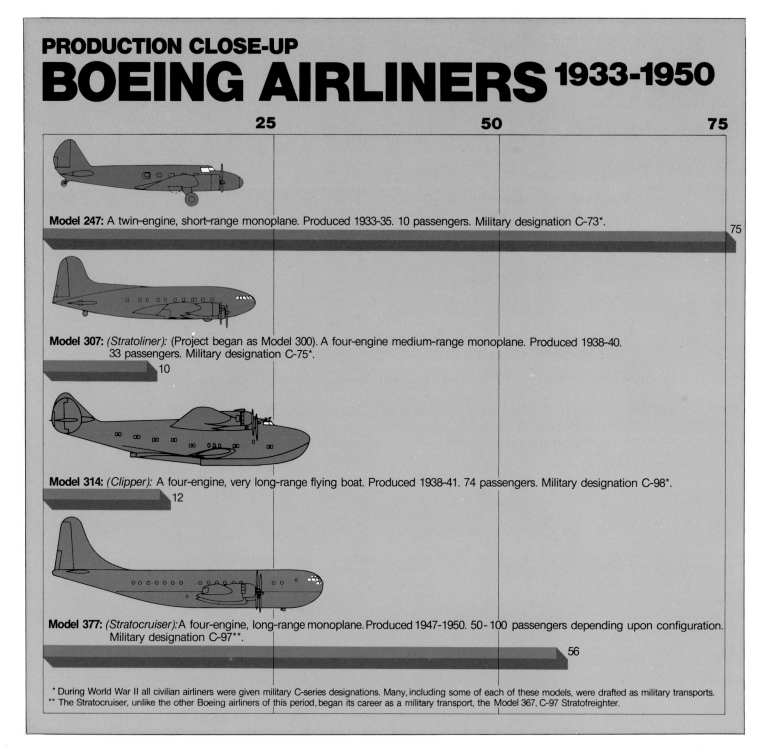

25   50   75

Model 247: A twin-engine, short-range monoplane. Produced 1933-35. 10 passengers. Military designation C-73*.

75

Model 307: *(Stratoliner):* (Project began as Model 300). A four-engine medium-range monoplane. Produced 1938-40. 33 passengers. Military designation C-75*.

10

Model 314: *(Clipper):* A four-engine, very long-range flying boat. Produced 1938-41. 74 passengers. Military designation C-98*.

12

Model 377: *(Stratocruiser):* A four-engine, long-range monoplane. Produced 1947-1950. 50-100 passengers depending upon configuration. Military designation C-97**.

56

* During World War II all civilian airliners were given military C-series designations. Many, including some of each of these models, were drafted as military transports.
** The Stratocruiser, unlike the other Boeing airliners of this period, began its career as a military transport, the Model 367, C-97 Stratofreighter.

In September 1945 Claire Egtvedt relinquished the presidency of the Boeing Airplane Company and William M Allen took over. Egtvedt, president since the death of Phil Johnson, became chairman of the board. William Allen had been Boeing's lawyer for many years, and was not new to the company. He was, in keeping with past presidents, a forward-looking man, and something of a gambler. A balding, thin man, Allen was down-to-earth, and when he took office, he made a number of rules for his personal guidance. Among them was this: 'Make Boeing even greater than it is.' This he proceeded to do.

In early September 1945 Boeing was facing another lean period. The Army Air Force had drastically cut back on production as the war wound down. There were 44,023 people on the payroll (down from a wartime peak of over 78,000), creating a huge expense. Wages had soared since Boeing's first days in 1916, when labor could be purchased for as little as 14 cents an hour.

The answer lay in returning to the commercial airliner business. Airline companies were calling for aircraft to match their growing needs. They wanted new planes, with the latest improvements, and rival builders were already responding to this need. Douglas could offer its trim and efficient DC-4, and 74 were delivered to airline companies after the war, followed by the DC-6. The DC-6 had a pressurized cabin, carried 50 passengers, and cruised at 315mph. More than 500 DC-6s were sold throughout the world, making Douglas a tough competitor indeed.

Lockheed had also entered the race with vigor. It put its Constellation, Model 49, into the sky on 9 January 1943. The Army Air Corps took over its production, calling the plane the C-69, and the 'Connie' became a military workhorse. After Paris was returned to Allied hands, the Connie broke speed records on a New York–Paris run of 14 hours and 12 minutes. It cruised at 327mph (100mph more than the Stratoliner), and carried 112 passengers in its pressurized cabin. Its speed and passenger capacity made the Connie, like the DC-6, a serious competitor.

Boeing never took its competition lightly. Company policy was to observe and then improve. During the war, the C-97,

Above: This **Model 377 Stratocruiser** served Pan American World Airways as the *Clipper Southern Cross.*

Boeing Model 367, had been developed. This large military transport was an offspring of the B-29 bomber and utilized the same wings and tail. It was the direct forerunner of the Model 377, the Stratocruiser, destined to be Boeing's next commercial airplane.

William Allen realized that Boeing's next venture into commercial aircraft would have to be something special. It would have to be big: very big. It would be fast, safe, and comfortable. The Pullman characteristics must prevail to attract passengers.

The Model 377 Stratocruiser was the airliner counterpart of the C-97, and the first commercial Boeing airplane produced since the 314 Clipper. Using adaptations of the proven C-97 airframe, and four 3500hp Pratt & Whitney Wasp Major engines the competitive advantages offered by the Stratocruiser were long range and passenger comfort.

In the midst of a postwar recession in the aircraft industry, Boeing decided to gamble its own money on the 377. It would be a big gamble, perhaps the largest ever, but William Allen ordered 50 of the Stratocruisers. At the same time he warned his sales force to sell the new airplane or Boeing would go broke! Boeing products were well known, and had a good reputation, but there was a hitch. The Stratocruisers cost over one million dollars each. Would customers buy at that price? The salesmen, and Boeing's reputation, had a job to do.

They were successful. On 28 November 1945 Pan American Airways placed an order for 20 Stratocruisers. The $24,500,000 contract was the largest ever given for commercial airplanes, but Juan Trippe, still president of Pan Am, had faith in the Boeing product. They had given him the efficient and graceful Clippers, and he planned on following the precedent by calling the new 377s Strato-Clippers.

Pan American Airways, however, couldn't afford to gamble on its planes – not to the tune of millions – but it held an ace. Officials knew that a C-97 AAF transport had, on 9 January 1945, flown from Seattle to Washington, DC in six hours and four minutes. The average speed was 383mph, with spurts to 400. That was speed, and fast time cut down on overhead. The C-97 was mother to the Stratocruiser and what one could do, so could the other. It was the simple logic of heredity, and Pan Am's reasoning helped pull Boeing out of trouble once more.

The Stratocruiser fuselage design was its own. It was a two-deck, figure eight shape, sometimes called the 'double-bubble.' Its wing, the Boeing-invented '117' airfoil, was considered the fastest wing of its time. Aerodynamic improvement over brute

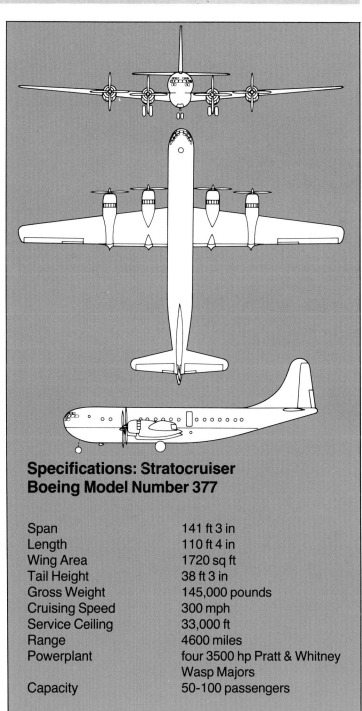

Specifications: Stratocruiser Boeing Model Number 377

Span	141 ft 3 in
Length	110 ft 4 in
Wing Area	1720 sq ft
Tail Height	38 ft 3 in
Gross Weight	145,000 pounds
Cruising Speed	300 mph
Service Ceiling	33,000 ft
Range	4600 miles
Powerplant	four 3500 hp Pratt & Whitney Wasp Majors
Capacity	50-100 passengers

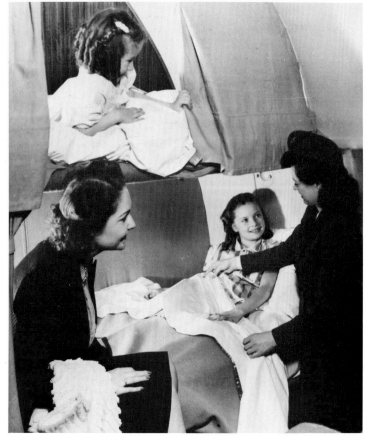

Above: Passengers relax in the air-conditioned comfort of the Stratocruiser's spacious cabin. The **Stratocruiser** could accommodate as many as 100 passengers, but then, as now, passengers were more comfortable when there were fewer seats.

Left: Bedtime in the clouds. The **377** was the last Boeing production airliner to offer Pullman-style berths.

engine power was nothing new to Boeing, who realized the importance of aerodynamics with the *Monomail* of the early 1930s.

Another important feature of the Stratocruiser was its wide cabin. It allowed extra room for passengers, who relieved the monotony of long flights by walking around. Passengers could descend to the lower deck via a circular staircase. There was a lounge on the lower deck, which sat 14 comfortably and where drinks were served. A nominal charge was set on the drinks, but talk was free and, according to those who were there, it was plentiful.

Two important additions helped increase passenger comfort on the Stratocruiser. They were air conditioning and altitude conditioning. At high altitudes, these features eased discomfort. Clean air, warmed to the proper temperature, was injected into the cabin. Supercharging equipment kept the air at the proper pressure, while the plane was cruising above the country's highest mountain peaks. Rapid changes in altitude could be effected with little or no change in cabin pressure. Soundproofing, as with the Stratoliner, reduced engine roar to a distant thrum. The interior of the Stratocruiser could be altered and equipped

Above: The gleaming **Stratocruiser** prototype, with Boeing markings, passes high over the Cascades.

to suit the needs of the purchasers. The standard version of the long-range ship was equipped to handle 75 seats. Fifty-six of these could be turned into berths, similar to the upper and lower berths of Pullman accommodations. Nineteen sleeper-seats provided night-time comfort for remaining passengers. The dressing rooms were arranged to provide ample space, and were tastefully decorated. When all available space was taken by seats, as many as 114 passengers were carried. A galley was located to the rear of the main deck, completely equipped for food preparation. It was considered to be as efficient as any modern kitchen. Because of all the luxury of first class accommodations, it was only natural that the nickname 'Statuscruiser' was soon given to Boeing's latest product.

Boeing, always eager to find the best design possible, which meant one that combined safety with performance, put in 4,000,000 engineering hours on the Stratocruiser. Though Pan Am ordered its ships in late 1945, the prototype did not fly until July 1947. The first 377s were delivered to Pan Am on 31 January 1949, a little over three years from the date ordered.

Pan Am, itself always conscious of safety, did not object. Boeing test-flew three of the 377s to cure imperfections. They put the trio through 250,000 miles of 'torture flights,' flying the big ships through every difficulty possible, while studying stress and performance. When Pan Am got the airplanes, their executives knew they could depend on them.

The 377s were built for easy maintenance and low-cost operation. They carried passengers for one cent per mile less than competitors, a fact airline accountants took into consideration. And engine mounts were designed so that powerplants could be changed quickly, a fact not lost on maintenance crews.

Although the safety record was excellent overall, several Stratocruisers were lost. Pan American Airways lost the *Good Hope* in the jungles of Brazil, and the *Clipper Romance of the Skies* went unromantically to its doom in the Pacific. Captain Richard Ogg landed his *Clipper Sovereign of the Skies* close to a Pacific weather ship. The seven crew members and all passengers were saved, but the airplane was lost. The great majority of the Stratocruisers, though, survived to end up in the junk dealer's yard, a sad end for a great skycruiser.

President William Allen's gamble paid off. Fifty-six Stratocruisers were sold and their ultimate performance was remarkable. As of March 1955, they had carried 3,199,219 passengers, crossed the Pacific and Atlantic 27,678 times and made 3597 transcontinental flights. In addition, they round-tripped to South America 822 times, bringing the total mileage for the Stratocruisers to 169,859,579!

The last of the 56 Stratocruisers was delivered to BOAC in May 1950. Wellwood Beall went along, and when he returned he had news for Boeing executives. Great Britain's jet-propelled De Havilland DH-106 Comet was making a hit. If Boeing wanted to remain competitive in the commercial airplane field, the next step was to design its own jet. Boeing designers went to work, for a new age in airliners had arrived, and Boeing certainly meant to catch up.

THE WAR YEARS

In May 1934, when the Boeing Airplane Company was surviving on military contracts, Claire Egtvedt received a letter from General Conger Pratt. General Pratt was Chief of the Air Corps Materiel Division. The letter requested Egtvedt to be present at a meeting to be held on 14 May at Wright Field. C A Van Dusen, a representative from the Martin Company, would also be present.

Leonard 'Jake' Harmon, an aide to Pratt, presented an exciting plan. He had long been an advocate of General Billy Mitchell's progressive ideas about the United States building a superior Air Force. Though Mitchell's ideas had fallen into disfavor, (airplanes, declared Navy brass, will never replace dreadnoughts), minds were changing.

'I want a big bomber,' said Harmon, in effect. 'It should have a span of 150 feet, and gross 60,000 pounds. It should have a range of 5000 miles in order to protect not only US coastlines, but those of Hawaii and Alaska, too.' These were still experimental times in the aircraft industry. Efficiency was equated with size. The bigger the better.

Both Egtvedt and Van Dusen were invited to submit plans for this mammoth by 15 June. The project was called XBLR-1, Experimental Bomber, Long-Range, No. 1. This was shortened to 'Project A,' and was top secret. Boeing designers went to work eagerly. Hard times still clutched the company's pursestrings, and any work meant paychecks. Midnight oil burned and the plans for Project A were submitted on time. Notice was eventually

Above: The giant **XB-15** was the largest landplane bomber in the world when it made its first flight on 15 October 1937.

Far left: The **XB-15's flight deck**, offering more than ample working space for the crew, resembled the interior of a large motor yacht. The double doors in the center lead to the bombardier's station in the nose.

PRODUCTION CLOSE-UP
BOEING MILITARY AIRCRAFT
1937-1946

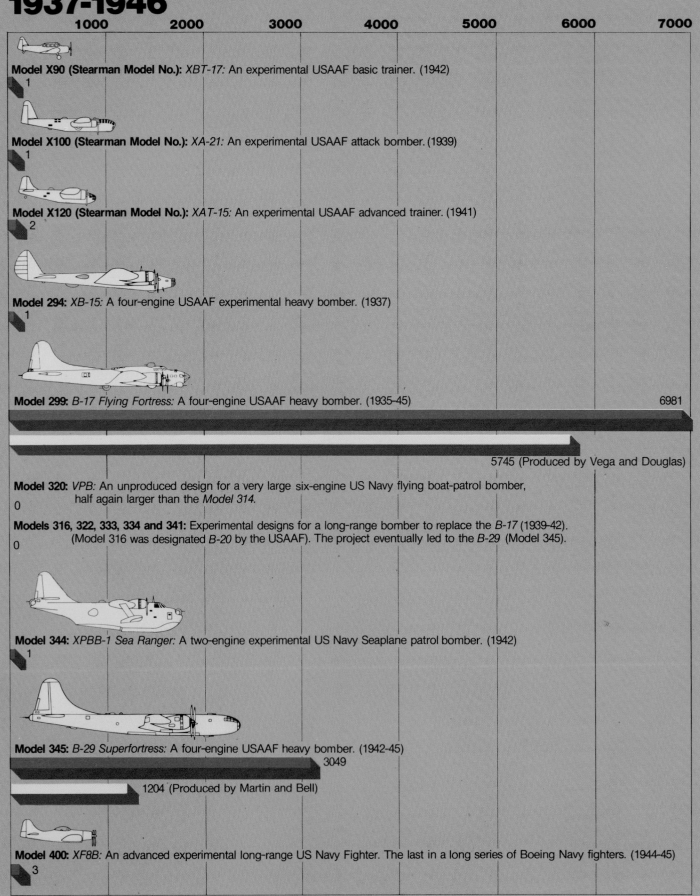

1000	2000	3000	4000	5000	6000	7000

Model X90 (Stearman Model No.): *XBT-17:* An experimental USAAF basic trainer. (1942)

1

Model X100 (Stearman Model No.): *XA-21:* An experimental USAAF attack bomber. (1939)

1

Model X120 (Stearman Model No.): *XAT-15:* An experimental USAAF advanced trainer. (1941)

2

Model 294: *XB-15:* A four-engine USAAF experimental heavy bomber. (1937)

1

Model 299: *B-17 Flying Fortress:* A four-engine USAAF heavy bomber. (1935–45)

6981

5745 (Produced by Vega and Douglas)

Model 320: *VPB:* An unproduced design for a very large six-engine US Navy flying boat-patrol bomber,
half again larger than the *Model 314.*

0

Models 316, 322, 333, 334 and 341: Experimental designs for a long-range bomber to replace the *B-17* (1939-42).
(Model 316 was designated *B-20* by the USAAF). The project eventually led to the *B-29* (Model 345).

0

Model 344: *XPBB-1 Sea Ranger:* A two-engine experimental US Navy Seaplane patrol bomber. (1942)

1

Model 345: *B-29 Superfortress:* A four-engine USAAF heavy bomber. (1942-45)

3049

1204 (Produced by Martin and Bell)

Model 400: *XF8B:* An advanced experimental long-range US Navy Fighter. The last in a long series of Boeing Navy fighters. (1944-45)

3

received that Boeing had been awarded the contract. This meant $600,000, and hard times eased their grip a little. Jack Kylstra was made project engineer and work went ahead on what Boeing called their Model 294. The Army, meanwhile, had changed its designation from XBLR-1 to XB-15.

It took nearly three and one-half years to finish the giant. One of the problems was the XB-15's sheer size. Nobody at Boeing had worked on an airplane so large before, and it became an experimental project for the work force as well as the engineers. Special tools had to be designed in order to make parts. A total of 670,000 man-hours went into its construction, and many of those hours were spent in testing components to destruction. Each section underwent thorough examination. A complete wing panel, for example, was weighted with lead far exceeding requirements. But technicians wanted to know the ultimate breaking-point and kept adding lead weights until the wing broke.

The bomber was so large that it was necessary to build it in sections. It was started in Seattle's Plant No. 1, but later barged up the Duwamish River to Plant No. 2, which was bigger and offered more space. When the sections had all been put together, the finished airplane was rolled across the street, Marginal Way, to Boeing Field.

The XB-15 was first flown on 15 October 1937 by Eddie Allen. He learned that the four 850hp Pratt & Whitney Twin Wasp radial engines were not going to make the XB-15 a speedy aircraft. It was simply too heavy, the design having outdistanced available powerplant technology.

Those who flew in the XB-15 were impressed by its size. Private R F Fowler of the 31st Bombardment Squadron, claimed that it would be necessary to establish radio communication between engines. This tongue-in-cheek remark was prompted by the fact that the wings contained passageways, enabling crewmen to make minor engine repairs while underway.

Its size brought other innovations. The endurance potential was far beyond that of a single crew, so bunks were installed to permit the carrying of two watches, nautical style. There was a kitchenette, complete with a hot plate, coffee pot, soup heater and a dry-ice box. Because many of its accessories were electrical, two auxiliary generators, driven by gasoline engines, were installed in the fuselage. This was a first for airplanes, and they helped deliver 110 volts through seven miles of wiring. The spacious living and working quarters were heated, ventilated and sound-proofed.

This was also the first Boeing military design with a flight deck instead of a cockpit. The flight deck was roomier, and was equipped with the latest technology. The fittings included an automatic pilot, controls for de-icing and a fire protection system. An aerodynamic improvement was the installation of large wing flaps to reduce landing speed.

The Army accepted the XB-15 prototype in March 1938, but it was to be the only one built. Although the B-17 (Model 299) had by then become the center of attention, it did not mean the end of the big ship. 'Grandpappy,' as the XB-15 was called, flew to Chile in February 1939, with a load of emergency supplies for earthquake victims. Piloted by Caleb Haynes, the big plane made the 3000 mile journey with two stops for fuel. Pilot Haynes flew the distance nonstop on the return, however, proving that Grandpappy's long-range potential was there. In that same year, 1939, skippered once again by Haynes, the XB-15 broke records by climbing to a height of 8200 feet with a load of 31,205 pounds. The load, plus the hefty 43,000 pounds of airplane, was a notable feat, though a little beyond the recommended gross of 70,706 pounds. Grandpappy was also notable for endurance, and could remain aloft for 24 hours before landing. Had there been air-to-

air refueling on a practical basis, the XB-15 could have broken more records.

Most airplanes are usually described in the feminine gender; like ships they are called she. Not Grandpappy. Because of its very size the XB-15 presented an undeniable masculinity, hence the nickname.

Though never used as a bomber, the XB-15 served in support of the Sixth Army in the South Pacific during World War II. Designated as the XC-105, Grandpappy carried troops and cargo into hostile skies for the duration. Perhaps the XB-15's most significant contribution to aviation was its usefulness as a test bed. The Army tested anti-drag cowlings, as well as various engines and electrical systems. Grandpappy also contributed its wing design to Boeing's Model 314 flying boat and its electrical system to the B-29.

A very important factor in building the XB-15 was the learning experience for Boeing. The company learned a lot about building big airplanes, and the experience put them far ahead of the competition.

In August 1934, not long after design work on the XB-15 began, Boeing received another letter from Wright Field. The Army was interested in developing yet another bomber concept. This one would carry a bomb load of 2000 pounds, with a range of 1020 miles, but with a *desired* range of 2200 miles. The required top speed would be 200mph, but the desired top speed was 250mph. It was to carry a crew of four to six men. Companies were invited to submit bids, and the successful bidder would build 220 airplanes!

This prize was worth going after, and Boeing entered a bid, though there was a tough stipulation: a flying bomber would have to be ready by August 1935. This meant company money would have to be spent, because there would be no financial aid from the military. None of the airplane builders of the mid-1930s were burdened with cash, but Claire Egtvedt went to the company's board of directors, which was, fortunately, composed of people who thought, as he did, that this was an important contract. He was voted an appropriation of $275,000 for the project.

The Army's plans for this newest concept called for 'multiple engines,' but multiple usually meant two. Boeing designers had been developing a wing capable of carrying four engines so Egtvedt phoned Wright Field, and asked if four engines would be accepted. The Army didn't mind. It was Boeing's money, anyway.

Specifications: XB-15
Boeing Model Number 294

Span	149 ft
Length	87 ft 7 in
Wing Area	2780 sq ft
Tail Height	18 ft 1 in
Gross Weight	70,706 pounds
Bomb Capacity	8,000 pounds
Top Speed	200 mph
Cruising Speed	152 mph
Ferry Range	5130 miles
Service Ceiling	18,900 ft
Powerplant	four 850 hp Pratt & Whitney R-1830-11 Twin Wasps
Defensive Armament	four 0.3 in and two 0.5 in machine guns

Above: The **XB-15** is prepared for the installation of the horizontal and vertical stabilizers.

Below: The rollout of the **XB-17**. Though there were to be numerous detail changes over the next 12,000 B-17s, the famous Flying Fortress profile was more than evident in this first glimpse in front of the hangar at Plant 1.

Four-engine bombers were not new. Four engines were then being planned in the XB-15 development. Up to then, however, additional engines were employed mainly to get more weight into the air. Boeing's idea was to give better performance, once the aircraft was aloft.

The new bomber was Boeing model number 299, and was conceived as a purely defensive weapon. This meant it was to protect the coastlines of the United States from foreign warships. When newsmen saw the Model 299 in flight for the first time they dubbed it 'a veritable flying fortress.' This was a nickname that would prove significant during World War II.

In size and configuration, the Model 299 was halfway between the Model 247 transport and the XB-15 bomber. Bombs were carried internally, and defensive weaponry consisted of machine guns installed in four streamlined blisters. The blisters were

Specifications: XB-17* Flying Fortress Boeing Model Number 299

Span	103 ft 9 in
Length	68 ft 9 in
Wing Area	1420 sq ft
Tail Height	18 ft 4 in
Gross Weight	32,432 pounds
Bomb Capacity	4800 pounds
Top Speed	236 mph
Cruising Speed	140 mph
Ferry Range	3010 miles
Service Ceiling	24,620 ft
Powerplant	four 750 hp Pratt & Whitney R-1690-E Hornets
Defensive Armament	five 0.3 in machine guns

*XB-17 was the unofficial designation of the Boeing-owned Model 299 prototype

placed on the back and belly of the fuselage, and one on either side about midships. A fifth gun protruded from the nose cone, and all of the guns could be either .30 or .50 caliber. Power for this fortress was provided by four 750hp Pratt & Whitney Hornet engines.

A year was not a very long time in which to design and build any airplane, but the 299 prototype was rushed to completion and first flown by Les Tower on 28 July 1935. After a series of shake-down flights, it was ferried to Wright Field on 20 August. Les Tower made the trip nonstop in nine hours. The new airplane averaged 232mph for the 2100 mile journey from Seattle, an unheard of speed. Boeing executives were hopeful, but other giants in the business were competing for the lucrative contract. Martin was showing a twin-engine ship, the B-12, and Douglas was flexing its muscles with another, the B-18.

Lieutenant Don Putt, who was assigned to test the 299 for the Army, recalled later, 'We thought it was one of the best ships that ever came across the board. Our inspection boys practically tore it apart, and I don't think there was a plane that ever went through with a better record.'

On 30 October, with Army test pilot Major Pete Hill in the cockpit, the 299 took off. The controls were inadvertently left in locked position, and the big plane spun into the ground. Control locks, which kept the rudder and flaps in place to prevent damage from the wind when the aircraft was on the ground, were not yet well known, so it was not uncommon for even experienced pilots to overlook them. Hill was killed, and Les Tower, along with a Boeing representative, died of burns later. The rest of the crew, including Lieutenant Don Putt, escaped, but the accident knocked Boeing out of the competition. Douglas's B-18 won the contract.

In spite of the accident, the Army had liked the way the 299 had performed. The accident had not been a fault of the airplane, but a tragic oversight. General Henry 'Hap' Arnold, of the Army Air Corps, gave permission on 17 January 1936 for Boeing to build 13 airplanes. In addition, an order was placed for a static test model, bringing the order up to 14 Model 299Bs.

The Army gave the Model 299B the designation YB-17, with the designation changing to Y1B-17 on 20 November as the planes were being purchased with 'F-1' funds. Boeing went into

Near right: A pair of **B-17Es** can be recognized by their faceted plexiglass noses. Later B-17Es were equipped with the ball turret that was standard equipment on the F and G models.

Above right: The **B-17C** was the first to be equipped with the 'bathtub' style gun fairing in the ventral position.

Below: The early **B-17s** were sent to Wright Field, Ohio, for evaluation by the Army Air Corps.

**Specifications: B-17C Flying Fortress
(RAF Fortress I)
Boeing Model Number 299H**

Span	103 ft 9 in
Length	67 ft 11 in
Wing Area	1420 sq ft
Tail Height	15 ft 5 in
Gross Weight	39,065 pounds
Bomb Capacity	4800 pounds
Top Speed	300 mph
Cruising Speed	227 mph
Ferry Range	3400 miles
Service Ceiling	36,000 ft
Powerplant	four 1200 hp Wright R-1820-65
Defensive Armament	seven machine guns, typically one 0.3 in and six 0.5 in

**Specifications: B-17E Flying Fortress
(RAF Fortress IIA)
Boeing Model Number 299-0**

Span	103 ft 9 in
Length	75 ft 10 in
Wing Area	1420 sq ft
Tail Height	19 ft 2 in
Gross Weight	40,260 pounds
Bomb Capacity	4200 pounds
Top Speed	318 mph
Cruising Speed	226 mph
Ferry Range	3300 miles
Service Ceiling	35,000 ft
Powerplant	four 1200 hp Wright R-1820-65
Defensive Armament	eight 0.5 in machine guns in turrets and waist positions and one 0.3 in in the nose

immediate production, and the first Y1B-17 was flown on 2 December 1936, a little over two years from the invitation to bid. The major change over the original Model 299 was the substitution of Wright Cyclone engines for the Hornets. The Wrights yielded 930hp, against the Hornets' 750.

Shortly after the first Y1B-17s went into service, the Army delivered specifications for the static test airplane, the fourteenth. It was to be a high-altitude bomber, with turbo-supercharged engines. This was delivered as the Y1B-17A and first flew in April 1939. This in turn resulted in a production order for 39 more slightly improved planes, which were called the B-17B. These were all delivered by March 1940. The B-17B featured 1200hp Wright Cyclone engines, and a redesigned nose. There was a navigator's blister above the cockpit, and constant-speed full feathering propellers. This model also introduced larger flaps and rudder.

The United States was aware it could become involved in World War II long before the Japanese attacked Pearl Harbor. German U-boats had been sinking Allied freighters off the east coast for some time. US Coast Guard escorts were assigned to the nearly helpless cargo ships, but German Wolf Packs lurked deep in international waters, where the Coast Guard had no authority, and picked off their targets. It was a ghastly slaughter, and it brought death so close that Washington, DC could not miss it. This arrogant nose-thumbing by the Axis served as a warning and led the United States to begin preparations for World War II

much sooner than might otherwise have been the case. President Franklin D Roosevelt did not wait for the Japanese to attack Pearl Harbor before increasing the forces of defense.

As the war in Europe gathered momentum, the 'Arsenal of Democracy' went to work. The Boeing Airplane Company was to be among the most important of the bomber manufacturers. Long before the US entered the war, the B-17 was on the way though it had inadequacies. These were not fully realized, however, until the B-17 came under actual combat conditions. Twenty B-17Cs were delivered to Britain's Royal Air Force, as Fortress Mark Is, in 1941. The RAF took them into combat, but the results were disappointing. Though the supercharged engines were efficient enough at high altitudes, the Browning machine guns froze up in the frigid atmosphere, and German fighters attacked from the rear, a blind spot. Eight bombers were lost in a short time, and instead of Flying Fortresses, the B-17s earned the less-confident nickname Flying Coffins.

Boeing had expected that changes would be needed, went back to the drawing board and came up with the B-17D. The electrical system was revised and self-sealing fuel tanks were added. More protective armor was added for the crew, and firepower increased. Cowl flaps opened the way for better engine cooling.

Most of the USAAF B-17Ds were delivered to the 19th Bombardment Group in the Philippines where they were caught largely off guard when the Japanese attacked Clark Field on 8 December 1941 (at the same time as their 7 December attack on

Leslie R Tower was born in Polson, Montana, in 1903. He saw his first 'flying machine' at the age of eight and thereupon dedicated his life to aviation. As soon as he graduated from high school he went to Seattle to study engineering at the University of Washington. After a year there, he joined the army as a flying cadet and served at Brooks and Kelly Fields before returning to his studies. In 1925 he joined the Boeing Aircraft Company as a draftsman. In 1927 he became chief test pilot for Boeing. Every plane developed by the company until 1935, from tiny pursuits to the giant Boeing 299 bomber, was taken on its first flight by Tower.

In addition to testing the new designs, Tower often ferried new military planes to Wright Field, Ohio, or Bolling Field in Anacostia, DC, as well as to west coast fields. He went as far as Japan, Spain and Brazil to demonstrate Boeing planes. He was in Spain with Major Erik Nelson demonstrating a Boeing ship in 1935 when he was recalled to test the bomber in which his career was brought to a premature end. He was severely injured in the wreck of the Army's newest Flying Fortress at Dayton, Ohio, in October, with another pilot at the controls. Tower died on 19 November 1935 after a hopeless fight against complications which resulted.

Les Tower was recognized as possibly the finest test pilot in the world. His record of eight years as chief pilot for Boeing without a single crackup is without equal.

Below: The **XB-17** prototype.

Pearl Harbor across the International Date Line in Hawaii). The aircraft that survived fought a valiant rear guard action as the Japanese advanced. They were, however, hampered by the same lack of defensive armament (particularly the absence of a tail gun) that had caused the British so much grief earlier against the Germans. Only one of the B-17Ds, nicknamed 'The Swoose' survived the campaign, returning to the States via Australia in 1942.

The tremendous stamina of the Boeing planes grew into legend. Many returned from raids with hundreds of bullet and flak holes in their bodies. Engines were shot out of action, wings and tail surfaces shattered, men killed and wounded, and yet the Fortress staggered home. Not all made it to safety, however, and a total of 4750 were lost. This of course reflects the B-17s large share of the fighting over Europe, Africa and, to a lesser extent, the Pacific.

The B-17's reputation as a powerful weapon grew after each encounter, whether in the Pacific or Europe.

On 14 December 1941, a B-17D commanded by Lieutenant Hewitt T Wheless, of the 19th Bombardment Group, was sent to attack a Japanese transport. The 19th BG had retreated from Clark Field under enemy pressure and were now stationed at Del Monte on Luzon, still in the Philippines. There were three Fortresses in the squadron that sallied out to sink the transport. Wheless became separated from the others in low clouds, so he continued alone. He found the freighter and was getting ready to

drop his bombs, when a force of 18 Japanese fighters dropped on him.

There followed a short, fierce battle that left one US airman dead and three Japanese fighters destroyed. The bombs were released on target, but the Japanese kept coming. The Fortress crew fought back until their guns jammed or ran out of ammunition. There was nothing they could do now but wait in grim silence. Lieutenant Wheless turned the bomber toward Del Monte.

The number one engine was dead and the radio out of commission. One fuel tank had been ripped apart, and the oxygen system shot away. The B-17s were not pressurized, and crews wore oxygen masks at high altitudes. However, in this case Wheless was flying low, and oxygen was not needed. In addition to the rest of the damage, the tail wheel was missing and the tires were flat. Two-thirds of the control cables had been damaged, and the fuselage was riddled with holes. Despite all this, the B-17D thrummed along on three engines, while the surviving crewmen waited. After 20 minutes more of Japanese attack, the enemy guns were quiet, out of ammunition. The Japanese pilots flew close for a look at this dauntless bomber, and later reported it as a 'four engined fighter.'

Below: War and peace. **B-17Bs** share the floor of Plant 2 with **Stratoliners** in this photograph taken in November 1939, ten weeks after the outbreak of the war in Europe.

B-17F FORWARD COMPARTMENTS

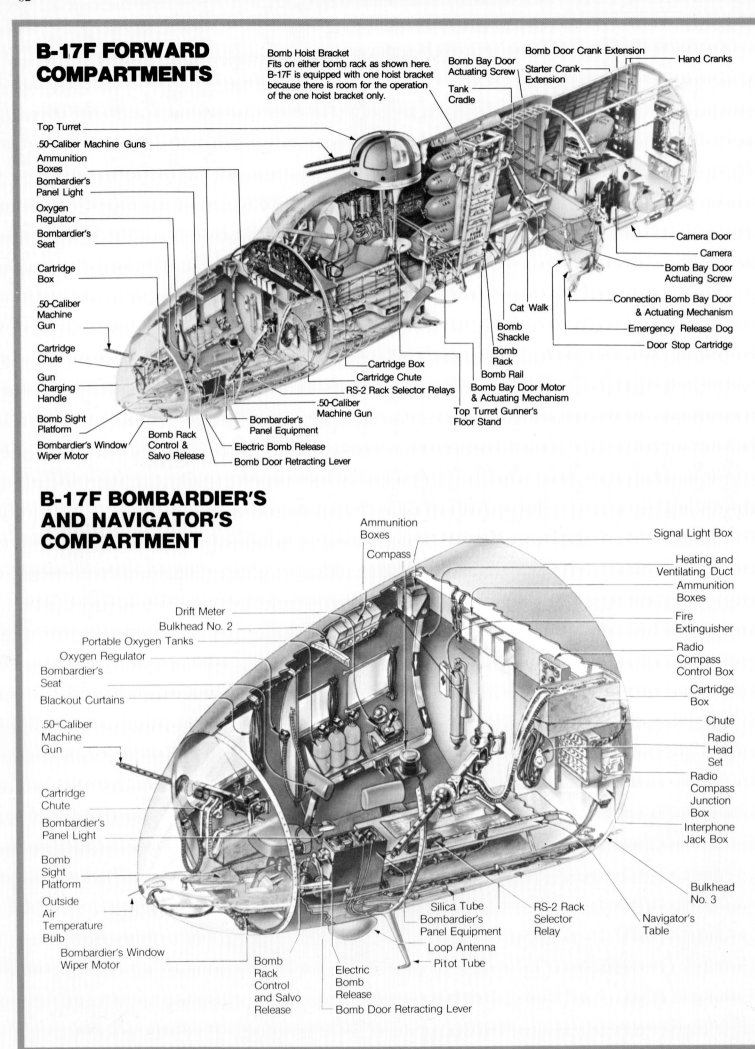

Bomb Hoist Bracket
Fits on either bomb rack as shown here. B-17F is equipped with one hoist bracket because there is room for the operation of the one hoist bracket only.

Bomb Bay Door Actuating Screw

Tank Cradle

Bomb Door Crank Extension

Starter Crank Extension

Hand Cranks

Top Turret

.50-Caliber Machine Guns

Ammunition Boxes

Bombardier's Panel Light

Oxygen Regulator

Bombardier's Seat

Cartridge Box

.50-Caliber Machine Gun

Cartridge Chute

Gun Charging Handle

Bomb Sight Platform

Bombardier's Window Wiper Motor

Bomb Rack Control & Salvo Release

Bombardier's Panel Equipment

Electric Bomb Release

Bomb Door Retracting Lever

Cartridge Box

Cartridge Chute

RS-2 Rack Selector Relays

.50-Caliber Machine Gun

Cat Walk

Bomb Shackle

Bomb Rack

Bomb Rail

Bomb Bay Door Motor & Actuating Mechanism

Top Turret Gunner's Floor Stand

Camera Door

Camera

Bomb Bay Door Actuating Screw

Connection Bomb Bay Door & Actuating Mechanism

Emergency Release Dog

Door Stop Cartridge

B-17F BOMBARDIER'S AND NAVIGATOR'S COMPARTMENT

Ammunition Boxes

Compass

Signal Light Box

Heating and Ventilating Duct

Ammunition Boxes

Fire Extinguisher

Radio Compass Control Box

Cartridge Box

Chute

Radio Head Set

Radio Compass Junction Box

Interphone Jack Box

Bulkhead No. 3

Navigator's Table

Drift Meter

Bulkhead No. 2

Portable Oxygen Tanks

Oxygen Regulator

Bombardier's Seat

Blackout Curtains

.50-Caliber Machine Gun

Cartridge Chute

Bombardier's Panel Light

Bomb Sight Platform

Outside Air Temperature Bulb

Bombardier's Window Wiper Motor

Bomb Rack Control and Salvo Release

Electric Bomb Release

Bomb Door Retracting Lever

Silica Tube

Bombardier's Panel Equipment

Loop Antenna

Pitot Tube

RS-2 Rack Selector Relay

B-17F REAR COMPARTMENTS

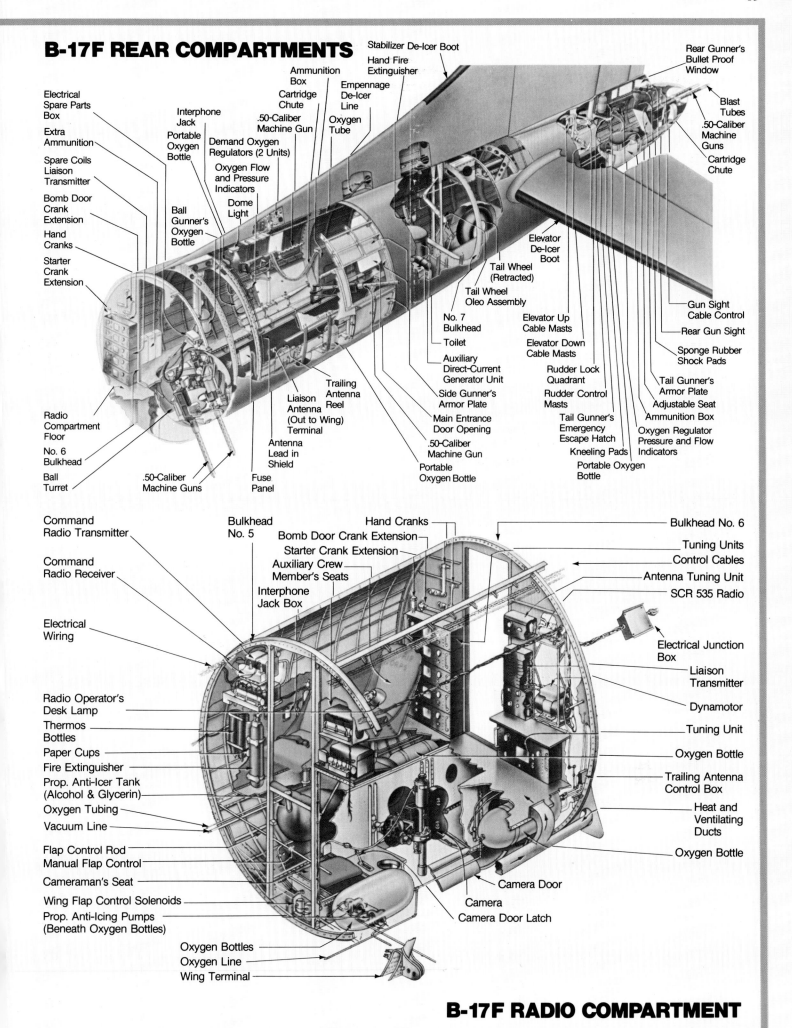

Electrical Spare Parts Box

Extra Ammunition

Spare Coils Liaison Transmitter

Bomb Door Crank Extension

Hand Cranks

Starter Crank Extension

Radio Compartment Floor

No. 6 Bulkhead

Ball Turret

Interphone Jack

Portable Oxygen Bottle

Ball Gunner's Oxygen Bottle

.50-Caliber Machine Guns

Stabilizer De-Icer Boot

Hand Fire Extinguisher

Ammunition Box

Cartridge Chute

.50-Caliber Machine Gun

Demand Oxygen Regulators (2 Units)

Oxygen Flow and Pressure Indicators

Dome Light

Empennage De-Icer Line

Oxygen Tube

Liaison Antenna (Out to Wing) Terminal

Trailing Antenna Reel

Antenna Lead in Shield

Fuse Panel

Elevator De-Icer Boot

Tail Wheel (Retracted)

Tail Wheel Oleo Assembly

No. 7 Bulkhead

Toilet

Auxiliary Direct-Current Generator Unit

Side Gunner's Armor Plate

Main Entrance Door Opening

.50-Caliber Machine Gun

Portable Oxygen Bottle

Elevator Up Cable Masts

Elevator Down Cable Masts

Rudder Lock Quadrant

Rudder Control Masts

Tail Gunner's Emergency Escape Hatch

Kneeling Pads

Portable Oxygen Bottle

Rear Gunner's Bullet Proof Window

Blast Tubes

.50-Caliber Machine Guns

Cartridge Chute

Gun Sight Cable Control

Rear Gun Sight

Sponge Rubber Shock Pads

Tail Gunner's Armor Plate

Adjustable Seat

Ammunition Box

Oxygen Regulator Pressure and Flow Indicators

Command Radio Transmitter

Command Radio Receiver

Electrical Wiring

Radio Operator's Desk Lamp

Thermos Bottles

Paper Cups

Fire Extinguisher

Prop. Anti-Icer Tank (Alcohol & Glycerin)

Oxygen Tubing

Vacuum Line

Flap Control Rod

Manual Flap Control

Cameraman's Seat

Wing Flap Control Solenoids

Prop. Anti-Icing Pumps (Beneath Oxygen Bottles)

Oxygen Bottles

Oxygen Line

Wing Terminal

Bulkhead No. 5

Bomb Door Crank Extension

Starter Crank Extension

Auxiliary Crew Member's Seats

Interphone Jack Box

Hand Cranks

Camera Door

Camera

Camera Door Latch

Bulkhead No. 6

Tuning Units

Control Cables

Antenna Tuning Unit

SCR 535 Radio

Electrical Junction Box

Liaison Transmitter

Dynamotor

Tuning Unit

Oxygen Bottle

Trailing Antenna Control Box

Heat and Ventilating Ducts

Oxygen Bottle

B-17F RADIO COMPARTMENT

PRODUCTION CLOSE-UP
B-17 FLYING FORTRESS

(Model 299)

| 1000 | 2000 | 3000 | 4000 |

XB-17-B-17A

Initial prototype series, including 13 *Y1B-17's*.

15

B-17B-D

Initial production series, saw the evolution of a redesigned nose and the addition of armament and self-sealing fuel tanks. 20 were transferred to Britain as *Fortress Mk I*.

119

B-17E

This model incorporated a redesigned rear fuselage and vertical tail surface, the addition of waist guns and 3 turrets. 46 were transferred to Britain as *Fortress MkIIA*.

512

B-17F

The *B-17F* standardized use of the Bendix ball turret introduced in later *B-17Es* and featured a one-piece plexiglass nose. 19 were transferred to Britain as *Fortress Mk II*.

2300 (Produced by Boeing/Seattle plant)

605 (Produced by Douglas)

500 (Produced by Vega)

B-17G

The principal production model, the *G* model was like the *F*, but with the addition of a chin turret and improved Superchargers. 112 were transferred to Britain as *Fortress Mk III*.

4035 (Produced by Boeing/Seattle plant)

2395 (Produced by Douglas)

2250 (Produced by Vega)

Other military aircraft designations with B-17 (Model 299) Airframes.

B-17H: Airborne lifeboat conversions of *B-17G*. 130 were planned, but only 12 were actually converted.

B-17L-P: Additional *B-17* conversions, used as target drones, target drone directors, etc.

XB-38: A single *B-17E* re-engined with 4 Allison liquid-cooled engines.

B-40: 25 *B-17Fs* equipped with a greatly increased number of machine guns, including additional dorsal & ventral turrets on some. The *B-40* saw limited service with the 8th AF as a long-range escort for bomber formations over Europe.

BQ-7: 25 used *B-17Es* & *Fs* were modified as radio-controlled bombs under Project Castor. Carrying up to 20,000 lbs of high explosives each, 11 one-way missions were flown against German targets before the project was cancelled because of the unreliability of the radio-control mechanism.

C-108: Four transport conversions from *B-17Es* and *Fs* including General MacArthur's personal executive transport "Bataan."

F-9: 29 *B-17Fs* and 9 *B-17Gs* converted to photo-reconnaissance versions with the addition of cameras in the nose, bomb bay and rear fuselage. In 1945 they were redesignated *FB-17F and G* and in 1948 they were redesignated again as *RB-17F and G*.

PB: 32 *B-17Gs* in US Navy service with APS-20 search radar added and defensive armament removed. An additional 17 *B-17Gs* became *PB-1Gs* in US Coast Guard Service.

Above: A Seattle-built **B-17F** with the one-piece plexiglass nose and ventral ball turret that became standard on the F model. The ball turret had first been introduced on the B-17E, but the one-piece nose was the feature that most distinguished the B-17F from its predecessor.

Lieutenant Wheless kept the ship on course, but gas was leaking from punctured tanks, and he realized the plane would run out of fuel before reaching home base. He changed course for Cagayan on Mindanao, but as he approached the airfield he saw it was covered with barricades. There was no way to avoid them, and not enough fuel left to reach another base, so the Fortress plowed across the field, coming to an abrupt halt tipped up on its nose. The crewmen leaped to safety, and the danger was over. They later counted over 1000 bullet holes in their ship.

Even before America was at war with Japan, Boeing had made radical improvements to the B-17D design. The next variant, the B-17E, which first flew on 5 September 1941, featured a major redesign of the rear fuselage and tail which considerably changed the outward appearance of the aircraft. The fuselage and tail surfaces were increased in size, which gave better control and stability in high altitude bombing. The B-17E was some six feet longer than the earlier models. The larger tail permitted the fitting of a pair of .50 caliber machine guns in that long-neglected position. Power operated turrets were also fitted in the dorsal and ventral positions and additional armor plate was carried. With all these changes the B-17E was considerably heavier than the original Model 299. During the next hectic months 512 B-17Es were built, 46 of which were delivered to Britain as Fortress IIAs.

Initially, the ventral turret was operated by periscope from below the waist hatches. This proved awkward in combat so the turret was replaced by the unique Sperry ball turret, an innovation that was to be maintained on later model B-17s.

In the summer of 1942 the first B-17Es arrived in Britain manned by American crews. These Fortresses were bristling with armament, quite different than earlier versions. The Es struck first on 17 August 1942. Their target was Rouen, a rail center northwest of Paris. Twelve Forts poured destruction on freight yards, trains, and round houses. Despite RAF experience of heavy losses in daylight raids in the early months of the war, the American leaders were still convinced that the Flying Fortresses could defend themselves against daytime fighter attack while bombing far more accurately than was possible at night. Although both these claims were later to come into question, on this occasion the B-17s came over at 25,000 feet, plastered their targets effectively and then returned safely to England.

The B-17F was introduced in April 1942 with a Wright Cyclone GR-1820-97 engine delivering 1380hp at 25,000 feet. In addition to the new engines and the now institutionalized ventral ball

Specifications: B-17F Flying Fortress (RAF Fortress II)
Boeing Model Number 299P

Span	103 ft 9 in
Length	74 ft 9 in
Wing Area	1420 sq ft
Tail Height	19 ft 2 in
Gross Weight	65,000 pounds
Bomb Capacity	9600 pounds
Top Speed	299 mph
Cruising Speed	200 mph
Ferry Range	3500 miles
Service Ceiling	37,500 ft
Powerplant	four 1200 hp Wright R-1820-65/97
Defensive Armament	nine 0.5 in machine guns

86

Below: A side-view interior cutaway of a Boeing/Seattle-built **B-17G** of the Eighth Air Force (1st Bomb Wing, 91st Bomb Group).

Above: A top view of an Eighth Air Force (1st Bombardment Wing, 351st Bombardment Group) **B-17G** taken on a mission over Germany.

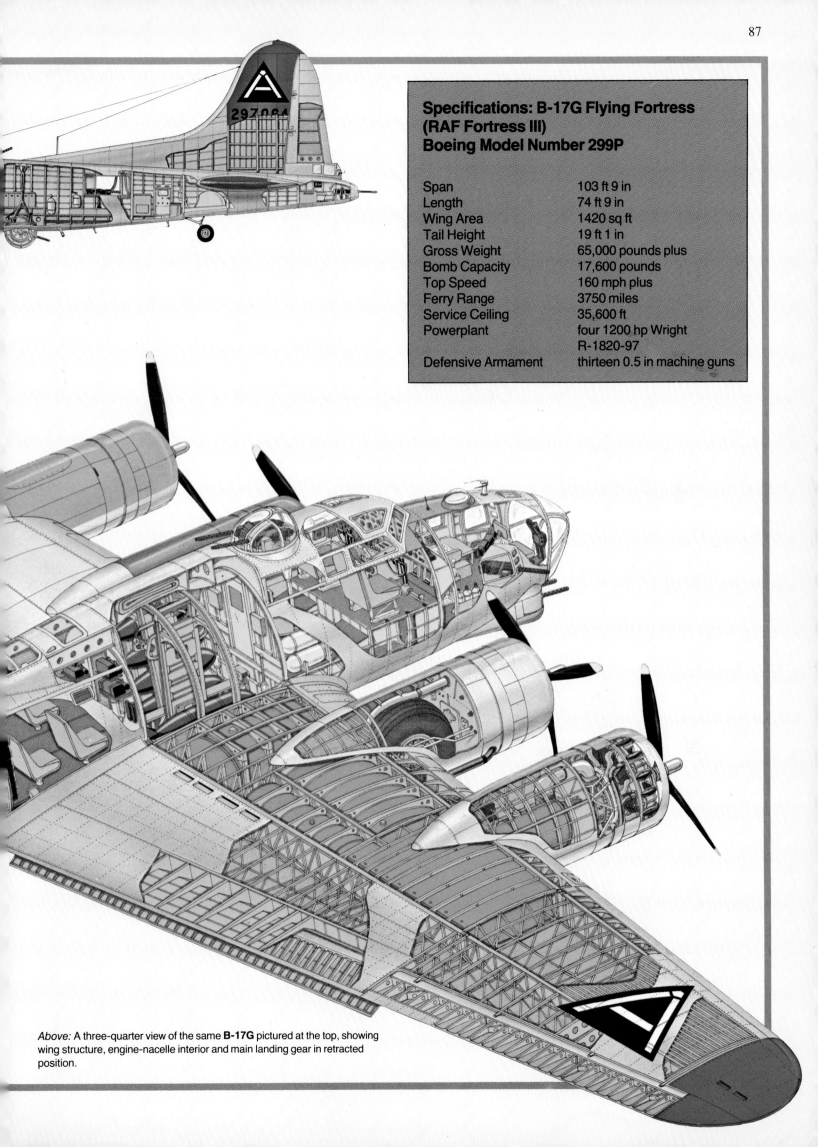

**Specifications: B-17G Flying Fortress
(RAF Fortress III)
Boeing Model Number 299P**

Span	103 ft 9 in
Length	74 ft 9 in
Wing Area	1420 sq ft
Tail Height	19 ft 1 in
Gross Weight	65,000 pounds plus
Bomb Capacity	17,600 pounds
Top Speed	160 mph plus
Ferry Range	3750 miles
Service Ceiling	35,600 ft
Powerplant	four 1200 hp Wright R-1820-97
Defensive Armament	thirteen 0.5 in machine guns

Above: A three-quarter view of the same **B-17G** pictured at the top, showing wing structure, engine-nacelle interior and main landing gear in retracted position.

Above: Eighth Air Force (1st Bomb Wing, 91st Bomb Group) **B-17Gs** in camouflage colors on their way to a target in Occupied Europe.

Below: The **B-17G** 'front office.'

turret, the F incorporated a one-piece molded plexiglass nose. The faceted nose of earlier models had inhibited visibility, making the one-piece nose a welcome improvement. The gross weight limit of the F was greatly increased over the E and extra 1100 gallon fuel cells, known as 'Tokyo Tanks' were added, extending the range considerably. It had been planned to have some of the B-17E production taken over by other manufacturers with surplus production capacity, but the B-17F superseded the E before the plan could be implemented. Over the course of the 15 months the F was in production, however, 605 Fs were built by the Douglas factories and another 500 by Vega. Boeing itself was to build a staggering 2300 in Seattle.

In May 1943 one B-17E was experimentally fitted with four 1425hp Allison V-1710-89 twelve cylinder liquid-cooled engines and redesignated XB-38. The idea was to determine whether the more powerful engines would increase the overall performance of the Model 299 airframe sufficiently to make it worthwhile to consider building a production series of B-38As. Performance was increased, but the single XB-38 was destroyed by fire in June before the tests were completed. With the Allison engines in great demand for the P-38 and P-40 fighters and the coming on line of the B-17F, it was considered less than prudent to divert precious production capability to an untested project, so the B-38 program was scrapped.

Meanwhile the B-17Es and Fs were swelling the ranks of the Eighth Air Force in England as a major part of the Allied Combined Bomber Offensive against targets in occupied Europe. The USAAF was given the daylight precision bombing role, while the RAF conducted area bombing by night. In flying to and from their targets it became evident that, despite their defensive armament, the bombers needed fighter escorts. The targets were generally beyond the range of Allied fighters so the German fighters found themselves free to attack the bombers without having to fight their way through a protective screen of fighters.

Below: The **B-17** gained a well-deserved reputation for being able to suffer severe damage and still limp back to base.

While longer range fighters were being developed, an interim idea evolved to take the basic B-17/Model 299 airframe, which certainly had the required range, and adapt it as a flying gun platform. Vega converted a B-17F and the result was designated XB-40. Twenty YB-40s followed. Though the specific armament varied from plane to plane, the result was a true 'flying fortress.' There were as many as 30 automatic weapons ranging from .50 caliber machine guns in multiple turrets to 20mm and in some cases 40mm cannons mounted in the waist positions. The first mission to be flown with a YB-40 escort was against St Nazaire in May 1943, and there were others to follow. It soon became evident that while the B-40s could keep up with the bomb laden B-17s on the way to the target, they could not, with the weight of all their guns and ammunition, match the speed and altitude of the empty B-17s on their way home. The project was deemed a failure and although four TB-40s would see service stateside as crew trainers, the program was scrapped in August 1943.

One innovation of the B-40 program was deemed successful however, and was incorporated into the later B-17Fs and the new B-17Gs that went into production in July 1943. That innovation was the Bendix power-operated chin turret. The B-17G was essentially similar to the B-17F except for the chin turret and a few other more minor armament modifications. The B-17G went on to be produced in larger numbers than any other model of any Boeing-designed aircraft before or since. In total 8680 B-17Gs were produced against less than half that for all other variants combined. Of the total, 4035 Gs were produced by Boeing with the rest coming off the Douglas and Vega lines, bringing the total B-17s of all variants to 12,731.

At the time Pearl Harbor was bombed, Boeing was producing B-17s at the rate of 60 a month. A year and a half later, as the B-17G was coming on line, production had more than quadrupled. The Boeing/Douglas/Vega pool went on to hit a peak B-17 production month in March 1944, when 578 B-17Gs rolled off the lines. After that, Boeing's contribution to the pool declined as emphasis was put on B-29 production.

Although the B-17 opened its campaign over occupied Europe in August 1942 with the attack on Rouen already mentioned, it was not until 27 January 1943 that a target in Germany, the port of Wilhelmshaven, was attacked. By the summer of 1943 the Eighth Air Force had begun to make deep-penetration daylight raids over Germany in considerable strength, giving the B-17s their most difficult assignment to that date. Although the Fortresses inflicted serious damage on German industry in these attacks, their losses became very severe as the German defenses increased their skill. Typical of this period were the particularly important and bloody attacks on Regensburg and Schweinfurt on 17 August. On 14 October Schweinfurt was visited again, this time by 291 Forts. After this raid 60 B-17s were missing, another 17 were critically shot up and many more were damaged.

Such losses could not be tolerated and, for a time, the Eighth Air Force limited its attacks to targets closer to home. However, with the introduction of the long-range escort version of the P-51 Mustang fighter at the end of 1943, the B-17s were able to resume their battle over Germany with growing success. The increase in Allied strength was such that, on Christmas Eve 1944, some 2000 American bombers were sent on missions over Germany. Of these, 1400 were B-17s. The Allies were well able to repeat this

Top: **'Aluminum Overcast'** was the term applied to the vast number of natural-metal finish B-17s that appeared over German targets in the last year of the war. This B-17G, individually named *Aluminum Overcast,* flew with the 1st Bombardment Wing of the Eighth Air Force and has been preserved in flying condition.

Left: An armada of Eighth Air Force (1st Bombardment Wing, 381st Bomb Group) **B-17Gs** with fighter escort leave England for their targets.

Above: After the war the USAF found little need for the USAAF's gallant bombers. A dozen B-17Gs, however, served the USAF as **B-17H** search and rescue aircraft.

Left: The arsenal of democracy. **B-17Gs** in the final phase of assembly on the floor of Plant 2.

performance, and such large numbers in the end ground Germany's resources to bits. Hitler had reason to fear the Flying Fortress.

These gallant ships and their crews served on the European front until 25 April 1945. On that day, 307 of them flew a final bombing mission. They attacked the Skoda armament factory and did their worst, or best, depending on point of view. American crews by this time were experts at the deadly work of dropping bombs. Six of the big ships were lost on the raid, however, so a price was paid.

The role played by the B-17 as part of the awesome Allied air armada that undertook the destruction of the war-making capability of the German Reich was tremendous. Of the more than one and one half million tons of bombs dropped on European targets by the USAAF, 640,036 fell from B17s compared to 452,508 tons dropped by Consolidated B-24 Liberators and 463,544 by all other aircraft combined.

After the war was over in both Europe and the Pacific, most B-17s went into the scrap heap, but not all.

It was fitting that the airplane would survive which prompted General Ira C Eaker to say, 'The B-17, I think, was the best combat plane ever built.' General Eaker was instrumental in developing offensive bombing tactics during the most critical period of the war and he knew his airplanes. The United States Air Force's first Chief of Staff, General Carl A 'Tooey' Spaatz, echoed Eaker's words when he said, 'I'd rather have the B-17 than any other.'

So the Flying Fortress did not perish outright. Foreign air forces, including those of Brazil and Israel, bought some. The Israeli Air Force took Fortresses into action during its 1948 War of Independence. Some B-17s were 'civilianized' by the Danish airline DDL, and flown as passenger/cargo carriers.

There were other uses. B-17s carrying underslung lifeboats which could be dropped by parachute were put to use with the designation B-17H (PB-1G in Coast Guard service). The Navy converted others for action in anti-submarine and weather reconnaissance work. Some Forts remained in military service as VIP transports and trainers. More were converted to radio-controlled drones, serving as targets. The last B-17 in US military service, a QB-17 drone, was destroyed in 1960. It was an incident touched with irony, because the destroying weapon was a Boeing developed Bomarc missile.

Below: After the war most of the **B-17Gs** that escaped the scrapyard ultimately had all their turrets deleted. The *Virgin's Delight* is preserved at the Castle Air Museum on the grounds of Castle AFB near Merced, California. Boeing KC-135 Stratotankers can be seen in the background.

Above: **The five thousandth B-17** was a Seattle-built G which was autographed by everybody who worked on it.

Below: The 'village' on the roof of **Plant 2** as photographed in 1945, after aerial photographs of the site were permitted. The 'roads' across Boeing Field, still visible in this photograph, were allowed to deteriorate later in the war as air attack became less likely.

he success of the B-17 and the enormous numbers of them produced were no accident. In 1939 Phil Johnson had been brought back into the company as president. Under his leadership and organizational ability, Boeing met the challenge of wartime production. To handle the enormous increase, thousands of workers were added to the payroll. Security was a constant worry. War jitters panicked sensible men, and every Japanese-American became suspect of spying. The Aleutian Islands were, after all, under attack, and enemy submarines had been sighted off the west coast with one shelling oil tanks near Santa Barbara, California.

To accommodate wartime production, the Boeing plants grew to an enormous 1,500,000 square feet of space, over 26 acres. If one Japanese submarine shell could cause trouble, a dozen would create a tangle it would take months to clear. Nor was there any doubt a raid was possible. The Boeing plants were on the Duwamish River, which flowed into Puget Sound, so close the fog horns could be heard on thick nights. And Puget Sound was deep enough to allow submarines access. There was also the threat of Japanese pilots flying long-distance one-way missions from a carrier and dropping destruction by the ton.

To prevent this, or at least to confuse the enemy, an ingenious marvel of camouflage was created. The Army Engineers, Passive Defense Division, were the instigators. They created a village over the roof-tops of Boeing's Seattle plants. From the air, the factory area looked for all the world like a small town. And who would bother about a helpless little town?

It was a huge task, covering a 26 acre site. Houses were made from canvas with painted windows. Trees up to twelve feet tall, shrubs and grass, were created from a million and a half feet of chicken wire covered with feathers and spun glass. They were colored whatever hue was necessary to lend an aspect of reality. Roads and streets were shaped with more canvas, covered with burlap. Where 'roads' crossed Boeing Field, which was directly

across the street from the factories, they were made of dirt soaked with oil.

There were 53 houses in 'town,' 24 garages, a corner service station, three greenhouses, and a store. There were three main streets, with numerous automobiles, and a cow grazing in a pasture. It was a real cow, eating real grass. There were even street signs with names like 'Synthetic Street,' and 'Burlap Blvd.' Two of the buildings, however, were genuine. They housed anti-aircraft guns with crews. Those who flew over the area in Army air transports recall that the camouflage was perfect, even at low levels, though it did seem weird to land on a country road. Occasionally, a pilot new to the area became confused, and had to be led down by another airplane.

The entire village was treated with a fire-retardent chemical as a precaution. There were, in addition, 67 sprinklers and 100 fire hydrants. One million board feet of lumber had gone into the construction of the village, an invitation to disaster by fire.

Security personnel were everywhere, in around-the-clock service. These included a company of Army Military Guards from the 41st Division as well as civilians. Among the civilian security people were women. Women were found to be especially good at such duties as traffic control, pass checking, and searching cars – and lunch pails – for pilferage. They were sharply dressed in blue-gray gabardine uniforms, but carried no firearms. Their duties did not take them to areas of possible violence, such as remote areas of the plants, where there were few, if any, people. But the women took their work seriously, and there was never a lack of applications. Being a guard was considered a top job.

It was a far cry from an occasion during World War I when E M Gott, General Manager, sent a typed letter to I M Ortman, Purchasing Agent, directing him to have a talk with the day watchman. The watchman was not showing enough authority at the gate. He should ensure that 'suspicious characters do not loiter in the vicinity of the gate or fence.'

Despite precautions, there were leaks. In order to obtain access to the B-29 assembly lines, it was necessary to get a special pass. The work was kept under wraps, secret, nobody other than workers directly involved knew a B-29 was in the making.

Top company brass were surprised, therefore, when a twelve-year-old boy from Wyoming wrote asking for more information on the B-29. He then proceeded to list amazing details about the hush-hush project, and made suggestions as to what information he would like to have. The leak was attributed to loose talk, and nothing was ever done to the boy.

There was little sabotage, however. A B-29 wing section was deeply slashed, but it had been done by an irate employee, not a saboteur. Some industrial diamonds were missing, but subsequent investigation turned them up at the home of another

Below: A stroll on Synthetic Street.

worker. The elaborate security system seemed to be working well.

However, not all systems are perfect. Though Boeing personnel managers made every effort to screen prospective employees, weeding out suspicious characters, some got by. The war had drawn Army contingents to many Alaskan towns. The Territory was considered vulnerable to Japanese air attacks, and defenses were bolstered. It happened that the Army contingent in Ketchikan closed the red-light district. The girls were sent to Seattle, where eventually, they found their way to Boeing payrolls. Alas for patriotism! The girls had to be fired, when it was learned that making arrangements for off-duty liaisons took precedence over building airplanes. All in all, though, Boeing security was very good.

The Seattle plants were awesome in their efficiency. Around-the-clock shifts involved a total of 40,000 men and women. The acres of overhanging fluorescent lights, the cavernous assembly halls whose floors were covered with gleaming metal wings, gave the scene a surrealistic atmosphere. The din of chattering rivet guns and clanking power tools added to the confusion. Yet it was here, in a larger-than-life setting, that the B-17 and B-29 were built, two airplanes which hastened the end of a terrible war.

Below: A shift change at **Plant 2** circa 1942.

Above: A **B-29** outside the big Renton plant at the foot of Lake Washington, where the majority of the B-29s were built.

Below: Technicians check out the engines of a **B-29** at the Boeing Field dispersal site.

Above: One of the first **B-29 Superfortresses** in formation with a **B-17G,** the last production model of the Flying Fortress. The early B-29s and B-17Gs were painted in camouflage colors but spent most of their careers in natural metal finish.

s first-hand combat experience and new technology brought improvements to the B-17, these improvements were extended to Boeing's second great World War II bomber, the B-29 Superfortress.

The story of the B-29, like that of the B-17, starts in the 1930s. In 1938 Claire Egtvedt and Ed Wells paid a visit to Wright Field. Colonel Oliver Echols, an Air Corps engineering chief, was an admirer of the Flying Fortress and Consolidated's B-24 Liberator as well. 'The trouble is,' said Echols in essence, 'we need airplanes with a longer range. Our present bombers can fly 3000 miles. We want one that will go four or five thousand.' There was no money, however, from the military for preliminary plans. Congress felt that larger bombers would show the world an untoward 'aggressiveness.' It might spark suspicions in unfriendly countries, and set off conflicts. In 1938, Congress did not want war. The Great Depression, which had laid the nation flat economically, was trouble enough. When Egtvedt returned to Seattle, he did not worry about money. Instead, he put designers to work on a superbomber study. Ed Wells was to oversee the project. 'Get the drag down,' he told engineers. 'It's the only way we can give Echols the distance he wants. The rivets must be flush, gun turrets cannot protrude, nacelles have to be skin tight.'

By late 1939, however, official opinion had changed and a specification for a long-range bomber was drawn up. Boeing had continued with unofficial design work on the long-range bomber idea and was thus well prepared to respond when the specification was issued to a number of aircraft manufacturing companies in February 1940. What was required was a bomber with 5333 miles range and an all-round performance considerably superior to the B-17 in speed and payload. The initial design had to be ready in one month. A revised design was submitted in April and after further work and consideration an official contract to produce prototype XB-29s was issued in September 1940.

What was wanted, Boeing concluded from the original specification, was an airplane with no more drag than a B-17, even though twice as large. It would have to have flight and landing performances never before achieved. Though Boeing had had experience in big planes like the XB-15, the Clippers, and the Stratocruisers, the new aircraft was in a class by itself, presenting problems never encountered.

One of the results of the experimentation that followed was a new wing for what was to be the XB-29, Boeing Model 345. Enormous wing flaps were originated, larger in themselves than the wings of many fighter planes, the biggest ever put on an air-

plane. They did the job, providing hoped-for lift and performance, yet keeping landing speed acceptably low. Drag was reduced to a minimum, and the resultant wing became known as the '117' wing.

An ingenious 'three bubble' system of pressurization for the crew spaces was developed. The pilots' cabin and the waist gunner's section were pressurized, and the two compartments were connected by a pressurized tunnel. The tunnel overrode the two bomb bays. The tail gunner's area was pressurized on its own.

There were two bomb bays. One was forward of the wing, and the other aft. This meant that one bay could not be emptied before the other, without throwing the bomber temporarily out of trim, its center of gravity having shifted. So an alternating system of dropping bombs was invented by the engineers to release the bombs first from one bay then the other. In this way, the center of gravity was maintained, and the bomber kept level flight.

With customary thoroughness, Boeing tested its work the hard way. A fantastic structural testing program was developed for this special airplane. Included were tests to destruction in which major sections of the XB-29 were torn to pieces. Changes were made because of these 'torture tests,' and no alternations were

Above: Boeing people not only built the bombers, they went overseas to supervise their servicing. **Ken Hamner** was a Boeing service rep with the Fifteenth Air Force in Italy in 1944.

Below: A veteran of the Battle of Kansas: a Wichita-built **B-29** goes to war.

Below: Eddie Allen's namesake, the **B-29** *Eddie Allen* of the 40th BG, 20th Bomber Command, nears the target on the 3 November 1944 raid on Rangoon, Burma.

required in the basic structure after the Model 345 was completed. The engineers had done their work well.

Even before the first XB-29 had been thoroughly tested, the Army ordered 990 of them. Ten were to be delivered in 1942, 450 in 1943 and 530 in 1944. It was an unprecedented act of faith, but Echols, who authorized the contract, had that faith.

There was to be a hitch, however. Competing builders tried to convince Echols that the B-29 would have too much drag. They knew little about the '117' airfoil, which had been kept secret. Don Putt, the Army man who had tested the military's first B-17, was sent to Seattle to meet with Wellwood Beall and other officials. After reviewing what had been done with the wing, plus the other anti-drag features, Putt convinced Echols to go ahead with the program. However, the Army did require a large number of detail changes throughout the design process. Particularly important was the decision made in late 1941 to fit a remote control gun-aiming system based around a General Electric computer. This involved considerable changes to the aircraft's electrical system and an increase in weight.

The Boeing work force expanded dramatically to handle production. In addition to the Renton plant near Seattle, other companies were asked to build what had now become the B-29. Bell erected buildings in Marietta, Georgia, expressly for the purpose. Martin did the same in Omaha, Nebraska. Mass production of the world's largest bomber was underway, and, as yet, the B-29 had not been flown!

On 21 September 1942 Eddie Allen, Boeing's chief test pilot, took the first one aloft. He liked what the big airplane did. It was as far ahead of its contemporaries as the Boeing B-9 had been in 1931. It handled well, was fast, and though there were minor problems, he landed and said briefly, 'She flies.'

There followed a series of flight tests with Allen and others at the controls. Then, on 18 February 1943, an engine on the second prototype XB-29 that he was testing caught on fire over Lake Washington. Allen headed for an emergency landing on Boeing Field, but the stricken bomber lost altitude rapidly and crashed into the four-storied Frye meat-packing plant on Seattle's south side, killing all those aboard.

The Boeing Airplane Company lost eleven of the most experienced Superfortress program personnel. Once again the B-29 program faltered, but General Arnold, Chief of Staff of the Army Air Force, was by now committed to them. He had arranged with Chinese leader Chiang Kai-shek to build a number of bases inside Chinese borders specifically to handle the B-29s. There was no turning back now. Boeing stepped up production, and by early 1943, there were 25,000 employees in the Wichita plant and another 33,000 in Renton.

In such a large undertaking, there were bound to be problems. Boeing was obviously not the only company involved in producing war products, and vital materials were being used in great quantities. Parts for the B-29s stopped coming, and work slowed down. There were particular problems with the supply of engines. General Arnold had promised the first bombers would leave for China by 10 March 1944. He sent General Orval Cook, military production chief, to Kansas to confer with Earl Schaefer, top man at the plant.

On investigation, Cook learned that each B-29 needed much final work before passing inspection. One of the foremen took him through a typical round of 'touch up' work. Everything from correcting crossed-up switches to recalibrating fuel gauges had to be done. Nothing was left to chance. Every switch, knob, dial and lever was manually checked to see if it responded properly. It was a time-consuming task, and technicians were in short supply.

General Arnold had a war to fight, and when he learned that the 10 March deadline could not be met, he said very definitely that he wanted the first batch of B-29s in the air by 15 April, no excuses. Thus began the 'Battle of Kansas.'

Six hundred specialists were flown in from Seattle, and they worked steadily for four weeks to get the B-29s ready for flight.

Edmund T 'Eddie' Allen was born on 4 January 1896 in Chicago, Illinois. In 1917, after he had completed his first year at the University of Illinois, he enlisted in the Infantry, but changed to the aviation branch and enlisted in the Signal Corps. Following his training, he was sent to England to learn how the British tested their planes, which led him into the test-pilot field.

Allen returned to McCook Field, Ohio, before the armistice and later resigned from the army to become the first test pilot of the National Advisory Committee for Aeronautics at Langley Field. In 1920 he entered MIT for two years' study of aeronautical engineering. In 1923 he began test piloting for various airplane manufacturers. He became a civilian test pilot at McCook Field and in 1925 a pilot of the Post Office airmail service. When Boeing Air Transport took over the Chicago-San Francisco airmail service in 1927, Allen became one of their leading pilots, and by 1929 he was one of the nation's top consulting test pilots.

Allen test flew Boeing's B-17, the B-15 and the Clipper. He was Boeing's best test pilot and he knew more about the infinite mechanical complexities of the giant airplanes than any other man. In 1939 he became head of Boeing's Research Division and directed the planning and testing that led to the B-29.

Below: On **18 February 1943**, Allen took off in the second prototype XB-29 (its three-bladed props visible here) for engine tests. Twenty minutes after takeoff, he notified Boeing Field that he was coming in with a wing on fire. Moments later, the plane hit the Frye Packing Plant.

W J Yenne, a welder working at the nearby Todd Shipyard, saw the plane moments after the crash. He remembered seeing a huge plane, unlike the familiar B-17, on the building 'like a hen on her nest.' Soon the windows were glowing orange as the flames spread, then the building was swallowed in billowing smoke.

It was an all-out battle, and the technicians won. Late in March 1944, the first one was flown to India by Colonel Leonard 'Jake' Harman. It was turned over to the 20th Bomber Command, which was led by General K B Wolfe. This unit had been formed some months previously but because of the shortage of B-29s its training had been less extensive than had been planned.

Other B-29s followed Harman's to India but more trouble waited. Engines overheated in the 120 degree heat and several aircraft crashed. Word was sent back to the States about the problem and baffles were designed and fitted to allow cool air to flow back over the engines. In addition, top cowl flaps, originally fixed, could be adjusted from the cockpit.

An immediate ferrying operation began to supply the Chinese bases from which the bombers would conduct operations. It was an urgent matter, and the B-29s themselves and other aircraft were pressed into service.

It was necessary to cross the Himalayas between Burma and China (fliers called it 'flying the Hump') and the cold air at altitudes of 25,000 feet could cause carburetors to freeze. It was a serious problem, until an enlisted man, Sergeant Leonard Egyed, developed a method of keeping them warm, and efficiency smoothed out.

The first two B-29s to surmount the Hump arrived safely on 24 April 1944. They landed at Chengtu, 1000 miles from their starting point, on an airfield made ready by 75,000 Chinese laborers. Chiang Kai-shek had kept his word although facilities were far from perfect.

On the 26 April Major Charles E Hansen took off for Chengtu. As he crossed over the Hump, he was challenged by a dozen Japanese Nakajima Ki-43 fighters (Allied code name Oscar). For the first few moments, the fighters flew along with the Superfortress, looking it over. Later writings by Japanese pilots called the B-29s 'monstrous bulls,' and 'stupendous giants.' As, indeed, they were. After their look, the Japanese opened fire, and the gun crews of the B-29 returned the greeting with a fusillade of .50 caliber bullets. Due to inexperience, things did not go well for the Americans, and several guns jammed. The Oscars had their own way with the 'monstrous bull,' until the tail gunner, whose guns were still working, shot one down. Pilot Hansen climbed to 18,000 feet and the Japanese declined to follow. After they disappeared, Hansen continued to Chengtu, landing with, it was learned, surprisingly little damage. News of the fight spread throughout the B-29 bomber commands, and was greeted with cheers. The big ship had had its baptism of fire, and had proven worthy.

On 5 June 1944 the B-29 made its first actual bombing mission. Some 98 planes steered for Bangkok to blow up railroad yards. The planes flew in a loose formation, the better to use radar bomb aiming, but accuracy was poor. Damage was minimal. Japanese fighters and antiaircraft guns defended the territory but no B-29s were lost to enemy action. Fourteen had turned back at the outset because of mechanical trouble, one had crashed on take off and two were forced to ditch in the Bay of Bengal as a result of bad weather.

Above: **Dorothy Bennett** at work in a B-29.

Though the raid on Bangkok was nothing to crow about, it did serve well in the experience department. The crews of the ditched bombers were rescued and reported that the B-29s 'ditched well.' Crews gained valuable insights in handling the giants; pilots sharpened their skills, gunners improved their aim. It had, on balance, been a worthwhile sortie.

On 14 June the 20th Bomber Command sent 75 B-29s against the Imperial Iron and Steel Works at Yawata, on the Japanese island of Kyushu. This was the first raid on Japan since General Jimmy Doolittle's daring B-25 attack from the aircraft carrier *Hornet* two years before. Each B-29 carried two tons of explosives and several news correspondents and photographers.

From the beginning there were problems. Seven B-29s were unable to get airborne, and one that did crashed. Four more returned because of engine trouble, but the remaining squadrons continued. They arrived over the target after midnight, and, under harassment from Japanese fighters and antiaircraft fire, made their runs. Many, unable to locate their target by sight, unloaded their bombs by radar. Once again, accuracy was poor and damage minimal. Several planes jettisoned their explosives because of mechanical difficulties, and the bombs went off harmlessly in the countryside.

Before the B-29s returned to Chengtu, seven more were lost, six to accident and one to enemy fire, the first B-29 so lost. Fifty-five men were listed as missing after this first strike against Japan. The United States hailed the raid as a victory, but the Japanese newspapers belittled it.

Although many important lessons were learned from this and later raids from Indian and Chinese bases, supply problems made these B-29 operations far less effective than had been hoped.

Below: Security was intense, with three different services guarding the **XB-29** as it was barged up the Duwamish on 21 July 1942.

However, the American drive across the Central Pacific had captured the Marianas Islands by mid August 1944, and bases for B-29s were quickly built there, within range of every part of Japan. Airfields were built on Saipan, Tinian and Guam and became operational from October. Under the command of General Haywood S Hansell, 21st Bomber Command began its attacks on Japan in November. All the attacks were made using high altitude, daylight precision bombing tactics but with only limited success. There were also many technical problems with the B-29s as a consequence of these tactics.

In January 1945 General Arnold moved General Curtis LeMay from 20th Bomber Command to replace Hansell. Despite his efforts Hansell had failed to produce the desired results. Losses were too high for the damage that was being inflicted to the Japanese war machine. Before LeMay arrived to take over, Hansell made two important changes. He centralized maintenance operations and took measures to reduce the weight of the bombers to cut down the strain on the engines and reduce the high rate of engine failures.

LeMay soon decided that the precision raids were not appropriate and that high explosives should be phased out in favor of incendiaries. The results of raids on 25 February and 4 March convinced LeMay that he was on the right track but he decided to make a more radical change. He had the B-29s stripped of most of their guns to save still more weight and ordered that missions should be flown at the much lower altitude of around 6000 feet and at night.

On the night of 9–10 March 1945 these tactics were tried out for the first time when LeMay sent 279 bombers to Tokyo in what was to be the most devastating bombing raid of the whole

Above: **B-29s** on the floor of the Renton plant.

Above: **Four 50-caliber machine guns** were standard equipment at first on the top forward B-29 turret, though later aircraft had the turret deleted entirely.

Above: A side view of the **B-29 Superfortress** *Eddie Allen.*

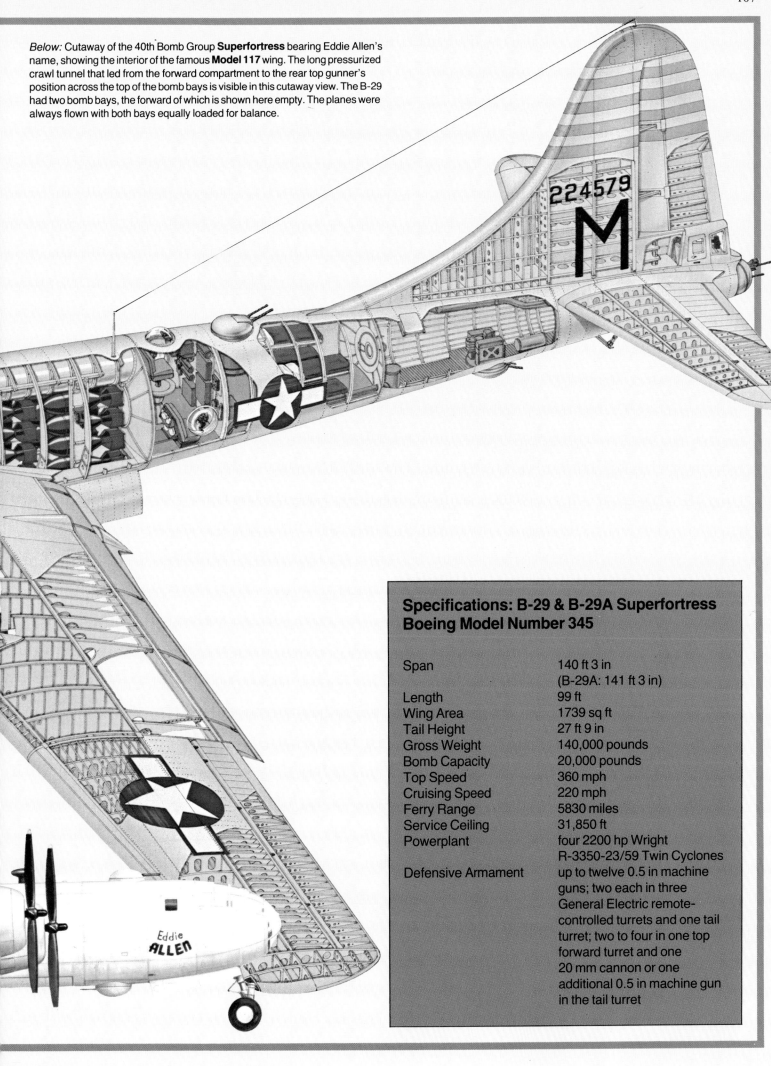

Below: Cutaway of the 40th Bomb Group **Superfortress** bearing Eddie Allen's name, showing the interior of the famous **Model 117** wing. The long pressurized crawl tunnel that led from the forward compartment to the rear top gunner's position across the top of the bomb bays is visible in this cutaway view. The B-29 had two bomb bays, the forward of which is shown here empty. The planes were always flown with both bays equally loaded for balance.

Specifications: B-29 & B-29A Superfortress Boeing Model Number 345

Span	140 ft 3 in (B-29A: 141 ft 3 in)
Length	99 ft
Wing Area	1739 sq ft
Tail Height	27 ft 9 in
Gross Weight	140,000 pounds
Bomb Capacity	20,000 pounds
Top Speed	360 mph
Cruising Speed	220 mph
Ferry Range	5830 miles
Service Ceiling	31,850 ft
Powerplant	four 2200 hp Wright R-3350-23/59 Twin Cyclones
Defensive Armament	up to twelve 0.5 in machine guns; two each in three General Electric remote-controlled turrets and one tail turret; two to four in one top forward turret and one 20 mm cannon or one additional 0.5 in machine gun in the tail turret

Above: A B-29 with the **20mm cannon** added to the tail turret and the top forward turret deleted.

war. The effect of the concentration of incendiaries was hellish. High winds fanned the flames into an inferno. Bombers coming in to drop their loads were rocked violently by the rising hot air, and some crashed.

A Japanese reporter told of the attack in these words:

'That bright starlight night will remain in the memory of all who witnessed it. After the first incendiary bombs fell, clouds formed and were lit up from below with a pink light. From them emerged Superfortresses, flying uncannily low above the centers of the conflagration, which gradually spread. A B-29 exploded before our eyes, almost over the center of the city. The fire-clouds kept creeping higher, and the tower of the Diet building stood black against the red sky. The city was as bright as sunrise; clouds of smoke, soot and sparks driven by the wind were flying over it. That night we thought the whole of Tokyo was reduced to ashes.'

The holocaust flattened nearly 16 square miles of the city. Nearly 25 percent of the city's buildings were destroyed, some 83,000 people were killed, over 40,000 wounded, and more than

one million left homeless. Neither Hiroshima nor Nagasaki, targets of the atomic bomb five months later, were to suffer as much damage. More similar raids followed, and their effects were cataclysmic. After the war, Rear Admiral Toshitane Takata said that America's airpower defeated Japan, and that the biggest single factor was the Boeing B-29.

However, the fighting continued throughout the spring of 1945, and into the late summer. The Axis powers in Europe had surrendered in May, so all the Allied military might was now centered on Japan. The Japanese were on the defensive, expecting an invasion from Allied ground forces, and, once again, they were correct. Plans for invasion were underway.

Two things stopped the invasion. On 6 August Colonel Paul Tibbets, commanding the specially rigged B-29, *Enola Gay*, (named for his mother), dropped the first atomic bomb (nick-named 'Little Boy') on Hiroshima. The effects were horrible and lasting. Under the menacing mushrooming clouds that soared 20,000 feet into the sky, 78,000 people lay dead, 51,000 more injured. The explosion and the resulting fire storm also com-

Above: The **Enola Gay** after her arrival at Tinian.

Below right: The **Enola Gay** takes off on her most famous mission.

pletely destroyed 48,000 homes and half wrecked 22,000 more. Radiation victims still survive and bear testament to the violence of the contaminated air.

Japan should have surrendered then. High officials urged it, but there was procrastination. It was hard for the warlords in Tokyo to adjust to the effects of the terrible weapon. So, on 9 August, another B-29, *Bock's Car*, left Tinian under Major Charles Sweeney. It had 'Fat Man' in its bomb bay, yet another atomic bomb.

The primary target of *Bock's Car* was Kokura, with the alternate target being Nagasaki. The weather proved too cloudy over Kokura, so the B-29 turned toward Nagasaki. The bomb was dropped at approximately eleven in the morning, and in a few seconds 35,000 more people were dead.

Japan surrendered formally on 2 September, the ceremony taking place aboard the battleship USS *Missouri*. The long, bitter war was over, and B-29s turned from missions of destruction to missions of mercy. They dropped tons of clothing and food to the thousands of Allied prisoners still in Japanese hands.

By the end of the war, the USAAF was capable of putting 1100 Superfortresses into the air with the last production B-29 coming off the line at Boeing's Renton plant in May 1946.

Losses, from all causes, came to 528, a stiff price which was paid in order to drop 64,190 tons of high explosives and 105,190 tons of incendiaries on Japan. In the aggregate Superfortresses had flown more than one hundred million miles as of 6 August 1945. After hostilities, B-29 manufacture was phased out, but unlike vast numbers of other USAAF aircraft which were scrapped, B-29s remained in service.

On 20 November 1945, the *Pacusan Dreamboat* flew nonstop from Guam to Washington, DC, a record distance of 8198 miles. On 5 October the following year, the same B-29 broke another nonstop record by flying from Honolulu to Cairo in 39 hours and 36 minutes.

The postwar years found the B-29s involved in military pursuits other than bombing. Like the B-17, a number were adapted to carry lifeboats (SB-29), while others served in reconnaissance (RB-29) and weather reconnaissance (WB-29) duties. One served as a flying powerplant laboratory (XB-29G), with a retractable jet engine mounted in one of the bomb bays. The Navy received 4 surplus B-29s which it designated as the P2B-1, one of which was used as a 'mother ship,' in supersonic research, carting the Bell X-1 Skyrocket aloft for launching. B-29s were

also taken into service with Britain's RAF after the war, designated in this role as Boeing Washingtons.

An entirely new career was opened for the Superfortress with the advent of aerial refueling as a means of extending the range of bombers and fighters. Under the designation KB-29M, 92 B-29s and B-29As were converted at Wichita to flying tankers. To keep the record straight it should be noted that the interim designation for the KB-29M was KB-29K. They carried a single large fuel tank in each bomb bay, along with a hose that could be unreeled and secured to the receiving plane. Some 74 B-29s were modified to receive fuel in this manner, adding an extra tank in one of the bomb bays. The modified aircraft were redesignated B-29M.

A drawback to that refueling system was the hose, which was difficult to control, so Boeing invented the 'flying boom.' This permitted direct mechanical connection between airplanes, and fuel could be transferred at a faster rate. One hundred and sixteen B-29s were modified at Renton, as KB-29Ps, carrying the flying boom refueling system.

After the war, United States strategic policy was built around the atomic bomb of which the United States enjoyed a monopoly. It was the ultimate weapon, the weapon that had won the war. The very threat of its use would deter any aggressor from contemplating any future Pearl Harbors, and the B-29 had shown itself to be the ideal delivery system. In 1947 the US Army Air Force (USAAF), which had in effect been largely autonomous since 1941, was abolished and replaced by the US Air Force (USAF), an entirely new service completely on a par with the

*Right: **Fifi**, the B-29 preserved by the Confederate Air Force, still flies and can be seen at many airshows around the United States every year.

Below: The B-29 **City of Philadelphia** is one of the aircraft preserved in the collection of the Pima County Air Museum near Tucson, Arizona.

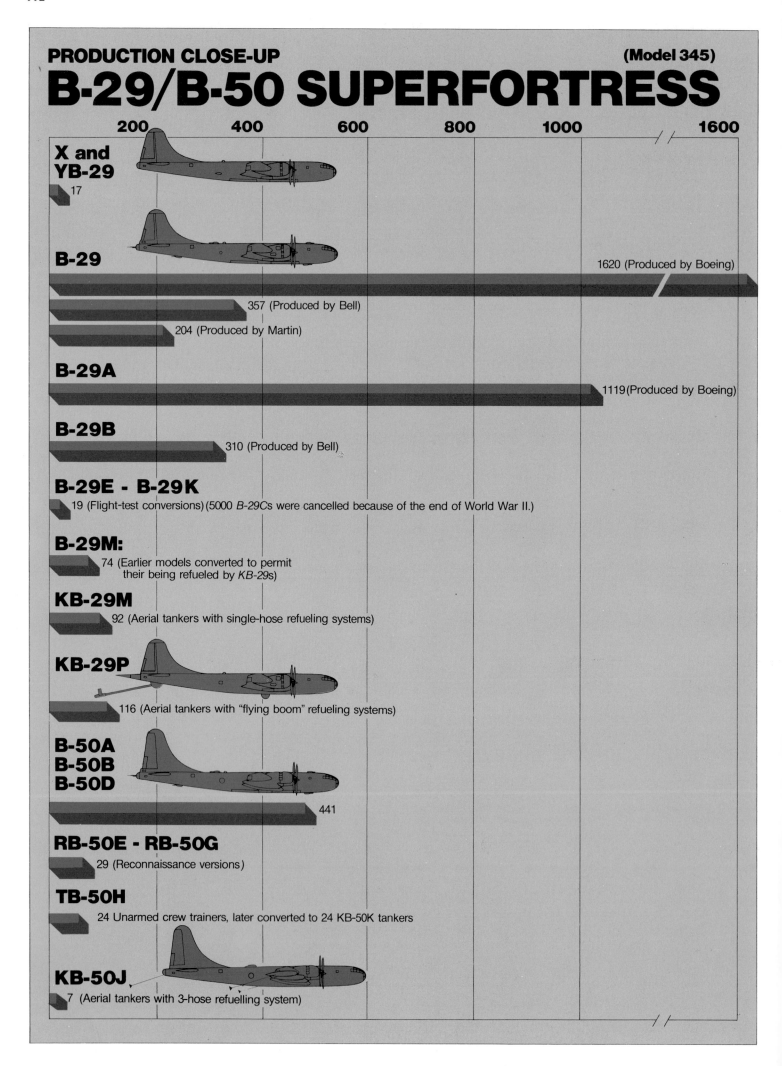

PRODUCTION CLOSE-UP
B-29/B-50 SUPERFORTRESS
(Model 345)

X and YB-29
17

B-29
1620 (Produced by Boeing)
357 (Produced by Bell)
204 (Produced by Martin)

B-29A
1119 (Produced by Boeing)

B-29B
310 (Produced by Bell)

B-29E - B-29K
19 (Flight-test conversions) (5000 B-29Cs were cancelled because of the end of World War II.)

B-29M:
74 (Earlier models converted to permit their being refueled by KB-29s)

KB-29M
92 (Aerial tankers with single-hose refueling systems)

KB-29P
116 (Aerial tankers with "flying boom" refueling systems)

B-50A B-50B B-50D
441

RB-50E - RB-50G
29 (Reconnaissance versions)

TB-50H
24 Unarmed crew trainers, later converted to 24 KB-50K tankers

KB-50J
7 (Aerial tankers with 3-hose refuelling system)

Above: A **KB-29P** refuels a Boeing B-50 in flight by means of the then-revolutionary flying boom.

Inset: Eighth Air Force **B-29s** (on temporary duty with the FEAF) on a bombing mission over North Korea circa 1950.

Army and Navy. The B-29s inherited by the new USAF were mostly allocated to the Strategic Air Command (SAC).

The confidence and complacency that marked US strategic thinking was to be shattered by two events. The first was the explosion of an atomic bomb by the Soviet Union in 1949, thus ending the US monopoly of such weapons. The second event was the June 1950 invasion of South Korea by the North Korean communists. The South Korean forces were in the process of being overwhelmed when the UN Security Council authorized the use of American Forces based in Occupied Japan to come to their aid. As part of the American commitment, B-29s found themselves at war again.

The B-29s were initially put into service in a tactical role, bombing bridges and searching for targets of opportunity. It was a role for which the big strategic bomber was not suited, and one which could be much better served by fighter-bombers and other tactical aircraft. The results were predictably poor. USAF Chief of Staff General Hoyt Vandenberg proposed sending two additional B-29 wings from SAC to Japan as part of the Far Eastern Air Forces (FEAF), and to employ them as strategic bombers. The additional wings and the change in tactics proved decisive. RB-29 strategic reconnaissance aircraft identified major strategic targets in North Korea, such as factories, rail hubs and oil refineries. FEAF B-29s went to work on strategic targets in late July and by early September all of the primary targets had been destroyed. They then began on the secondary strategic targets bombing them until late September, by which time UN forces under General Douglas MacArthur had pushed the North

Koreans back so far that the strategic targets were being captured by UN forces. On 27 October FEAF was disbanded and the B-29s returned to their stateside SAC units in triumph.

Suddenly the UN victory evaporated. The UN troops had successfully defeated the North Korean forces and had occupied nearly all of the Korean Peninsula when hordes of Communist Chinese troops swarmed across their Yalu River border with Korea. By sheer force of numbers, they drove the UN forces back to the general area of the prewar demarcation line between North and South Korea at the 38th Parallel.

From then on it was a very different war. Prohibited from hitting at true strategic targets within Communist China itself, the returning B-29s were largely relegated for the next two and a half years to tactical operations. As those painful years of the Korean war dragged on, it became evident that the B-29's days were numbered. A technological marvel in the mid 1940s, the Superfortress was now being rendered obsolete by advances in air defense technology and the sheer speed of the communist MiG-15 jet fighters.

During the Korean conflict, a total of 21,000 B-29 sorties dropped 167,000 tons of bombs on enemy targets. Thirty-four Superfortresses were lost, of which 20 went down under enemy fire. The last B-29s in squadron service were retired in September of 1960, over 16 years after the first one had been flown to China. The *Enola Gay*, the bomber that was pivotal in ending World War II, was given a permanent home with the Smithsonian Institution in 1949, while *Bock's Car* now resides in the US Air Force Museum near Dayton, Ohio.

Specifications: XF8B-1
Boeing Model Number 400

Span	54 ft
Length	43 ft 3 in
Wing Area	489 sq ft
Tail Height	16 ft 3 in
Gross Weight	20,508 pounds
Bomb Capacity	3200 pounds
Top Speed	432 mph
Cruising Speed	190 mph
Ferry Range	3500 miles
Service Ceiling	37,500 ft
Powerplant	one 2500 hp Pratt & Whitney R-4360-10 Wasp Major
Defensive Armament	six 0.5 in machine guns or 20 mm cannons

Above: The **F8B** was Boeing's last fighter-aircraft design. Although it was advanced for its time, it was quickly rendered obsolete by turbojet fighters. Note the contra-rotating propellers.

During the course of World War II, while all-time Boeing production records were being set with the B-17 and B-29 programs, several Boeing projects did not fare so well. One such design was the Model 320, a massive flying boat with a 200 foot wingspan. It had a twin fuselage layout like that of the popular P-38 fighter, with the flight deck located on the huge wing section between the fuselages, which had a profile similar to that of the Model 314 Clipper. The big craft would have had a range of over 7000 miles, a mixed bomb and torpedo payload of nearly 44,000 pounds, with a speed of just under 200mph. The 320 was a victim of advancing technology and never got off the drawing board.

There were, however, high hopes for the Model 344 flying boat, which the Navy designated XPBB-1. Indeed, the big plant site at Renton on the shore of Lake Washington was acquired by Boeing as the manufacturing site for the XPBB-1. Dubbed Sea Ranger, the big patrol bomber first flew on 9 July 1942, taking off from Lake Washington. Boeing employed a wing similar to that of the B-29 and the hull was all-metal. There was a crew of ten, and because of the long-range duties, living quarters were provided.

It was an efficient airplane, Boeing having drawn on its Clipper experience in planning the design. With a gross weight of 62,000 pounds (101,129 with JATO, Jet Assisted Take-Off), she rose from the water in a quick 43 seconds. Her two engines were capable of carrying the Sea Ranger nonstop for 72 hours, enough time to take her from Seattle to Great Britain and return, going via New York both ways.

After the battle of Midway had demonstrated that carrier and land-based bombers could destroy an enemy task force at sea, the Navy cut back its interest in flying boats. The 57 production models, PBB-1s, were therefore not built, and the Sea Ranger remained one of a kind.

The last of these short-fall airplanes was the XF8B-1. It was also built for the Navy. Given the Boeing designation Model 400, engineering began in March 1943 and the initial test flight took place on 28 November 1944.

The XF8B-1 employed two contra-rotating propellers powered by its single engine. The props, each 13½ feet in diameter, spun in opposite directions, greatly reducing torque. In spite of its ten tons of weight, it flew in excess of 450mph, according to a press release of 1945. Lieutenant Walter J McAuley, an Army Air Technical Service pilot, said of the XF8B-1, 'It has lots of power, and seems to have fine possibilities.'

With a service ceiling matching that of the B-29, the XF8B-1 gained the nickname 'Five-in-One,' because of its versatility. It

Above: The **XPBB Sea Ranger** was Boeing's last flying-boat design. Manufacture of the first 57 was postponed by the need for Boeing to concentrate on B-17s. In 1944 the program was revived with production to be farmed out to Martin since the Renton plant purchased for the PBB program was now being used for building B-29s. However, no production aircraft were built and this single prototype remained an only child.

Specifications: XPBB-1 Sea Ranger Boeing Model Number 344

Span	139 ft 8 in
Length	94 ft 9 in
Wing Area	1826 sq ft
Tail Height	34 ft 2 in
Gross Weight	62,006 pounds (101,129 pounds with JATO)
Bomb Capacity	20,000 pounds
Top Speed	219 mph
Cruising Speed	158 mph
Ferry Range	4245 miles
Service Ceiling	18,900 ft
Powerplant	two 2000 hp Wright GR-3350-8 Twin Cyclones
Defensive Armament	eight 0.5 in machine guns

served equally as a fighter, interceptor, dive bomber, torpedo plane or horizontal bomber. By the time the 'Five-in-One' was ready for production, though, Germany had startled the world with its first jet fighter, the Messerschmitt Me 262, signalling the end of piston-engined fighters. Only three XF8B-1s were delivered, and the design was retired. It was to be the final installment in the series of Boeing Navy pursuit aircraft that stretched back to 1923 and the FB-1.

While during the war Douglas, Vega, Bell and Martin all produced the Boeing designed B-17s and B-29s, just prior to the war the reverse had been true. In 1940 during the Battle of France, Boeing contracted to build 240 Douglas DB-7B attack bombers for the French Air Force. By the time they were completed, France had fallen to the Germans, and the aircraft were transferred to Britain as Boston Is. An additional 140 were built for the USAAF under the designation A-20C.

During the war, the Boeing-Canada factories in Vancouver, which had produced a small number of British Blackburn Shark torpedo planes for the Royal Canadian Air Force during 1938–39, were expanded as aircraft repair and conversion facilities. These facilities also produced 55 Consolidated PBY-5A flying boats for the RCAF and 307 PBY-5 and PBY-6 Catalina flying boats for the US Navy as well as various British Empire services.

These aircraft were given the Navy designations PB2B-1 and PB2B-2 (Patrol Bomber, Boeing), even though they were Consolidated designs.

Though the Stearman Aircraft Company became the Wichita Division of Boeing in 1939, there were three prototype programs designed before the transition, but produced afterward, that retained the Stearman model numbers. These were a single prototype of the Model X90 primary trainer designated XBT-17 by the Army, a single prototype of the Model X100 attack bomber designated XA-21 by the Army and a pair of prototype Model X120 twin engined advanced crew trainers which were designated XAT-15 by the Army.

Below: Though the **B-50** is very similar to the B-29 at first glance, it can be readily distinguished by its higher tail and revised engine nacelles.

A s the B-17 had been the subject of re-engining experiments resulting in the XB-38, so too was the B-29 the subject of re-engining trials. The first such experiment was the XB-39, a single YB-29 named *Spirit of Lincoln* and equipped with four Allison V-3420-11 2600hp liquid-cooled engines. The second experiment involved a single B-29A re-engined with four Pratt & Whitney R-4360-33 air-cooled engines delivering 2500hp. The first experiment was dropped but the second was the object of high hopes. Initially the aircraft was redesignated XB-44, but when it was decided to perpetuate the design the prototype was again redesignated, this time to XB-29D. First flown in May 1945, the new bird showed great promise and became the prototype for a sort of Super Superfortress and Boeing's first postwar bomber, the B-50.

Though similar in appearance to the B-29, from which it was developed, the B-50 was covered with a tougher new aluminum skin. The wings were 16 percent stronger, 26 percent more efficient, and 650 pounds lighter. B-50s also had 59 percent more horsepower with the installation of four 3500hp P&W Wasp Major engines. A Boeing designed ball-bearing actuator made it possible to retract the undercarriage in 11 seconds, improving takeoff performance. Conventional rubber de-icer boots were replaced with hot-air de-icing systems. These kept the leading edges of the wings and empennage free of ice at all times.

With all of these improvements, Boeing engineers were not finished. They added steerable nose wheels, reversible-pitch propellers and the tail was five feet taller than that of the B-29. The tail could be folded down to permit entry into hangars. When the B-50 was finished, though it kept the 345 model number, it was a 75 percent new airplane.

One of the B-50s, the *Lucky Lady II*, made history's first nonstop flight around the world. Leaving Fort Worth, Texas, on 6 February 1949, the *Lucky Lady II* flew eastward via the Azores to Saudi Arabia and thence to the Philippines, Hawaii and back to Fort Worth. The journey took 94 hours and 1 minute, and the plane was refueled at three different points while aloft by KB-29 tankers.

The B-50D provided for the installation of a droppable 700 gallon tank under each wing, or a 4000 pound bomb. Important, too, in this model was the single-point fueling system, which allowed every tank to be refueled quickly from a single external fitting. This was especially valuable during air-to-air fueling maneuvers.

Eleven B-50Ds were delivered to the Air Force as 'Flying classrooms,' designated TB-50D. The planes were used by the Air Training Command in schooling potential B-47 Stratojet crew: multipurpose navigator/radar operator/bombardiers. The last of the 'Super Superfortresses' were 24 TB-50H crew trainer

Above: A **B-50 bombardier's view** of another Eighth Air Force B-50.

conversions completed in 1952. The arrival of the B-47 jet bomber was making the internal combustion B-50 obsolete. The B-50 was the last piston-engined bomber Boeing ever built for the Air Force.

A *Super* Super Superfortress was for a time considered. The prototype would have been the YB-50C with a longer fuselage and a ten-foot greater wingspan. Before the program was terminated without any aircraft actually being built, the USAF went so far as to order 73 under the designations B-54A and RB-54A.

A total of 346 B-50s were built but even after the B-47 practically killed them, they did not give up. A Boeing design was meant to last, and most of the remaining airplanes were converted to KB-50J and KB-50K, three-hose aerial tankers for the Tactical Air Command, between 1957 and 1959. The engines were supplemented by a single jet pod under each wing to increase speed and altitude performance.

An interesting footnote regarding the size of bombers goes as follows: In 1944, the B-29 was called a 'very heavy bomber.' Only a few years later, the B-50, which outweighed the B-29 by 30,000 pounds, was called a 'medium bomber.' In 1952, when Boeing's jet powered B-52 appeared, it was called a 'heavy bomber,' and weighed over 300,000 pounds. This was a far cry from the B-9 of the early 1930s which weighed only 13,919 pounds.

Specifications: B-50D Superfortress
Boeing Model Number 345

Span	141 ft 3 in
Length	99 ft
Wing Area	1720 sq ft
Tail Height	32 ft 8 in
Gross Weight	173,000 pounds
Bomb Capacity	28,000 pounds
Top Speed	400 mph
Cruising Speed	300 mph
Ferry Range	4900 miles
Service Ceiling	40,000 ft
Powerplant	four 3500 hp Pratt & Whitney R-4360-35 Wasp Majors
Defensive Armament	various armament schemes, up to 13 machine guns in some versions, KB-50D tankers unarmed

POSTWAR MILITARY AIRCRAFT

Boeing's first postwar military aircraft was certainly the B-50, which served to fill the gap in Boeing's lineage of USAAF/USAF aircraft between the B-29 which had been the ultimate bomber of the war years and the jet bombers that were soon to render piston-engined bombers forever obsolete. However, simultaneously with development of the B-29 and later the B-50, Boeing engineers were working on a military transport aircraft, the Model 367 Stratofreighter. The Model 367 (military designation C-97) bore the same structural relationship to the Model 345 (B-29) that the Model 307 Stratoliner had to the Model 299 (B-17). Boeing had pioneered the perfectly circular fuselage with the B-17 and much more evidently with the Stratoliner. They used the same circular design again on the B-29, but went a step farther with the Model 367. Its cross section consisted of two fuselages, two circles, in a sort of inverted figure 8, with the larger circle on top (the passenger section), and the smaller circle on the bottom (the cargo hold). The XC-97, which first flew on

15 November 1944, had wings, engines and tail surfaces almost identical to those of the B-29. The six service test aircraft did not fly until March 1947, by which time the B-50 program had overtaken the C-97 program and had made available a wealth of new technology which could be incorporated into the C-97A.

If the structural relationship of the B-17 had been to the 307 as the B-29 was to the XC-97, so the structural relationship of the C-97A was to the B-50. The C-97A adopted the B-50's tail (five feet higher than that of the B-29 and XC-97) as well as the 3500hp Wasp Major engines. The basic C-97A airframe also became the Model 377 Stratocruiser commercial airliner, which, as we have seen earlier, was Boeing's last propeller driven commercial passenger plane.

Outstanding features of the C-97, in addition to the double-deck pressurized fuselage, were the large clamshell cargo doors beneath the tail, and an integral ramp and cargo hoist system that permitted unassisted loading of standard 2½ ton trucks, and even

Above: Most Stratofreighters served as KC-97 flying-boom tankers. Here a **KC-97** refuels a **B-50D**.

Below left: The US Air Force **C-97,** *Shrimp Boat,* landing at Boeing Field. The C-97 was the workhorse of the Military Air Transport Service throughout the early 1950s.

small airplanes such as the L-15 Scout. In all, there were 6140 cubic feet of usable cargo space, more than twice the volume of any transport then flying.

The Army Air Force was impressed by the design and a contract was issued for three prototypes which became XC-97. Test pilot A Elliott Merrill had this to say after his first flight:

'Control characteristics are excellent. The cockpit arrangements and vision are very fine. These are features which you can't be certain of until you have the airplane in the air, and can subject it to flying conditions.'

It seems a rather subdued statement for what was to become a, very significant aircraft. If the pilot was reticent, Wellwood Beall, then a Boeing vice president in charge of engineering, was more enthusiastic. 'This new ship,' he declared, 'has better flying characteristics than any airplane we have ever built, even the B-29.'

Proof of his statement came on 9 January 1945. The XC-97 made a nonstop flight from Seattle to Washington, DC in six hours and four minutes. It was a record for transport aircraft. The big plane flew at 30,000 feet, taking advantage of favorable winds for the entire distance. It averaged 383mph for the 2323 mile trip, which was 20 miles faster than the B-29's top speed, and faster than some piston-engined fighters of the time. Military strategists took note.

System by system, the production Stratofreighters matched the advances of the B-50, with only outside dimensions and basic loading facilities remaining the same as the original XC configuration. The 117 airfoil of the B-29 was retained, but wings utilizing new metals and a refined internal design 16 percent

stronger and 26 percent more efficient became standard. The wings weighed 650 pounds less than those of the B-29/XC-97.

The first three production models were designated YC-97A, while the fourth was tagged YC-97B. This one was built for passenger service, with cargo provisions deleted in favor of air-liner seats, windows, and other interior appointments similar to the commercial Model 377 Stratocruiser. It saw service with the Military Air Transport Service's Pacific Division. The others cut their service teeth with Strategic Support Squadrons of SAC, MATS and the Air Materiel Command. Nine YC-97As were built.

In 1948–9 some of the SAC Stratofreighters gave the world an idea of what they could do. The Soviets cut off ground transport routes through East Germany to West Berlin, then under Allied jurisdiction. The only way to reach the city was by air. One C-97 made 27 flights to the besieged city, carrying a record million pounds of such diverse cargo as coal, baby food, dehydrated potatoes, iron pipe and steam boilers.

In the meantime, additional contracts had been issued for more C-97s. On 6 June 1949 the first of 50 production C-97As to be built took to the air. In September of the following year, the first SAC command transports were delivered under the designation of C-97D. Five months later, the C-97C appeared, featuring flush-mounted antennae and strengthened fuselage structures. A total of 14 C-97Cs rolled off the production line.

Testing the work limits of the C-97 was a never-ending task. It became another workhorse, reminiscent of the Douglas DC-3s and DC-4s, only with much larger capacities and more endurance. The KC-97A was a natural outgrowth. Three prototypes were

built to show the multipurpose versatility of the modified internal design. The KC-97 could be used as a tanker, a troop or cargo carrier, or as a hospital ship. Quick convertibility from basic freighter to aerial tanker was made possible by the design of the tanker equipment. The controls of the flying boom, a Boeing invention, were assembled in a single pod attached beneath the KC-97's fuselage. It occupied the same space normally occupied by the loading doors.

Boeing had experimented with air-to-air refueling in 1929, using a Model 95 mail and freight biplane receiving from a Model 40B. In those tests, a hose was extended from the tanker, and the two airplanes were flown into position. A crew member on the 95 grasped the nozzle, and stuck it into the fuel tank filler pipe. The experiments were soon discontinued, but the idea was not abandoned. When the need for tankers came up, Boeing was ready with the KB-29W and then the KC-97.

The flying boom became a vital component in air-to-air refueling. Boeing and the Air Materiel Command had conducted Operation Drip in March 1948. The purpose was to test the feasibility of passing fuel between two B-29s in flight. AMC had requested Boeing to undertake the program, incorporating a British-developed 'hose-type' refueling arrangement for B-29s. In May of that year, Boeing tested the hose-type operation. AMC was not satisfied with the results and asked Boeing to develop another system. Company engineers proposed the use of a flying boom and began tests with a 'dry boom' to check the feasibility of the idea.

There followed a period of experimentation in which B-29s were modified to serve as both tankers and recipients. More than

Above left: Engineering Chief **Wellwood Beall** (Left) and Company President **Bill Allen** discuss military application of the Model 367 with **General Eisenhower** during the General's 13 August 1947 visit to Boeing Field.

Below: Stripped of the village that camouflaged its roof during the war, **Plant 2** evolved into the manufacturing site for the B-50 and C-97.

Specifications: KC-97G Stratofreighter Boeing Model Number 367

Span	141 ft 3 in
Length	117 ft 5 in
Wing Area	1769 sq ft
Tail Height	38 ft 3 in
Gross Weight	175,000 pounds
Top Speed	375 mph
Cruising Speed	300 mph
Range	4300 miles
Service Ceiling	35,000 ft
Powerplant	four 3500 hp Pratt & Whitney R-4360-59B

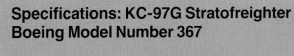

PRODUCTION CLOSE-UP
BOEING POSTWAR MILITARY AIRCRAFT

200	400	600	800	1400

Model 345: *B-50 Superfortress:* A four-engine USAAF/USAF heavy bomber (advanced *B-29*). (1947-53)

346

Model 367: *C-97 Stratofreighter:* A four-engine USAAF/USAF transport, ultimately used primarily as a tanker. (1944-1956)

27 C-97

808 KC-97 tankers

Model 424: Boeing's first jet-aircraft design, the *Model 424* was straight-winged medium bomber. (1943)

0

Model 432: A further elaboration of the *Model 424,* which internalized the pair of underwing jet engines. (1944)

0

Model 448: This model, essentially a sweptwing version of the *Model 432,* provided the final link in the series of stepping stones that led from the *B-29 (Model 345)* to the *B-47 (Model 450).* (1945)

0

Model 450: *B-47 Stratojet:* six-engine USAF medium-range jet bomber & reconnaissance aircraft. (1947-56)

1373

667 (Produced by Lockheed and Douglas)

Model 451: *L-15 Scout:* A small US Army liaison aircraft. (1947-48)

12

Model 462: A designation for a six-engine turboprop heavy bomber. (Program eventually evolved into Model 464). (1946)

0

Model 464: *B-52 Stratofortress:* An eight-engine USAF long-range heavy bomber. (1952-62)

744

Model 474: *B-55:* The designation for a USAF heavy bomber with 4 pylon-mounted turboprop engines. (1948)

0

Model 479: *B-55:* The final elaboration of the *Model 474* design, in which the 4 turboprops were replaced by 6 turbojet engines.

0

Model 701: *B-59:* Designation for a four-engine USAF mach 2 supersonic medium bomber.

0

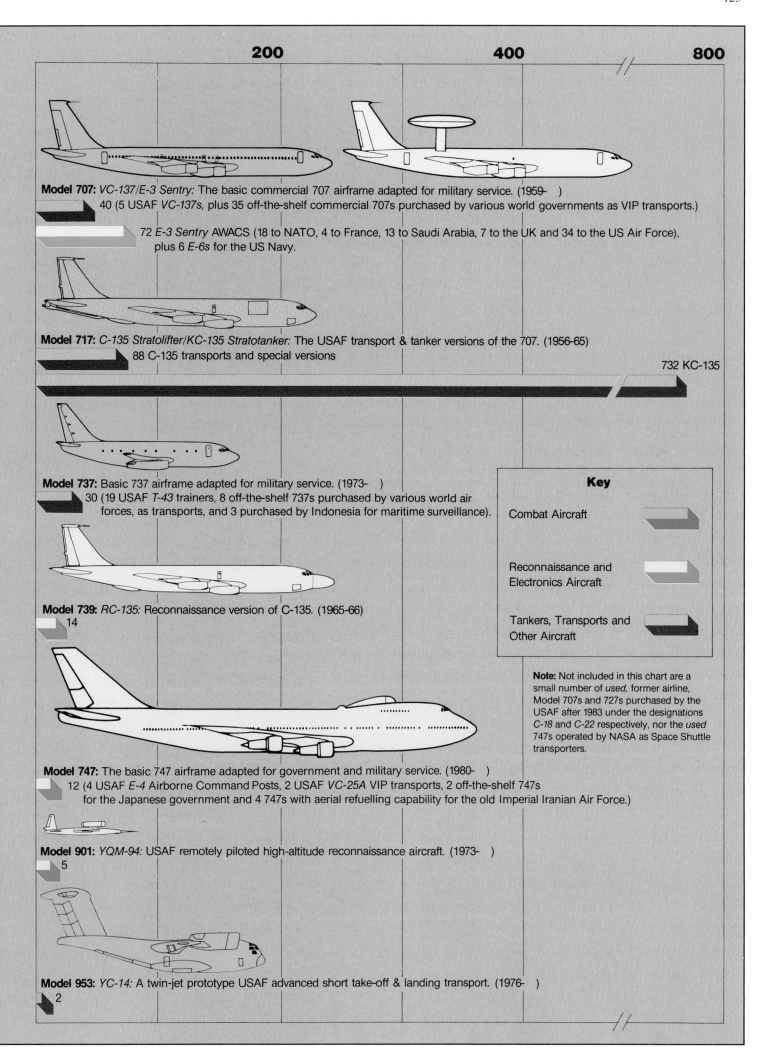

200   **400**   **800**

Model 707: *VC-137/E-3 Sentry:* The basic commercial 707 airframe adapted for military service. (1959–)

40 (5 USAF *VC-137s*, plus 35 off-the-shelf commercial 707s purchased by various world governments as VIP transports.)

72 *E-3 Sentry* AWACS (18 to NATO, 4 to France, 13 to Saudi Arabia, 7 to the UK and 34 to the US Air Force), plus 6 *E-6s* for the US Navy.

Model 717: *C-135 Stratolifter/KC-135 Stratotanker:* The USAF transport & tanker versions of the 707. (1956–65)

88 C-135 transports and special versions

732 KC-135

Model 737: Basic 737 airframe adapted for military service. (1973–)

30 (19 USAF *T-43* trainers, 8 off-the-shelf 737s purchased by various world air forces, as transports, and 3 purchased by Indonesia for maritime surveillance).

Model 739: *RC-135:* Reconnaissance version of C-135. (1965–66)

14

Model 747: The basic 747 airframe adapted for government and military service. (1980–)

12 (4 USAF *E-4* Airborne Command Posts, 2 USAF *VC-25A* VIP transports, 2 off-the-shelf 747s for the Japanese government and 4 747s with aerial refuelling capability for the old Imperial Iranian Air Force.)

Model 901: *YQM-94:* USAF remotely piloted high-altitude reconnaissance aircraft. (1973–)

5

Model 953: *YC-14:* A twin-jet prototype USAF advanced short take-off & landing transport. (1976–)

2

Key

Combat Aircraft

Reconnaissance and
Electronics Aircraft

Tankers, Transports and
Other Aircraft

Note: Not included in this chart are a
small number of *used,* former airline,
Model 707s and 727s purchased by the
USAF after 1983 under the designations
C-18 and *C-22* respectively, nor the *used*
747s operated by NASA as Space Shuttle
transporters.

Specifications: L-15 Scout
Boeing Model Number 451

Span	40 ft
Length	25 ft
Wing Area	269 sq ft
Tail Height	8 ft 8½ in
Gross Weight	2050 pounds
Top Speed	104 mph
Cruising Speed	95 mph
Range	250 miles
Service Ceiling	15,000 ft
Powerplant	one 125 hp Lycoming 0-290-7

100 hours of flight testing were devoted to the program, in which the dry boom was tried with the B-29 and the XB-47 as well. Since fighter airplanes were also to be serviced by air-to-air refueling, experiments were extended to an F-86 Sabre.

The flying boom concept of refueling was an improvement in that the operator had more control of the apparatus than with the dangling hoses. He was able to 'fly' his boom to the receiving airplane's fuel inlet. While he was operating the boom, he was in command of the tanker, giving directions to the pilot by an inter-communications system. The operator himself fell heir to the nickname 'Clancy,' after the hero of a popular tune, which featured the line 'Clancy lowered the boom.'

Sixty tankers ordered by the Air Force were designated KC-97E, and the first one was delivered in July 1951. They were followed by an order for 159 KC-97Fs, which featured improved Pratt & Whitney engines.

After the Fs came the Gs, the last production model, of which 592 were built. This airplane was fitted with external wing tanks, and a different arrangement of internal tanks. This shuffling around of internal tanks permitted the carrying of troops or cargo without removing the refueling equipment.

Two of the KC-97Gs were taken from the production line in 1953, and modified at the request of the Air Force to serve as test beds for a new Pratt & Whitney turboprop engine, the T34. The new engines boosted the power up to 5700hp, 2200hp more than delivered by the old Wasp Majors. These YC-97Js were tested by MATS out of Kelly AFB, Texas, and one of the airplanes set

records for crossing both the Atlantic and Pacific oceans. However, the model was never put into production because, by then, the Air Force was eyeing an exciting new Boeing airplane, the jet powered 717.

During their lifetime, the KC-97s transferred millions of gallons of fuel in air-to-air operations. Operations involving air fuelings averaged 2880 contacts per week, or one aerial servicing every three and a half minutes. The Strategic Air Command's table of organization called for each 45-plane wing of Boeing B-47 Stratojets to be complemented with a 20-plane tanker squadron of KC-97s.

As an example of use and efficiency, the 2nd Air Refueling Squadron, at Hunter AFB, Georgia, conducted tests in early 1955. The refueling squadron transferred a total of 563,270 gallons of fuel to SAC B-47s in 16 scheduled days of flying – setting a record. Since its creation four years previously, the 2nd ARS had transferred more than 6 million gallons of fuel in mid-air.

The KC-97 made the transformation to refueling jets easily. It serviced bombers, fighters and freighters with equal aplomb. In an experiment, one KC-97 was equipped with J47 jet engines and its efficiency was substantially improved in altitude and speed. Despite its adaptability, the KC-97 was, in the final analysis, an airplane made for piston engines, and inevitably it was to be replaced by the KC-135 jet.

The last KC-97G rolled out of the factory in June 1956, concurrent with the completion of the first Boeing Model 717, KC-135 Stratotanker. The roll-outs were only minutes apart, and the end of an era had arrived. A total of 835 C-97s in all configurations had been manufactured.

In the immediate post-World War II period, when Boeing was building some of the largest aircraft the world had yet seen and was contemplating even larger planes, it is interesting to note that they were designing a plane so small that it could be folded up and carried in a truck. While really of moderate size by pre-war standards it was, and is, the smallest plane built by Boeing since the late 30s.

The L-15 Scout, Boeing Model 451, was a monoplane designed for the Army ground forces as an observation platform. Twelve were to be delivered to the Army during 1947–48 before production was terminated.

Below: The **L-15 Scout**, Boeing's smallest postwar plane, could be readily disassembled and could be converted easily from a seaplane to a landplane.

Above: Boeing's sleek **B-47** was the backbone of the Strategic Air Command throughout the mid 1950s.

The observer had good visibility by virtue of a tubular tail boom, eliminating the conventional bulk of the rear fuselage. The L-15 carried a crew of two, the pilot facing forward and the observer to the rear.

The Scout was a versatile little ship, at home on wheels, skis or pontoons. Extremely slow flight was achieved through the use of a thick airfoil and unique full-span 'Flapperons,' that combined the functions of flap and aileron. They were mounted below the wing instead of being built into its trailing edge.

The Scout was designed for rapid assembly and disassembly in the field, and could be carried complete in the back of a standard 2½ ton Army truck. Inward-turning landing gear struts permitted a further width reduction, and allowed the dismantled Scout to be rolled into a C-97 cargo plane for transportation by air.

Eventually the Scouts came into private hands. Doctor Ed Kraft of Point Barrow, Alaska, flew his over the Brooks Range to Fairbanks in the spring of 1957. The distance was approximately 550 miles, and, with stops for fuel, the flight used up an entire day, dawn to dusk. Speed may not have been the L-15's prize possession, but durability was no problem.

Boeing's first jet bomber, the B-47, grew out of the tremendous advances in aircraft technology that occurred during World War II. The war had begun with some pilots going into combat in open-cockpit biplanes and ended with Germany fielding a variety of jet propelled aircraft including over 1000 Me 262s. While jet propulsion had been experimented with in both Britain and the United States before the war, it was not until the technological success that the Germans were enjoying became apparent that there came a mad scramble to get jet aircraft into allied air forces. Though vastly outnumbered in the last years of the war and almost certainly doomed, the Luftwaffe had pulled way ahead of the Allies technologically. Both Britain and the United States had jet combat aircraft flying before the war ended, but only Britain's Gloster Meteor saw even limited action.

As early as 1943–44, Boeing engineers were toying with the idea of a jet bomber. Their first design, Model 424, was really nothing more than a B-29 with a pair of jet engines mounted under each wing. Their Model 432 was similar to the 424, with the engines moved into the fuselage.

When the war ended, Boeing's chief aerodynamicist, George Schairer, was in Germany with Dr Theodore von Karman and a group of American scientists who constituted the US Army Scientific Advisory Group. Their function was to seek out and evaluate the scientific and technical records amassed by the Germans in the course of their development of such things as jet propulsion. Among the most important results of the inquiries was Schairer's determination that the 18.5 degree sweep of the Messerschmitt Me 262 wing improved performance to a significant extent. The theory of swept wings had been proposed as early as 1935 by the German scientist Adolf Buseman. Schairer had interviewed and been impressed with Buseman, and the results of the Me 262 program provided the practical corroboration of the theory.

Schairer wrote to the Seattle bomber team that it would be well to investigate the possibilities of a bomber with swept wings.

Above: A Lockheed-built **B-47E** with its tail guns and its JATO pack removed and with the addition of external fuel tanks. Lockheed's Marietta, Georgia, division built 386 B-47Es.

The team at that time was working on the Model 432, a design in which the four jet engines were mounted on the fuselage above a straight mid-section wing. When Schairer's letter arrived, the Model 432 was junked, and the design team, including Wellwood Beall, Ed Wells, Lysle Wood, and George Schairer, on his return, put their heads together and drew up Model 448.

By September 1945 the Model 448 design had turned into a beautiful ship, with laminar-flow wings and tail, both in a 35 degree swept-back configuration. Four jet engines would be mounted in two pods, one pod on either side of the fuselage. They hung from the wing on nylon struts, but because early jet engines had a limited thrust, two more were later added in a single pod at the tip of each wing.

The airplane, now called the Stratojet, was a satisfactory design as far as Boeing was concerned, and a wooden mock-up was built. In April 1946 Army Air Force officials were invited to take a look. With some reservations, which Boeing was able to iron out, the USAAF was impressed and gave the go-ahead for an improved Model 448, which Boeing had designated Model 450.

A tandem bicycle landing gear was adopted, which raised up into the belly of the aircraft, and the engines were moved to mid-wing positions, away from the fuselage. The two outrigger engines remained in place. Giving the Model 450 their designation of XB-47, the USAAF issued a contract for two prototypes. Work began at once, and the first XB-47 was rolled out of Plant 2 in Seattle on 12 September 1947.

The world had never seen an airplane quite like the XB-47. The wings were as slender as 'fine steel blades,' according to an

Below: The **Super Guppy** was the offspring of the **Pregnant Guppy**. both of them having been in their time, in the early to mid 60s, the largest-capacity aircraft in the world. The turboprop-powered *Super Guppy*, like its predecessor, was a modified Boeing Model 377 designed to airlift rocket and missile sections from their manufacturing site to their launch sites. Using the *Guppies* cut the transit time from several weeks to a matter of hours. It is ironic to note that the *Guppies* are now being used to transport subassemblies for Boeing's chief commercial rival, Airbus Industrie.

observer, and they swept out, back and gently down. Six General Electric J35-GE-2 turbojets, rated at 3750 pounds of thrust, jutted from under the wings. The second prototype was equipped with GE J47-GE-3s delivering 5000 pounds of thrust.

Because of its high wing loading and the slow acceleration characteristics common to early jets, 18 jet-assisted takeoff rocket units were built into the sides of the fuselage. On later models, the 'JATO' rockets were carried on a jettisonable external rack, as a weight-saving measure. The heavy weight of the fixed JATO units also resulted in higher landing speeds with severe braking problems. This was handled by deploying a ribbon-type parachute from the tail just as the wheels touched down. On later models, this practice was modified to trail a small drogue parachute while in the landing pattern. The main braking chute popped out just before the airplane landed.

Although much heavier than the B-29, the heaviest World War II bomber, Stratojet was classed as a medium bomber. It was normally operated by a three man crew – the pilot and copilot, who were seated tandem style under a fighter-type canopy, and a bombardier/navigator nested in the nose. The bomber's only defensive armament was a remotely operated tail turret.

The first XB-47 made its maiden flight on 16 December 1947. The flight plan called for the XB-47 to take off from Boeing Field and land at Moses Lake Air Force Base, in central Washington, a distance of 145 miles. The weather was overcast and cold, not an ideal day for testing any airplane, let alone one with so radical a design. The takeoff was delayed, waiting for weather. At 12:45 p.m., Captain James Fitzgerald, an F-80 pilot who had been sent from Wright Field to take pictures, offered to scout Moses Lake, and bring back a weather report. He returned in the speedy time of 27 minutes, and recommended the XB-47 give it a try.

Test pilot Robert Robbins, and Scott Osler his co-pilot, swung the B-47 out on the field, and started down the runway. When the B-47 hit 90mph, a fire warning light blinked on. It was the No. 2 engine. Robbins quickly throttled back and started to brake. As he said in his report, 'I elected not to take off, and with the far end of the field racing toward us, it seemed minutes before we slowed down.' By now, Osler had a chance to read the millivoltmeter and determine that the warning was false. 'We'd both felt it was false from the first, but this was no time to take chances . . . We headed for the north end of the field again, taking it easy so the brakes and tires would have a chance to cool down. Osler watched the millivoltmeter on No. 2 as we taxied.

'Then we were ready to take off again. The plane started its roll down the field. It seemed to accelerate slowly at first, then more rapidly. The performance figures I had studied in the cockpit that morning flashed through my mind. They were telling me when we'd reach the speed and the point on the field when it would no longer be possible to stop. The fire warning light flashed on No. 2 again. Another false alarm.

'We had planned that the plane would roll on the nose wheel first, then lift completely off the runway. I'd requested the tower to notify us when they saw light under either wheel. We reached the critical speed. I lifted the guard off the JATO switch, preparing to fire the first six of the plane's eighteen units if necessary. We were now going too fast to stop.

'Then the plane came off. Before I knew it we were 60 feet in the air. The tower started to shout that we were airborne, but I was well aware of it. From that moment, I was happy with the plane. It became apparent that we would have no trouble. Call it intuition, or whatever you want, we knew we had it in the bag. The plane felt mighty good.'

Robbins summed up his flight in these words: 'The best way to tell about the performance of the Boeing Stratojet is to say that

PRODUCTION CLOSE-UP
B-47 STRATOJET

(Model 450)

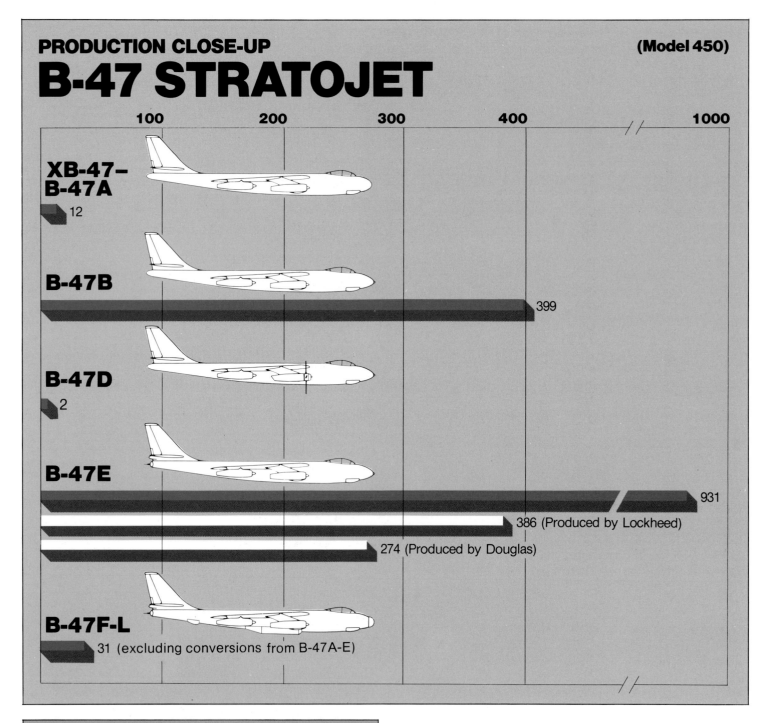

100   200   300   400   1000

XB-47–B-47A   12

B-47B   399

B-47D   2

B-47E   931

386 (Produced by Lockheed)

274 (Produced by Douglas)

B-47F-L   31 (excluding conversions from B-47A-E)

Specifications: B-47E Stratojet
Boeing Model Number 450

Span	116 ft
Length	107 ft
Wing Area	1428 sq ft
Tail Height	28 ft
Gross Weight	206,700 pounds
Bomb Capacity	20,000 pounds
Top Speed	606 mph plus
Cruising Speed	525 mph plus
Ferry Range	4100 miles
Service Ceiling	40,500 ft
Powerplant	six 7200 pound thrust General Electric J-47 Turbojets
Defensive Armament	two 20 mm cannon in radar-directed tail turret

any good crew could have flown it. It took no unusual ability or education. Neither Osler nor I deserve any real credit for the flight. Rather, the credit should go to the men who envisioned this plane, the men who carried out these visions on the drafting boards, and the factory workers who made the visions a reality. It is their airplane.'

The plane went on to prove itself. In 1949, it set a speed record by crossing the continent in 3 hours and 46 minutes. This was a long jump from the days when the Boeing 247's top speed was 200mph, and the range was 800 miles.

On 20 September 1951, the Stratojet made the first jet flight over the North Pole, paving the way for what is now common practice. On 28 July 1953 the B-47 set a transatlantic record, crossing the ocean in 4 hours and 45 minutes. Its average speed was 617.4mph, but on 23 December of the same year, the jet bomber crossed the Atlantic again, averaging 650.5mph. And on 16–18 November 1954 a B-47 flew 21,000 miles nonstop, with mid-air refueling.

The first production models of the B-47A and B retained the six J47-GE turbojets, upgrading them to J47-GE-11 and -23,

Above: The turboprop-powered **XB-47D**.

delivering 5200 to 5800 pounds of thrust. In addition to the bomber variants, the B series included 74 DB-47B drone directors, 24 RB-47B reconnaissance aircraft, 66 TB-47B crew trainers and one WB-47B conversion was made for weather reconnaissance. One B-47B was delivered to Canada as a test bed for the 20,000 pound thrust Canadair Orenda Iroquois turbojet engine. This aircraft, done up in RCAF markings (even though leased rather than sold), became the only postwar Boeing combat aircraft to be delivered to a foreign country.

The single B-47C, a converted B-47B, was intended to be the prototype of the B-56/RB-56A program. The B-47C would have been re-engined with four YJ-71-A-5 engines and redesignated XB-56, but the program was dropped without the initial conversion being made.

Two B-47Bs, however, were re-engined experimentally with a pair of 9710 pound thrust Curtiss Wright YT49-W-1 turboprops in place of the inboard turbojet engine nacelles and redesignated XB-47D. The engines were, at the time, the most powerful turboprops ever built.

The B-47E was the standard production B-47. It incorporated ejection seats, 20mm tail cannons, JATO pack and upgraded engines. The series included 24 DB-47E drone directors, 14 QB-47E drones, 240 RB-47Es and 34 WB-47Es.

The last B-47s were a series of experimental conversions. One F and one G were converted for probe and drogue refueling tests, with the B-47G the tanker. Thirty-five B-47Hs were electronic reconnaissance conversions while the B-47J was an MA2 radar bombing test bed and 35 EB-47Ls were B-47E conversions for electronic communications.

Over 2000 B-47s were produced by a pool of Boeing, Douglas and Lockheed, with the last one rolling off the Lockheed assembly line on 5 February 1957.

By that time improvements in Soviet air defenses meant that the B-47s could no longer make bomb runs over the Soviet Union at extremely high altitude without the threat of surface to air missiles (SAMs) and interceptors. New tactics had to be developed if the B-47s were to be able to fulfill their mission. The tactics that were devised are similar to those that would be used by B-52s in the 1980s if a strike against the Soviet Union was to take place. They involve penetration of enemy air space at very low levels, with either a rapid climb at the release point or a roll off a half loop after the release of the bomb, to avoid the nuclear blast. The B-47 may have reminded some of a fighter when it first appeared,

but the tight turns and fighter style maneuvers did not suit the B-47 airframe, which was not designed for such contortions. Airframe failures inevitably followed, and planes crashed. In one 30 day period in 1958, six B-47s went down. The day of the Stratojet was coming to a close.

Ironically, the B-47 phase out began in 1957, the same year as the last one was produced. By 1962 their numbers had dwindled to 880. Three years later the remaining 114 were put into mothballs or sold for scrap.

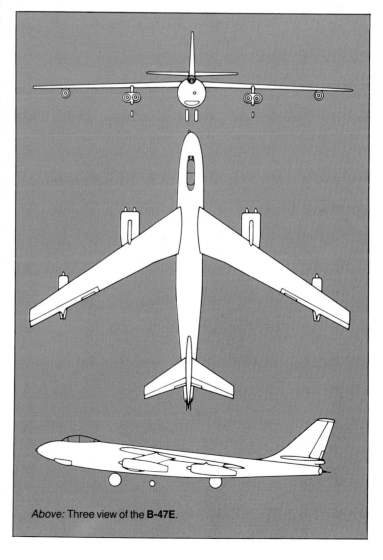

Above: Three view of the **B-47E**.

Boeing president William Allen should have been pleased with his company's financial gains by the close of 1952. Sales of the Stratocruiser, the B-50 bomber and the B-47 had hitched up Boeing's economy by a considerable margin.

In 1951 sales reached a nifty $337,300,566 worth of Boeing products. By the end of 1952 sales totalled $739,010,214. One of the big reasons for this jump over the previous year was the B-47. Though it had become one of the most expensive airplanes in history, with a unit price of about three million dollars, both Boeing, Seattle, and Boeing, Wichita, were rolling them out by the dozen. In July 1952, General Hoyt S Vandenberg, Air Force Chief of Staff, announced that the Boeing B-47 'Is now the back-bone of SAC.' General Vandenberg also mentioned that the Boeing B-52, then in development, would be at least of equal importance. He also denied that the Air Force owned any flying saucers!

When the General alluded to the B-52, he was referring to an airplane that was so secret, it had been kept, literally, under wraps. The B-52 prototype was rolled out of the Seattle plant on 29 November 1951, at nine in the evening. Air Force people were

so nervous about letting their secret out they demanded it be covered with muslin as a disguise. Boeing staff spent frantic hours rounding up enough cloth to cover an airplane with a wingspan of 185 feet and a fuselage 157 feet long.

Security was tight. Troops were brought in from nearby Fort Lewis as guards. Streets were closed to the public and special Air Force passes were required of anybody entering Boeing country. The Air Force also wanted a revetment built on Boeing Field high enough to hide the bomber from curious eyes. They also demanded that the test flight be made at night.

Carl Cleveland, Director of Public Relations for Boeing, was irritated. For one thing a revetment would be useless. Boeing Field was surrounded by high hills. There were houses on the hills, and people living in them. They could easily see over the tallest revetment. Further, no sane test pilot would take a brand new airplane up for the first time at night. This was especially true of the largest jet bomber America had ever built. The pilot wanted to *see* what was happening. In any case the instruments for night flying should themselves be tested – in broad daylight – before any night flying was tried.

On top of this, the Pentagon had stipulated that the negatives of all photographs taken of the event must be sent to Washington for developing and classification. Since hundreds of photos were taken, many rolls of film were exposed. There was scarcely time to find a darkroom in order to change rolls, so special light-proof black bags were used. The cameraman placed his camera in the bag and performed the entire operation of removing and replacing the film by feel. Upon viewing one of these fumbling operations, a security officer from Fort Lewis immediately thrust his hands in the bag, too, to make certain there was no hanky-panky.

The big airplane, crouching in its cocoon of white, resembled a giant moth. There was no doubt what was under the cloth, since its shape gave it away. People had seen the B-47, with swept wings such as those on the B-52, so what else was new? This foolishness, plus the revetment idea, the night testing and the nearly impossible orders to send all exposed film to Washington, DC finally got the best of Carl Cleveland. And the fact that he was run off the field, because he had a camera but no 'camera pass,' may have also helped to snap his patience.

He got on the phone to Colonel Arno Lehman in the Public Information Office of the Secretary of Defense. Lehman, a man with a clear, logical mind, flew to Boeing Field the next day. The

results of his visit made Boeing happy, at least. All restrictions were lifted, the plane was uncovered, and it would fly at a normal time for new airplanes, in daylight.

Though the security seems today to have been overdone, back in 1951 it was, unfortunately, somewhat justified. The United States was in a bitter Cold War with the Soviets who would have loved to have had B-52 aeronautic advances for themselves. The US was also in the grip of Communist-hunting Senator Joseph McCarthy and the Committee on Un-American Activities. It was a time of jitters both nationally and internationally, and in the light of such dangers, real and imagined, the Air Force was acting in what it perceived to be a responsible manner regarding the B-52.

The Boeing B-52 appeared on the scene overnight, or so it seemed, but events leading to that dramatic roll-out began in 1946. Boeing, in competition with Consolidated Vultee, Martin and other airplane builders, had been asked to submit designs for a long-range bomber. It was to be much larger than existing heavy bombers and, at Air Force request, would be powered by turboprop engines. Turboprops were still considered mighty muscle, and not to be overlooked. The secrecy surrounding the project reminded long-time Boeing engineers of Project A of the 1930s that resulted in the XB-15, another long-range bomber.

The design team went to work. It was headed by such men as Wellwood Beall, Ed Wells and George Schairer, all old airplane hands. The objective was to design and build the eventual successor to the Consolidated B-36 heavy bomber that would be brought on line in 1948 as the replacement for the B-29s and B-50s which were in 1946 the backbone of the strategic bomber force. The first design Boeing submitted was the Model 462 which resembled an enlarged six engine B-29, with a B-17 style flight deck arrangement. The design had by 1948 gradually evolved into the model 464-35 with swept wings and four turboprop engines with contra-rotating propellers. However, these designs were

Above: The **XB-52**.

Specifications: XB-52 & YB-52 Stratofortress
Boeing Model Number 464

Span	185 ft
Length	153 ft
Wing Area	4000 sq ft
Tail Height	48 ft 4 in
Gross Weight	390,000 pounds
Bomb Capacity	10,000 pounds
Top Speed	600 mph
Cruising Speed	525 mph
Ferry Range	7000 miles
Service Ceiling	50,000 ft
Powerplant	eight 8700 pound thrust Pratt & Whitney YJ57-P-3 Turbojets
Defensive Armament	none

Above: The **YB-52**.

running into trouble because, with turboprop propulsion, the performance could not exceed that of the new B-36 by a significant degree.

It is interesting to note that, at the same time the Boeing engineers were evolving a swept wing turboprop based ultimately on the B-29, Russian engineers of the Tupolev design bureau were developing a swept wing turboprop based on the B-29. Their aircraft, the Tu-95 (later NATO codename 'Bear') was developed out of their experience producing the Tu-4, which was virtually a bootlegged copy of B-29s that had made forced landings in Russian territory during World War II. The career of the Tu-95 has closely paralleled that of the B-52, and today it is the mainstay of the Soviet equivalent of SAC, the *Dalnaya Aviatsiya* or Long Range Aviation.

Ed Wells and George Schairer argued for an all-jet aircraft. After all, the B-47, their all-jet medium bomber, was proving to be a success on her early test flights. Colonel Pete Warden of Wright Field, long a Boeing advocate, managed to get them an OK to try a jet design. 'But,' he told them, 'keep the turboprop in mind.' In October 1948 plans for the new airplane were submitted to officials at Wright Field. The bomber now had a 20 degree sweepback and it was to be powered by Pratt & Whitney jet engines. The gross weight stood at 300,000 pounds, speed 500mph.

Pete Warden looked the plan over with a critical eye, and was doubtful. 'Give it more speed,' he advised in effect. 'You need a faster wing, something like the B-47.' It was Friday, and the end of the work-week, so the Boeing engineers that had come along for the presentation returned to their hotel for a talk. Top men were present, including Ed Wells, George Schairer, Bob Withington and Vaughn Blumenthal from the aerodynamics department. Art Carlsen and Maynard Pennell represented preliminary design.

They worked all weekend, revising the plans for their Model 464-49, which they now called the Stratofortress. They gave the bomber more sweep, angling the wings back 35 degrees like those of the B-47. They added two more engines, making a total of eight, two to a pod. It was known that Pratt & Whitney was experimenting at that time with a more powerful jet engine, the J57, which the Boeing men proposed to incorporate into the Stratofortress, which now weighed 330,000 pounds but whose range outdistanced the B-47 and whose speed was more than 600mph.

To make their new concept more eye-appealing and graphic, the planners built a balsa wood model, and took it to Wright Field for a Monday meeting with the military brass. The results pleased the officers. They read the 33 page report and studied the clean lines of the balsa model. Based on what they read and saw, Boeing was authorized to build two prototypes of the Model 464, given the Air Force designation B-52. Thus was history shaped over a weekend in a hotel room, for the B-52 was destined to make much history in the years to come.

With its contract in hand, Boeing got set to build the two prototypes, the XB-52 and YB-52. They were equipped with eight P&W J57 engines (as had been Convair's failed YB-60) and each was able to develop 10,000 pounds of thrust. That made them 10 times more powerful than the B-29. The B-52s could fly higher than the B-47s and required only five crewmen – as against the Convair B-36's 22.

Above: The third Wichita-built **B-52G** is refueled by Boeing **KC-135A** Stratotanker.

The first prototype to lift from Boeing Field was the YB-52. In the cockpit were test pilot Tex Johnson and co-pilot Lieutenant Colonel Guy Townsend. It was 15 April 1952.

A crowd had gathered for the event, and as the J57s wound up, they split the air with an eerie wail. As one reporter put it, 'the sound was like a piercing cry.' It made the audience jittery, causing a mechanic to mutter, 'Tex Johnson will chop off the engines if they don't sound right to him.'

But all was well in the cockpit, and the YB-52 lifted off at 11:09 a m She flew for two hours and 51 minutes, anxiously observed by George Schairer and Wellwood Beall from the ground. Their design, the result of an inspired weekend four years before, had become a beautiful reality.

The YB-52 cut through the sky smoothly and the test went well. After Johnson landed he said, 'The airplane functioned very satisfactorily with no trouble at all with basic systems. Its performance appears to be just what was predicted by Boeing engineers.' Then he added, 'It landed just like any airplane.'

The other prototype, the XB-52, made its first flight on 2 October 1952. The same two pilots took her through two hours and 42 minutes of tests. After landing, they reported no serious problems, and the B-52 bomber was 'in.'

Representatives of the Air Force were at both test flights, but they were as much observers as critics. The Air Force had already signed a contract for 13 B-52As in February of 1951 even before the prototypes flew. The big bombers were needed and the military had faith in the Boeing product. The Cold War with Russia had intensified and nobody knew for sure which way it would go. The US was also deeply involved in the Korean War, which was seen as part of the effort to resist Soviet communism.

The size of the Air Force's new long-range bomber was striking. Its tail stood 48 feet in the air, nearly five stories high. The wings spanned 185 feet and the body was 156 feet 6 inches long. The wing area of 4000 square feet was larger than a good-sized house. In fact, this latest Boeing aircraft was so large that the 'world's biggest doorway' was built into a new hangar just to accommodate it.

The terrific noise, noted on the first test flight of the YB-52, was causing problems. Flaps installed between engines were cracking. Consequently the largest noise suppressors yet invented were added. The fuel load of 29,645 gallons (more in later models) was so heavy that outrigger wheels were pressed hard against the ground. Indeed, the plane was so hefty that it sagged both in the air and on the ground. Because of this, the problem of reinforcement against sag became an on-going engineering battle. Engineering won, but the present day B-52 is a different airplane structurally than its prototypes. Extended tests were made on the structure of a B-52G, one of the last models. An entire airplane, except for engines, instruments, wiring and other accessories, was subjected to Boeing's famous 'torture test.' It was systematically destroyed while several thousand gauges and instruments recorded the stresses and strains on different components from wings to empennage. The testing lasted for approximately nine months, and as a result major structural changes made it virtually a new bomber.

The B-52A, nominally the first production model, but actually a flight test model, was flown in August 1954. It and all successive Model 464s differed from the prototypes in having adopted a traditional flight deck with the pilot and co-pilot seated side-by-side, as in a commercial airliner. Below were the bombardier and radar operator, while a gunner occupied a separately pressurized compartment in the tail. The compartment could be jettisoned if necessary, but until that fateful moment, the gunner was in charge of four .50 caliber machine guns.

PRODUCTION CLOSE-UP
B-52 STRATOFORTRESS

X-YB-52: The series prototypes had a *B-47 style* flight deck with tandem seating for the pilot & co-pilot and eight 8700-lb. thrust Pratt & Whitney turbojet engines.

X-YB-52 — 2

B-52A — 3

B-52A-F: The early production models adopted a traditional flight deck with side by side seating for the pilot & co-pilot, added provisions for aerial refueling & external fuel tanks and added defensive armament in the form of a manned tail turret with four .50-caliber machine guns. The F model introduced 13,750-lb. thrust turbojet engines.

B-52B — 50

B-52C — 35

B-52D — 101 / 69

B-52E — 42 / 58

Produced by Boeing/Seattle plant
Produced by Boeing/Wichita plant

B-52F — 44 / 45

B-52G: This later model incorporated a shorter tail and moved the tail gunner to the forward crew area to operate the tail turret by radar. As with the *B-52H*, the G model has been retrofitted with elaborate electronic counter-measures (ECM), as well as FLIR (forward-looking infrared sensors) and terrain-avoidance radar which are displayed to the crew on EVS (electro-optical viewing system) video screens in the cockpit.

B-52G — 193

B-52H — 102

B-52H: On the final production model the turbojets were replaced with eight 17,000-lb. thrust Pratt & Whitney turbofan engines. The four .50-caliber machine guns in the tail turret were replaced with a Vulcan 20mm six-barrel rotary cannon.

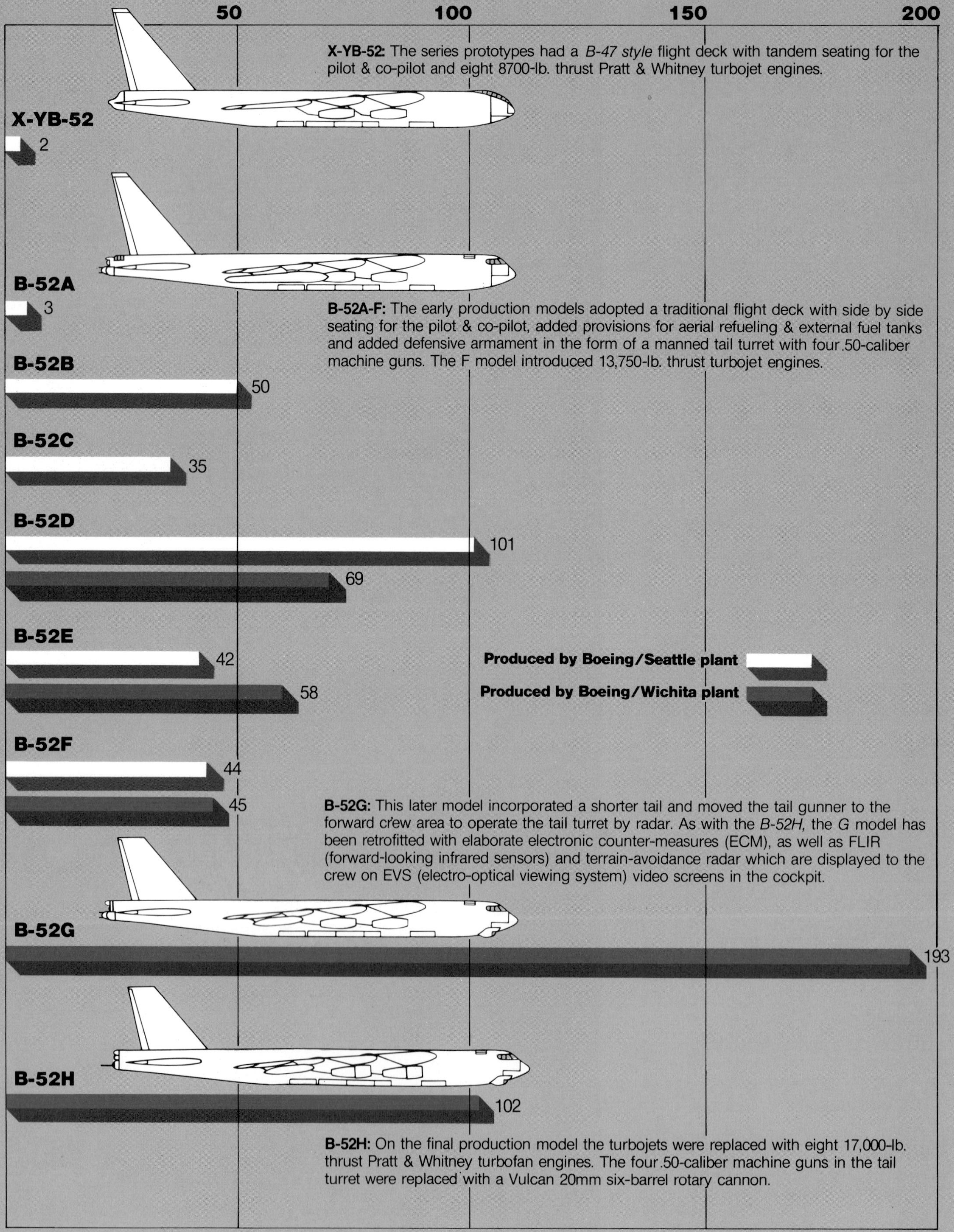

The fuel capacity of the B-52A had been increased by the addition of 1000 gallon drop tanks under each wing. Provision had also been made for flying boom refueling, which greatly increased the range. Pratt & Whitney J57-P-9Ws replaced earlier engines, yielding a thrust of more than 9000 pounds each, and the gross weight of the airplane reached a staggering 415,000 pounds.

Even before the 3 flight test B-52As first flew, the Air Force issued a contract for 50 B-52Bs. Photo-reconnaissance or electronic capsules could be installed in the bomb bay. Twenty-seven were built with the capsules and designated RB-52B.

Next off the line were 35 B-52Cs also with J57-P-29W turbojets. Quite similar to the B-52B, the Cs were also to serve dual purposes, but were built to higher load factors, grossing 450,000 pounds. Fuel capacity had been increased to 3000 gallons by installing larger drop tanks.

The next version, the B-52D, was to be used only as a bomber. Because of the winding down of the B-47 program and their desire to have strategic aircraft produced inland rather than near a coastline, the Air Force chose Wichita as the primary source of production. The first of 69 Wichita-built B-52Ds and 58 B-52Es rolled out in December 1955. Seattle, however, still rolled out 101 B-52Ds and 42 B-52Es from its production lines. Seattle's direct involvement with manufacturing the B-52 ended with the 'F' model. Forty-four were built in Seattle, and another 45 in Wichita. One of the principal changes over earlier models was

Above: The installation of **Pratt & Whitney J57 engines** on a B-52 assembly line.

Specifications: B-52D Stratofortress Boeing Model Number 464

Span	185 ft
Length	157 ft 7 in
Wing Area	4000 sq ft
Tail Height	48 ft 4½ in
Gross Weight	450,000 pounds
Bomb Capacity	54,000 pounds conventional explosives, or four free-fall nuclear weapons
Top Speed	585 mph
Ferry Range	7500 miles
Service Ceiling	50,000 ft
Powerplant	eight 10,000 pound thrust Pratt & Whitney J47-29W Turbojets
Defensive Armament	four 0.5 in machine guns in tail turret

Below: A **B-52D** of Strategic Air Command's 43rd Strategic Wing (Third Air Division) at Andersen AFB, Guam, in August 1979. The black-bottomed B-52Ds, with their enlarged bomb bay, flew frequent missions from Guam against targets in Southeast Asia throughout most of the Vietnam War years.

Above: Boeing test pilot **Chuck Fisher's B-52H** during its final approach into Blytheville AFB, 700 miles after it lost its tail to clear-air turbulence.

the engine. Eight P&W J57-43W turbojet engines gave the B-52F over 13,750 pounds of thrust for each engine. As the B-52 increased in weight because of added structural metal, larger fuel tanks and other innovations, the engines provided more power. Pratt & Whitney kept pace.

Significant innovations were first seen in the B-52G. In this version, the gunner was moved from the tail to a forward position with other crewmen for greater team efficiency. He monitored a television screen in his forward position which was fed images by a scanning camera. Enemy fighters could be fired on by remote control. The armament remained unchanged – 4 deadly .50 caliber machine guns.

The B-52G's exterior appearance was also modified by decreasing the height of the tail. One of the most important improvements was a redesigned wing in which wing fuel bladders were eliminated in favor of integral tanks, which reduced overall weight and opened the way by strengthening the wing, to the mounting of two supersonic AGM-28 Hound Dog missiles. Hound Dogs were long-range air-to-surface weapons, among the first of their kind. The AGM-28 was a 9600 pound, winged missile, powered by an underslung turbojet. It had a range of 690 miles and its mission was to increase the range of strategic bombers. The missile flew on, after firing, as the bomber turned away in what was called a stand-off situation. The missile continued to the target, but the bomber would be spared the danger.

The B-52H was fitted with eight 17,000 pound thrust P&W TF-33-P-1/3 turbofan engines, increasing the unrefueled range by 30 percent over the G. The .50 caliber machine guns were replaced by a six-barreled 20mm Vulcan gun, capable of virtually shredding any would-be attackers.

From its inception the B-52 has been an outstanding aircraft, most notably for its range. On 18 January 1957, three B-52s landed at March AFB, California after flying nonstop (with inflight refueling) around the world in 45 hours, 19 minutes. They averaged over 530mph during the 24,325 mile flight from Castle AFB, also in California. This cut the previous record in half, a record set by another Boeing bomber, the B-50A, 'Lucky Lady II.'

On 10 January 1962 a B-52H took off from Kadena AB, Okinawa and flew *unrefueled*, nonstop, the 12,532 miles to Madrid, setting a world distance record.

As recently as November 1981, SAC B-52s, taking part in a Rapid Deployment Force exercise codenamed operation 'Bright

Star' flew nonstop to a bombing range south of Cairo, dropped their bombs and returned to their home bases in North Dakota. Earlier, in March 1980, a B-52 from K I Sawyer AFB in Michigan flew nonstop around the world in 45 hours, repeating the feat of the three B-52s in 1957. Thus the B-52 proved to the world time and again that it had the right stuff.

Even this excellent bird has had its moments of stress. In 1964 a B-52H was being tested for low-level flying performance over the Rockies. A Boeing crew was taking the bomber through a variety of tests, of structural design in high turbulence. Cruising at an altitude of 500 feet, moderate turbulence was encountered and it was decided to discontinue low-level trials. The B-52H climbed to 14,300 feet, finding smooth air, but after several minutes rough turbulence suddenly rocked the ship. It was jabbed from the side severely, then tossed up and down. The crew noted high vertical G-forces and lateral motion of the airplane. It was as if the plane had been shoved to the right by a heavy blow. The aircraft came through the encounter, but almost all of the tail fin had been ripped off!

In the words of pilot Chuck Fisher, 'I gave orders to prepare to abandon the airplane, because I didn't think we were going to keep it together. We didn't know what was damaged, but control was difficult. We cut our speed to 225 knots, and dropped to about 5000 feet. Everybody was ready, should the need come to leave the ship. We figured we'd put a little more altitude between us and the ground, so we climbed to 16,000 feet very slowly. We kept trying to figure out the reason for our control problem. We had all eight engines, and all leading edges, but the plane would suddenly pitch or tuck in response to control. When this happened, control was very marginal and we didn't hold out much hope for getting it in in a landable condition. But we headed for Wichita.

'As soon as we got into a range where we could rendezvous with another airplane, Dale Felix came up in a fighter, and reported our damage. Most of our vertical fin was gone, but the horizontal stabilizer was intact. There was a chance.

'Because of the heavy population around Wichita, we decided to divert to Blytheville. We proceeded with a KC-135 and a T-33 escorting us. Arriving at Blytheville, we lowered our landing gear, experiencing yaw, but only during transition from up to down. The landing was not my best one, but the airplane was drifting left off the runway, and the only way to stop it was to get

it on the ground. Our weight at touchdown was 250,000 pounds, and we were going at 158 knots. We stopped at 5000 feet, and we were safe. So was the airplane.'

There have been close calls of another nature. In January 1961 two 24-megaton thermonuclear bombs came loose from a B-52 over Goldsboro, North Carolina. One of them was found in a marsh; five of its six interlocking safety devices had failed. Part of the second bomb was never found.

In 1966 a B-52 crashed into another airplane off the coast of Spain and four nuclear bombs fell. One was found intact on the ground. Two exploded on impact, and the last was pulled from the sea after a four month search. As a result of this accident, 5000 barrels of contaminated Spanish soil were shipped to South Carolina. Total cost of the tragedy, 50 million dollars.

The B-52's service record can be broken into three parts, the first part being the decade from 1955 to 1965 when it was the high flying cutting edge of SAC's nuclear deterrent force, constantly patroling the skies, waiting to be called upon to take part in a nuclear counterstrike against the Soviet Union. The final part is the period from 1973 when upgraded B-52s have shared the

Above: B-52s of the 93rd Bomb Wing depart Castle AFB on their 1957 **nonstop round-the-world flight**.

Below: **B-52s** share the flight line at Boeing's Wichita plant with their little brothers, the **B-47s**.

nuclear deterrent roles with land-based and submarine-based ballistic missiles. In between, the B-52 went to war.

The war in Southeast Asia began for the B-52 on 18 June 1965 when 27 stateside based B-52Fs flying from Andersen AFB on Guam struck Vietcong positions in South Vietnam. The missions were code named 'Arc Light,' and they were to continue until the US withdrawal from Vietnam. The controversial Arc Light carpet bombing raids were flown pretty much continuously from Andersen AFB, and later also from U Tapao Royal Thai Air Base, 12 to 14 hours closer to the target than Guam. The big bombers would come in at very high altitude from which they could be neither seen nor heard on the ground and drop their bombs by radar on preselected Vietcong targets in South Vietnam. They would then begin the long haul back to Andersen or the shorter one to U Tapao without having seen their targets or

Above: A Wichita-built **B-52F** drops 750-pound general-purpose bombs against a Vietcong target. When the B-52s went to war in 1965, they kept the natural-metal finish with the previously white undersurfaces painted gloss black for night operations.

Above: By October 1966 the **B-52Ds** with the three-tone camouflage system and black bottom and tail were replacing the silver Fs in the skies over Vietnam. The era of natural-metal Air Force bombers that began with the B-17Gs around 1944 was over.

Above: A **B-52G** lumbers down the flightline at **Andersen AFB** on Guam's north shore. During the Vietnam war, Andersen was an important base for B-52D strikes into Southeast Asia. In December 1972, during operation Linebacker II, they were launched at a rate of three per hour.

Above: Loading **general-purpose bombs** onto a B-52D at U Tapao AB, in Thailand.

Above: Armorers use a hoist to position bombs on one of a B-52D's **external weapons pylons**.

Above: A Guam-based **B-52D** unloads its bombs over the target.

the enemy below. A year after the beginning of Arc Light, they were averaging 8000 tons of bombs a month and though their results against the guerrilla targets were often hard to determine, intelligence reports generally stated that the B-52s were the weapon that the Vietcong feared most.

Arc Light constituted day-in day-out drudgery for the B-52 crews. They lived for up to six months at a time in sticky heat, flying long, boring missions against an unseen enemy. The planes themselves were designed for strategic missions. Indeed they came from a long line of strategic bombers. They found themselves, however, flying routine tactical support missions.

But in December 1972 all that changed. The US was finally trying to disengage itself from an increasingly unpopular war.

American diplomats were at the Paris Peace Talks trying to negotiate a settlement that could allow them to withdraw, and North Vietnam was dragging its feet.

It was decided at the highest levels of the US Government that North Vietnam must be forced to negotiate. SAC was ordered to prepare to undertake massive strategic bombing raids over North Vietnam, striking the capital of Hanoi and the major port city of Haiphong.

In what has since been called their finest hour, the B-52s finally went to war as strategic bombers in the operation code-named 'Linebacker II.' All the B-52Ds in SAC's arsenal, except those already at U Tapao, were flown out to Andersen where they were supplemented by additional B-52Gs. The battle plan

Below: A **B-52D** drops 1000- and 750-pound bombs on a target 25 miles from Bien Hoa AB, Vietnam, on 1 December 1966.

called for a series of nighttime raids over a three night period with over 80 aircraft from both bases taking part the first night and that number growing to nearly 100 by the third night.

On 18 December wave upon wave of the big planes lumbered off the two fields. Navy and Air Force fighter bombers had preceded them, and Boeing KC-135 tankers were standing by to top off B-52 fuel tanks enroute. The North Vietnamese had assembled an awesome concoction of SAM missiles and anti-aircraft defenses in the Hanoi-Haiphong area, and the B-52s found the going tough. After three days the aerial armada was suffering losses at the unacceptable rate of 7 percent. In World War II, when a B-17 went down, there were three or four coming off the assembly line to replace it. In SE Asia when a B-52 went down, that was it, there was no longer an assembly line. The

enemy, however, was suffering as well. When the decision was made to continue the raids past the third night and to go after the SAM sites that had proved so costly, the loss rate went down to a very acceptable zero percent for the next three nights.

Captain David R Rusch, a Boeing KC-135 tanker pilot with the 99th Air Refueling Squadron based at U Tapao airbase in Thailand, flew in support of the final operations of Linebacker II. Except for 24 hours during Christmas, there was constant activity over North Vietnam during the raids.

Circling the Tonkin Gulf, Captain Rusch had this view of the second night's raid: 'The B-52s came in high over the gulf, as the Navy aircraft went down after antiaircraft artillery sites, which opened fire as they were attacked. Then came SAM calls over the radio, and attack planes went in to hit the missile launchers. I

saw the B-52s begin their bomb runs, when suddenly the whole sky lit up. A B-52 had taken a direct hit from a SAM. Although the B-52s were protected by fighters, and had their own superb electronic jamming equipment, the North Vietnamese found a way to determine the bomber's altitude. One or two MiGs would dart through the formation, not shooting at anybody, but just up there to determine the altitude, which the pilot would radio to the ground. Then the North Vietnamese would fire several missiles timed to go off about that altitude and hope for a lucky hit, which they occasionally scored.'

At the end of 11 days of bombing, the overall loss rate was down to 2 percent, North Vietnamese air defenses had been all but wiped out and Le Duc Tho and the North Vietnamese team at the Paris Peace Talks were back at the negotiating table.

The last B-52H rolled off the assembly line at Wichita on 26 October 1962. Since then the Stratofortress has seen itself outlive a whole lineage of would-be successors. First there was the Convair (formerly Consolidated-Vultee, later General Dynamics) B-58, the supersonic high altitude bomber of the late 1950s. Then there was the huge Mach 3 Rockwell (formerly North American) B-70 of the middle 1960s that never got past the flight test stage. Finally there was the Rockwell B-1A in the mid 1970s which, though it died a political death, was considered to be no more of an improvement over the B-52 than the Boeing 462 had been over the B-36.

It is a compliment of the highest order to the men who developed the B-52 that their design was so sound and forward looking as to allow it to extend its service life into its fourth decade. It has survived far past the point at which an aircraft brought on line in the mid 50s should have been expected to be phased out. In fact, it is generally accepted that when the B-1B, the much improved offspring of the B-1A, comes on line in the mid 80s it will operate side by side with updated B-52s.

Updating, and the flexible systems that allow updating, are indeed the underlying reasons for the B-52's continued success. Today the B-52 fleet within SAC has been simplified to just three models, the D, G and H. (The D is on the point of retirement.)

When it was decided to commit B-52s to combat in SE Asia in 1965, it was almost exclusively the B-52F that went into service. Simultaneously, SAC initiated a project called 'Big Belly' in which the bomb bay capacity of B-52Ds was dramatically increased. Gradually the Fs were pulled out, mothballed and replaced with Ds. Before the Big Belly program, B-52s generally could carry 27 500-pound conventional bombs in their bays. Afterward, with the expanded bomb bay and two underwing pylons, the B-52D's bomb carrying capacity quadrupled.

While the B-52D became SAC's principal bombing platform for conventional high explosive or 'iron' bombs, the more advanced G and H have been designated as the principal carriers of nuclear weapons in the form of internally carried gravity weapons (bombs), or the underwing mounted Boeing Short Range Attack Missile (SRAM), successor to the earlier Hound Dog. As the B-52s ply the uncertain skies of the 1980s and 90s, they will gradually become the launch platform for yet another Boeing product – the Air Launched Cruise Missile (ALCM).

All three in-service B-52 models have been structurally strengthened and have been retrofitted with advanced electronics. In an important change of tactics necessitated by advances in radar and surface to air missiles (SAMs) that have made traditional high altitude strategic bombing impractical, bombers have had to switch to practicing extremely low-level bombing runs to allow them to come in under the enemy's radar. To permit this, B-52s have been equipped with ACR (Advanced Capability Terrain Avoidance Radar) that allows the giant bombers to fly, hugging the lay of the land, at 300 feet (500 for B-52D) for extended periods. In addition to ACR, B-52s are equipped with Phase VI (Phase V on B-52D) Electronic Counter Measures (ECM) which allow them to counter or defend themselves against enemy radar and radar-guided missiles fired from either the ground or hostile aircraft.

The newer and more advanced B-52s, the G and H, have received the more advanced electronics packages. Most important is the AN/ASQ-152 Electro-optical Viewing System (EVS). The EVS consists of two steerable cameras, one a TV

B-52G MAJOR INTERNAL SYSTEMS

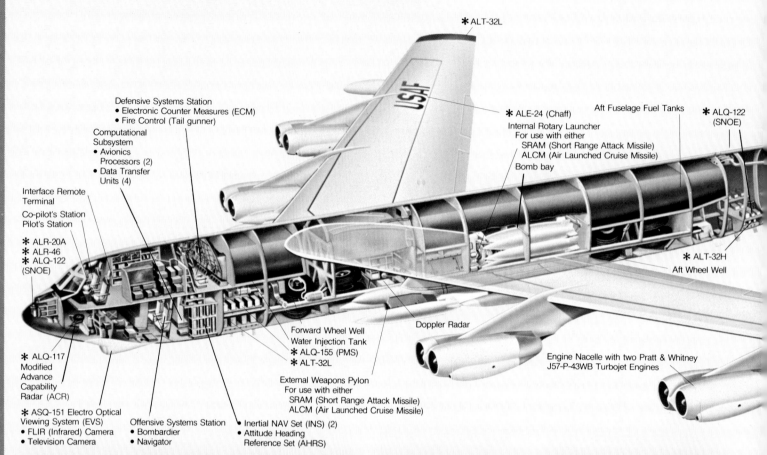

✳ ALT-32L

Defensive Systems Station
• Electronic Counter Measures (ECM)
• Fire Control (Tail gunner)

Computational Subsystem
• Avionics Processors (2)
• Data Transfer Units (4)

Interface Remote Terminal
Co-pilot's Station
Pilot's Station
✳ ALR-20A
✳ ALR-46
✳ ALQ-122 (SNOE)

✳ ALQ-117 Modified Advance Capability Radar (ACR)

✳ ASQ-151 Electro Optical Viewing System (EVS)
• FLIR (Infrared) Camera
• Television Camera

Offensive Systems Station
• Bombardier
• Navigator

✳ ALE-24 (Chaff)
Internal Rotary Launcher
For use with either
SRAM (Short Range Attack Missile)
ALCM (Air Launched Cruise Missile)
Bomb bay

Aft Fuselage Fuel Tanks
✳ ALQ-122 (SNOE)

✳ ALT-32H
Aft Wheel Well

Forward Wheel Well
Water Injection Tank
✳ ALQ-155 (PMS)
✳ ALT-32L

External Weapons Pylon
For use with either
SRAM (Short Range Attack Missile)
ALCM (Air Launched Cruise Missile)

• Inertial NAV Set (INS) (2)
• Attitude Heading Reference Set (AHRS)

Doppler Radar

Engine Nacelle with two Pratt & Whitney J57-P-43WB Turbojet Engines

Above: The appearance of the nose of the B-52G and H, the youngest of the B-52 fleet, has been completely transformed. Visible under the chin are the **Hughes AAQ-6 forward-looking infrared sensor (FLIR)** and **Westinghouse AVQ-22 low-light television (LLTV)** cameras with their covers in the closed position. The FLIR sensors provide a daylight-type image at night and during periods of low visibility due to fog or storms. The LLTV cameras provide a clear image during daylight and even under starlight. The combination permits low-altitude operations in all visibility conditions.

Above: **The flight-deck interior** of the B-52G and H has been transformed by the addition of the green electro-optical viewing system displays. The EVS displays are the terminal for both FLIR and LLTV as well as the Advanced Capability Terrain-Avoidance Radar System (ACR). The displays also provide the pilot with such information as air speed, radar altitude, artificial horizon (with horizontal reference line) and heading error. In the foreground, the B-52's eight throttle levers are visible. The B-52 is the only jet flying with eight engines.

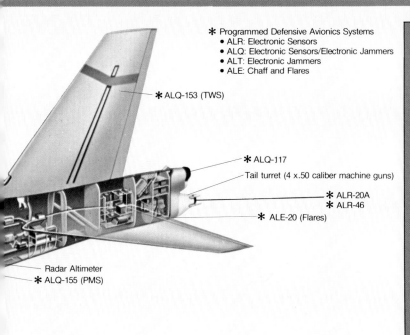

* Programmed Defensive Avionics Systems
  • ALR: Electronic Sensors
  • ALQ: Electronic Sensors/Electronic Jammers
  • ALT: Electronic Jammers
  • ALE: Chaff and Flares

* ALQ-153 (TWS)

* ALQ-117

Tail turret (4 x.50 caliber machine guns)

* ALR-20A
* ALR-46
* ALE-20 (Flares)

Radar Altimeter
* ALQ-155 (PMS)

* ALE-24 (Chaff)

* ALR-20A

Fixed External Fuel Tank (700 gallons)

Specifications: B-52G Stratofortress
Boeing Model Number 464

Span	185 ft
Length	160 ft 11 in
Wing Area	4000 sq ft
Tail Height	40 ft 8 in
Gross Weight	488,000 pounds
Bomb Capacity	13,500 pounds (conventional), or eight nuclear bombs, or twenty SRAM
Top Speed	595 mph
Ferry Range	8400 miles
Service Ceiling	55,000 ft
Powerplant	eight 13,750 pound thrust Pratt & Whitney J57-P-43WB Turbojets
Defensive Armament	four 0.5 in machine guns in tail turret

Left: A **cutaway drawing of a B-52G** in its original natural-metal finish showing its major internal systems, particularly the **Defensive Avionics Systems** and the position of **Boeing SRAM missiles**, on the external weapons pylons and within the bomb bay.

Below: A **B-52G** of the 328th Bomb Squadron (93rd Bomb Wing) based at Castle AFB in California. The 93rd Bomb Wing was the first to receive B-52s in 1955.

camera, the other infrared (FLIR), mounted side by side under the chin of the aircraft. The cameras are in turn connected to three video screen monitors on the flight deck. There is one each for the pilot, co-pilot and navigator.

In broad daylight, the TV camera shows the viewer exactly what he can see out the front window. In times of low and marginal visibility, the FLIR camera shows the viewer exactly what he could see out the front window if it were broad daylight. In addition to the visual picture (and the reason for viewing the screen rather than looking out the window), the EVS gives the pilot all the critical data he needs to fly the aircraft. Like the Head Up Display (HUD) now being used in fighters that projects instrument data on the front of the canopy so that the pilot does not have to look down during a dogfight, the EVS allows the

B-52 pilot to fly the aircraft while looking in only one place. While the TV or FLIR shows him visually what is outside, numbers on the top of the screen give him his airspeed, heading and time to go on the mission. An altitude indicator is on the right, while the artificial horizon is in the center.

In addition to flight information, the EVS monitor, via the terrain avoidance radar, 'paints' the terrain profile in the form of a graph across the screen. The graph is constantly changing so that the pilots' graphic perception of the terrain is constantly updated. This is critical when flying a mission in bad weather at 500mph, 300 feet off the ground.

Further planned and scheduled improvements will allow the B-52 systems to serve until the end of the century. Many newer electronic and weapons systems are under consideration as is a possible re-engining with larger, jumbo-jet type turbofan engines, such as the 47,800-pound thrust Pratt & Whitney JT9D-7R4D that is now being used on the 767 Airliner. One B-52 has in fact been flown with the huge General Electric XTF-39 turbofan engine.

In the early stages of the B-52 development Boeing was also working, as has been noted, on turboprop designs. In the late 1940s some authorities felt that turboprops might ultimately prove superior to pure jets because the combination seemed to offer a solution to the drag problems encountered by jet engines at high speed. However, by 1948 the idea had been rendered largely obsolete by advancing wing and engine technology. This ensured the demise of the Boeing Model 474, an unproduced four-engine turboprop design that was a parallel development to the Model 462 which turned into the 464/B-52 program. The progress of the B-52 also put an end to a development of the 474, the larger swept-wing Boeing Model 479. The Air Force issued a contract for the 479 on 1 July 1948 and gave it the designation XB-55. It was to have six Pratt & Whitney J-40 engines arranged in the same pylon arrangement as the B-47 and some of the structural design was similar to that of the B-52. The success of the B-52 led to the abandonment of this program, however.

No sooner had jet bombers succeeded piston engine bombers than the Air Force began to set its sights on a supersonic bomber. Supersonic flight, long a mysterious theory, was now a reality, and both the United States and the USSR were building supersonic fighters. In order to compete with supersonic interceptors, it was reasoned, one needed a supersonic bomber. The idea was that a supersonic bomber would replace the B-52 as the B-52 had the B-47. Boeing first began work on a supersonic bomber design in 1951. The original conception of a supersonic bomber revolved around the Model 450-65 which was a variation on the B-47. The Model 450-65 design was similar in profile to the B-47, with shorter, broader wings and the engines buried in the wing.

Eventually Boeing evolved a series of designs for a sleek Mach 2 aircraft which they proudly designated Model 701. In its various metamorphoses, the 701 (which the Air Force had designated XB-59) had a swept, canard and even a delta wing configuration. Ultimately, Boeing lost the supersonic sweepstakes to Convair's B-58 Hustler, of which over one hundred went into SAC inventory as supersonic replacements for the B-52s. In the mid-1960s the B-58 itself came by a potential successor in North American's gigantic B-70, which flew at three times the speed of sound.

Finally, both the B-58 which had made it into production, and the B-70 which never got past the prototype stage, fell victim to much the same kind of changing Air Force requirements that had earlier killed the B-47. In the end, both planes were replaced by updated versions of the B-52, the plane that they had been supposed to replace.

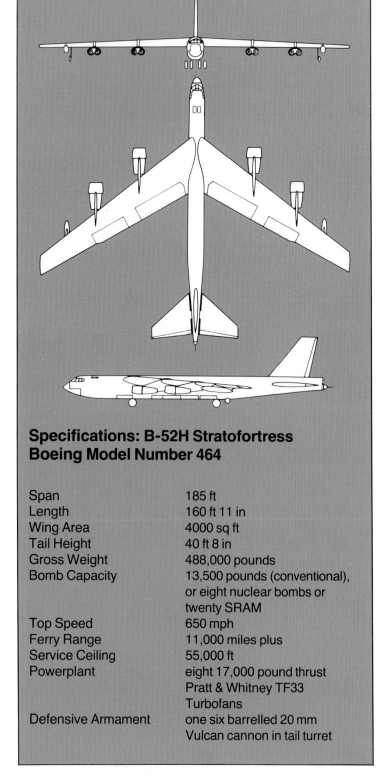

Specifications: B-52H Stratofortress
Boeing Model Number 464

Span	185 ft
Length	160 ft 11 in
Wing Area	4000 sq ft
Tail Height	40 ft 8 in
Gross Weight	488,000 pounds
Bomb Capacity	13,500 pounds (conventional), or eight nuclear bombs or twenty SRAM
Top Speed	650 mph
Ferry Range	11,000 miles plus
Service Ceiling	55,000 ft
Powerplant	eight 17,000 pound thrust Pratt & Whitney TF33 Turbofans
Defensive Armament	one six barrelled 20 mm Vulcan cannon in tail turret

We have already seen that even as the last KC-97 was being rolled out, production of its Boeing successor the C-135 Stratolifter/KC-135 Stratotanker was just beginning. For reasons of corporate security this new jet program had been camouflaged under the Stratofreighter model number 367 at first. The Model 367-80 or 'Dash Eighty' as it came to be known around the drafting tables at Boeing, would be the immediate prototype for both the Model 707 jetliner and the Model 717.

The C-135/KC-135 story is still unfolding today but there were no assurances at first that the 717 would arouse Air Force interest. The KC-97G was doing well, but military orders would be important if the $15 million price tag for the new ship was to be paid. Both William Allen and Wellwood Beall campaigned for Air Force orders, but without results. As work on the Dash Eighty progressed, and more money was pumped into the enterprise, the Boeing company faced another difficult period. Layoffs threatened the work force and stockholders were not going to take such a huge loss happily.

In the spring of 1954, however, Boeing's luck changed. The Strategic Air Command let it be known that a jet tanker was going to be needed and Air Force interest in the 717 accordingly increased. Air Force Secretary Harold Talbot was impressed with the airplane, but no decision to buy was made.

On 14 May 1954, the 367-80 prototype was rolled out of the Renton plant. Air Force representatives were present for the roll-out, and liked what they saw. On 15 July the prototype made its first flight, and shortly thereafter, on 5 August, the Air Force announced it would purchase a limited number of the jet tanker/transports. Boeing was in business.

The 717 had only a single large cargo door and, because the fuel tanks were located in the lower portion of the two-deck body and in the wings, this allowed an unobstructed upper deck for passengers and cargo. In tanker versions the flying boom, now a telescoping, streamlined apparatus, operated from the lower deck. The crew consisted of the pilot, co-pilot, navigator and boom operator.

The first production Stratotanker rolled out on 18 July 1956 at Renton, and its test flight took place on 31 August. As R L Loesch, Senior Experimental Test Pilot for Boeing, said, 'The KC-135 should be one of the best-liked airplanes in the Air Force. I would predict that any difficulty that arises will not be in getting pilots in the KC-135s, but in keeping them out.'

The new jet fitted into its refueling duties with ease. It is still in service. It can operate at altitudes up to 40,000 feet and cruises at 530mph, a comfortable match for the jets it refuels. Its principal strategic mission lies in refueling long-range bombers. For this reason, the active duty tanker fleet is owned and managed by SAC. Another 128, flown by National Guard and Reserve forces, support SAC missions.

The KC-135 is a powerful airplane. Four turbojets, mounted under the 35-degree swept wings, thrust it skyward at weights grossing 297,000 pounds. All internal fuel, save for 1200 gallons, can be pumped through the flying boom, and time spent during the transfer of fuel is not critical. A KC-135, piloted by Colonel K H Kalberer, and a B-52, skippered by Captain W W Leesburg, once kept in transfer position for an even 60 minutes, while 10,000 pounds of fuel were transferred. After the test, Captain Leesburg reported that the two airplanes could have gone on indefinitely.

KC-135s were used extensively in the Vietnam War, demonstrating that the tactics of air war had changed for all time. Combat aircraft were no longer limited by onboard fuel. Fighter pilots, knowing a Stratotanker could be tapped for more fuel, could spend more time in a combat area. Far-flung bomber targets were brought within reach thanks to KC-135 refueling facilities.

Through the years, the C-135/Model 717 became the true workhorse of the Air Force, a real jack of all trades. Beginning with C-135A there have been more designation variations of this plane than with any other aircraft in USAF service, taking the alphabetic nomenclature system up to RC-135W. It will likely be the first aircraft to go past Z. The overwhelming majority of C-135s though, have been KC-135 Stratotankers. Most of these, 724, were KC-135As, while 17 KC-135Bs were built and three KC-135As were converted to KC-135R (sometimes referred to as RC-135R) reconnaissance/tanker aircraft. A number (classified, but probably in excess of 40) of KC-135As were also modified to carry JP-7 fuel for the SR-71 strategic reconnaissance aircraft. These were redesignated KC-135Q.

Of the others, 53 were built as transports, 18 C-135As, 30 C-135Bs and 5 VC-135s. An additional 11 were completed as

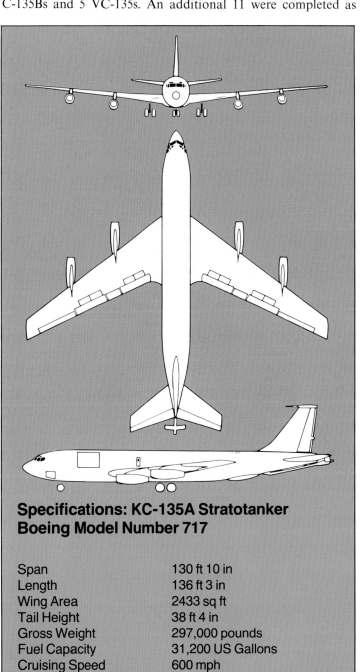

Specifications: KC-135A Stratotanker Boeing Model Number 717

Span	130 ft 10 in
Length	136 ft 3 in
Wing Area	2433 sq ft
Tail Height	38 ft 4 in
Gross Weight	297,000 pounds
Fuel Capacity	31,200 US Gallons
Cruising Speed	600 mph
Ferry Range	5000 miles
Service Ceiling	41,000 ft
Powerplant	four 13,750 pound thrust Pratt & Whitney J57 Turbojet

Above right: A receiving aircraft's view of the **KC-135** refueling boom. The linkup between the two planes can take place in just a few minutes; thereafter the two can remain linked for close to an hour. In this view the boom operator's window can be clearly seen just forward of the boom root.

Top: A SAC **KC-135** of the 93rd Air Refueling Squadron based at Castle AFB in California.

WC-135B weather reconnaissance aircraft. The remaining C-135 designations include EC-135A, B, J, K and L electronic reconnaissance and flying command post aircraft, many of which are conversions from other C-135s. Because conversions are continually taking place, and because much of the electronic gear and many of the aircraft missions are classified, it is not always certain which aircraft are designated as which, and when. The same is true of JC-135, JKC-135, NC-135 and NKC-135 aircraft which are used for various types of classified and unclassified testing of assorted electronic devices and laser weapons.

Finally, there were 14 RC-135A and B reconnaissance and photo-reconnaissance aircraft built in the mid-1960s under the Boeing model number 739. These had a distinctive large radome

in the nose and have since been upgraded and redesignated RC-135D, G, M, W etc.

Boeing's KC-135 became an important part of the Air Force. The last of them was delivered in 1965, and a year later its Boeing predecessor, the last active-duty KC-97, was phased out – nearly 24 years after it was originally conceived. The present-day KC-135 expects an even longer life than the KC-97. Like its teammate, the B-52, it will see use until the close of the 20th century.

While the 717 model number was assigned to the military and the 707 model was reserved for commercial programs, the USAF has adapted the slightly larger 707 airframe for a couple of unique functions.

Designated VC-137A (later re-engined with TF33P turbofan engines and redesignated VC-137B), three Model 707s were acquired in 1959 for use as VIP transports. Five VC-137s, now including VC-137Cs, are operated by the 89th Military Airlift Wing based at Andrews Air Force Base near Washington. One of the VC-137Cs, when used as the VIP transport of the President of the United States, is designated 'Air Force One.' The interiors of the VC-137s are fitted out with offices, sleeping quarters and the complicated communications equipment required by the President and his entourage whether they are flying to Europe for a summit conference or to Iowa for a political rally.

The Air Force is also obtaining Model 707s as Airborne Warning And Control System (AWACS) aircraft. Originally designated EC-137, the AWACS aircraft are now given the designation E-3A.

The idea for an AWACS aircraft goes back to 1963, but the theory behind it is as old as radar. Normal ground-based radar has an inherent blind area near the ground where surface features

Specifications: C-135B Stratolifter Boeing Model Number 717

Span	130 ft 10 in
Length	136 ft 6 in
Wing Area	2433 sq ft
Tail Height	41 ft 8 in
Gross Weight	275,000 pounds
Cargo Capacity	60,000 pounds
Cruising Speed	600 mph
Ferry Range	5000 miles
Service Ceiling	41,000 ft
Powerplant	four 18,000 pound thrust Pratt & Whitney TF-33-P5 Turbofans

Above: This **EC-135C (Boeing Model 717)** began life as a **KC-135B** tanker but had its refueling boom removed when it was converted into an airborne command post. Now identical in outward appearance to a standard C-135B in matt-gray finish, this plane confirms that you really do need a detailed listing to tell 135s apart. Aircraft may be modified and subsequently redesignated on more than one occasion.

While the 707 airframe is produced (as are all 707 airframes) by the Boeing Commercial Airplane Company, the responsibility for the E-3A AWACS part of the program falls to Boeing Aerospace. They received an Air Force contract in July 1970 to flight test two competing radar systems, which included one designed by Hughes Aircraft, in addition to the Westinghouse system that eventually was adopted. After the radar was proven, there came the System Integration Demonstration (SID) phase of the AWACS evaluation. The SID was followed by a series of Initial Operational Test and Evaluation (IOT&E) flights. These testing programs complete, the decision was made in April 1975 to begin production of the E-3A. All the test aircraft were refurbished and delivered as operational systems, the first one being delivered on 23 March 1977.

All of the USAF E-3A aircraft are assigned to the 552nd AWACS Wing at Tinker AFB in Oklahoma, but serve temporary duty all over the world from Okinawa to Iceland. They play a critical role in North American and Western European air defense. When tensions heated up in the Middle East in the early 1980s with the fall of the Shah of Iran and the Iran-Iraq war, Saudi Arabia asked for and received assistance from the United States in the form of several USAF E-3As to be based in Saudi Arabia to keep track of Iranian aircraft. The Saudi Air Force has since decided that they would like to purchase E-3s of their own. This has aroused an angry response from the Israelis who feel that Saudi E-3s could be used to track Israeli aircraft for hostile Arab countries.

In December 1978 the NATO Defense Planning Council, made up of the defense ministers of member nations, gave the go-ahead for acquisition of a fleet of 18 E-3 AWACS for the NATO airborne early warning requirement. Boeing Aerospace is leading an international team of American, Canadian and German firms to develop the electronics and support package for the NATO E-3A. The NATO AWACS program contract was signed in 1980, and deliveries began in early 1982.

In addition to the VC-137s and E-3s for the USAF and NATO, 707 airframes have been acquired by several foreign Air Forces as military transports and tankers. The Canadian Armed Forces use five 707s (designated CC-137) of which two have been converted for use as hose and drogue tankers. The Federal German Luftwaffe has acquired 707s for use as transports, while the Imperial Iranian Air Force (before it became the Islamic Iranian Air Force) received 14 707s, some of which were completed as tankers. It is worth noting that Iran's Air Force was the only one to purchase a tanker version of the 747. The IIAF had also ordered a number of E-3s, but the order was terminated when the Shah's government was overthrown in 1979.

such as trees and hills interfere with the radar's ability to 'see.' Hence the term 'flying under the radar' is used to refer to an aircraft flying low to the ground to avoid detection by enemy radar. The AWACS incorporates a new technology in radar called 'look down radar' which is able to look into the blind spot near the ground and separate targets from the kind of ground clutter that confuses conventional radar.

The most distinctive feature of the E-3A is its unique 'skunk-striped' Westinghouse rotodome. The rotodome, perched over the rear fuselage, measures 30 feet across and is six feet thick. It rotates at 6rpm while in operation, but is rotated at $\frac{1}{4}$rpm while not operating, to prevent the bearing lubricant from congealing. The active ingredients of the rotodome are the AN/APY-1 surveillance radar, IFF (Identification, Friend or Foe), and data link fighter-control (TADIL-C) antennae.

Specifications: VC-137C Air Force One
Boeing Model Number 707

Span	145 ft 9 in
Length	152 ft 11 in
Wing Area	3050 sq ft
Tail Height	42 ft 5 in
Gross Weight	328,000 pounds
Cruising Speed	626 mph
Service Ceiling	38,500 ft
Range	7000 miles
Powerplant	four 13,000 pound thrust Pratt & Whitney TF33-P Turbofans

Specifications: E-3A Sentry (AWACS)
(Formerly EC-137 D)
Boeing Model Number 707

Span	145 ft 9 in
Length	152 ft 11 in
Tail Height	41 ft 4 in
Gross Weight	325,000 pounds
Cruising Speed	600 mph
Service Ceiling	29,000 ft plus
Mission Endurance	11 hours plus (unrefuelled)
Powerplant	four 21,000 pound thrust Pratt & Whitney TF33-PW Turbofans

Above: A **KC-135A (Model 717)** in the high-visibility orange markings common in the late 50s and early 60s.

Above: This **VC-137 (Model 707)**, tail number 27000, has served as *Air Force I*, the US president's personal transport, since 1972.

Below: Twelve **KC-135Fs** were supplied to France to serve its strategic bomber force. They have since been modified to use the probe-and-drogue method of refueling (not shown here).

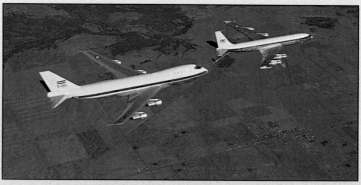

Above: An Imperial Iranian Air Force **Model 707** tanker refuels an IIAF **747**. Canada and Iran operate 707 tankers, while the IIAF has the only 747 tankers.

Above: The US Air Force **E-3A Sentry (Model 707)** Airborne Warning And Control System (AWACS) aircraft is the most advanced radar aircraft in the world.

Right: Avionics equipment in the **E-3A** includes surveillance radar, navigation, communications, data processing, identification and displays.

Above: One of 19 **T-43A** crew trainers (Model 737) supplied to the USAF Air Training Command. Fifteen remain with ATC while four now serve the Air National Guard.

Above: The plane that might have been. Boeing's **'C-5A'** design strongly resembled the later 747 but incorporated the same high wing as the winning Lockheed C-5A design.

While it had been a common practice during and shortly after World War II for commercial airliners all to lead to military variations, Boeing's commercially successful 700 family has seen little military service. The 717 has been a significant exception of course, because the 717 designation was specifically earmarked for the military. The 707, as has been shown, is in service in VIP transport and AWACS roles while of the others, 19 Model 737s were purchased as crew navigation trainers and given the designation T-43A (*see* page 185).

The story of Boeing's Jumbo Jet, the Model 747, presents a variation on this theme. It was born as a result of a USAF requirement for a very large transport for oversized cargo. Boeing failed to win this contract but put the experience to good use with the 747. The story has now come full circle and Boeing is proposing the 747 for military use.

The project (originally designated CX-HLS) would eventually evolve into the C-5A project, and the resulting aircraft would be the biggest airplane in the world. Boeing, Douglas and Lockheed all submitted designs and in September 1965, Lockheed was given the contract. While the Air Force generally felt that Boeing's design was superior, it was regarded as too costly. Though the Lockheed bid was lower, design flaws and cost overruns have made the Lockheed C-5A one of the most costly aircraft in USAF service.

The Boeing-Lockheed C-5 controversy was to rear its head again 17 years later. At the onset of the 1980s the Military Airlift Command of the Air Force found itself with a Rapid Deployment Force to support. Rapid deployment of forces means deployment by transport aircraft, and the RDF requirement for outsize airlift capacity (*big* transport planes) outstrips the capacity of MAC's 70-odd Lockheed C-5As. In 1982 Congress was faced with the dilemma of whether to ask Lockheed to gear up its long-dismantled production lines to produce a line of new C-5Bs, or whether, as Boeing has suggested and Senator Henry Jackson of Washington State has proposed, simply to go into the used-airplane market and buy the Air Force already existing 747 cargo planes. The advantage to the C-5 design is that its cargo area is larger, large enough to handle the Army's bulkiest equipment such as the new M-1 Abrams Main Battle Tank; and that both ends of the aircraft open so that equipment can be driven on one end and off the other. The C-5A or B can also land on short semi-improvised runways in remote or front line areas. The 747, on the other hand, can carry almost anything that the C-5 can and a greater volume. The 747 can also fly farther and faster than the C-5 and has a far better maintenance record. The principal advantages of the 747 as far as Congress is concerned are that the used 747s are immediately available at a fixed cost that is much lower than the estimated cost of the C-5B, which would not come on line for years.

Some 747 aircraft are presently in service with the USAF with the designation E-4A and E-4B. They serve as Airborne Command Post Aircraft, successors to the older EC-135s. Airborne command posts add the flexibility of movement and altitude to the functions performed by command posts situated on the ground. They serve as a communications hub from which a commander can communicate with superiors and subordinates and direct the forces under his control. The E-4 Airborne Command Post aircraft is a modified 747 equipped with extensive electronics which would be the critical communication link between national command authorities and the nation's strategic retaliatory forces during and following an attack upon the United States.

The E-4s would be used by the National Command Authorities and by the Commander-in-Chief of the Strategic Air Command to direct USAF strategic forces during a nuclear conflict. One E-4 is always kept on the alert at Andrews AFB near Washington DC for use by the President of the United States as his airborne command post in case of an attack. They can be used to order the

Specifications: T-43A
Boeing Model Number 737

Span	93 ft
Length	100 ft
Wing Area	980 sq ft
Tail Height	37 ft
Gross Weight	115,500 pounds
Cruising Speed	575 mph
Service Ceiling	35,000 ft
Range	2995 miles
Powerplant	two 14,500 pound thrust Pratt & Whitney JT8D-9 Turbofans
Capacity	twelve students (or four advanced students) and three instructors

Above: An **E-4A (Model 747)** is refueled by a **KC-135 (Model 717)**. The first E-4As were supplied to the USAF in 1974 to support the National Emergency Airborne Command Post (NEACP, known as 'kneecap') and serve as the presidential airborne command post. Eventually the E-4As will all be converted to E-4Bs and assume all of the airborne command-post functions of NEACP and SAC.

firing of intercontinental ballistic missiles if ground control centers become inoperative.

Boeing built and delivered to the US Air Force three 747-200s which were modified to an interim E-4A configuration by E-Systems, Inc, of Dallas, Texas. These interim systems utilize older command, control and communication equipment from EC-135s. Boeing has since developed an advanced version, the E-4B, which entered service in January 1980. The E-4B is able to operate in a nuclear environment where nuclear explosions usually disrupt currently used communications equipment.

Following competitive bidding Boeing Aerospace Company was awarded a contract in June 1980 to modify one of the existing E-4A systems to the improved E-4B configuration. A second E-4A/E-4B modification was added to the program in December 1980. Plans call for the Air Force to modify a third system and to acquire two additional 747-200 airplanes and equip them as E-4Bs to make up a fleet of six advanced command posts.

The E-4 will replace the EC-135, which is much smaller. The principal advantages of the E-4B over the EC-135 are improved communications capability, increased protection from nuclear bursts, greater endurance and more room to accommodate battle staff and new equipment. The E-4 is designed for missions as long as 72 hours while carrying nearly three times the payload of the EC-135.

The aircraft's main deck is divided into six functional areas: the command work area, conference room, briefing room, battle-

Specifications:
E-4A/B Airborne Command Post
Boeing Model Number 747

Span	195 ft 8 in
Length	231 ft 10 in
Wing Area	5500 sq ft
Tail Height	63 ft 5 in
Gross Weight	803,000 pounds
Cruising Speed	600 mph
Service Ceiling	45,000 ft
Unrefuelled Endurance	14 hours plus
Mission Endurance	72 hours plus
Powerplant	four 52,500 pound thrust General Electric CF6-50E Turbofans

Above: The **E-4B (Model 747)** differs from the E-4A in outward appearance by the addition of the radomes at the rear of the upper deck.

Below: One of 18 **E-3As** supplied to NATO is seen with an F-16 fighter, one of the planes that it would control in the event of a war in Europe. Originally given NATO markings, these E-3s will eventually wear the national markings of Luxembourg, which ironically has no other air force (OTAN is NATO in French).

STATES OF AMERICA

Below: USAF **E-3As** are prepped for delivery at the south end of Boeing Field. Visible top left is the **Red Barn**, Boeing's first headquarters building, now being restored as a museum (see p 17).

staff work area, communications control center and rest area. The flight deck houses the cockpit, navigation station and flight-crew rest area. Cargo areas beneath the main deck house communications and power supply equipment, spares and on-board maintenance facilities. Equipment on the E-4B includes thermal shielding, advanced command and control electronics, a 1200-KVA generator which is the largest power generation system ever flown, and both SHF (super high frequency) and VLF/LF (very low frequency/low frequency) communications systems. The VLF system requires trailing wire antennae up to five miles in length. In all, the E-4B carries 13 external communications systems employing 50 antennae. To cool this large array of equipment, it has an air conditioning system with an output up to 8000 cubic feet of air per minute.

The total program for equipping all six command post aircraft is expected to be completed in the mid-1980s. The E-4B program is under direction of the Electronic Systems Division of the US Air Force Systems Command. The E-4 Airborne Command Posts are based at Offutt Air Force Base, Nebraska, headquarters for the Strategic Air Command, which is the operating command.

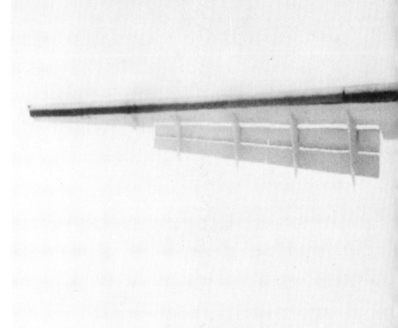

Right: Boeing's **YC-14** short-field transport takes off during tests at Edwards AFB, California. Using new technology such as Upper Surface Blowing, the YC-14 was one of two planes considered to replace the USAF C-130 Hercules transport.

Below: The second prototype **YC-14** in camouflage colors.

In November of 1972, Boeing and McDonnell Douglas were selected to build prototype aircraft as part of the US Air Force's Advanced Medium STOL (Short Take Off and Landing) Transport (AMST) program competition. The military requirement was for a transport that could operate from short semi-prepared fields, yet still have the cruising capability of a modern jet transport. Each company built a pair of aircraft. The McDonnell Douglas entry was powered by four 16,000-pound thrust UAC JT8D-17 turbofan engines and was designated YC-15A. Boeing's Model 953, designated YC-14A, was powered by a pair of 50,000-pound thrust GE CF6-50D turbofans, mounted above and forward of the high wing. The YC-14A was the first large aircraft to employ the concept of Upper Surface Blowing (USB). USB uses the thrust of the engines to blow high speed air over the wing and flaps, creating powered lift. The high positioning of the wing and engines also minimizes the possibility that the YC-14 would be damaged by debris and dirt on remote landing strips. The YC-14 is capable of lifting 27,000 pounds or 150 troops from 2000 foot runways and 69,000 pounds from normal runways. The aircraft also utilizes an advanced electronic flight control system and high flotation, lever type rough field landing gear.

The first YC-14 flew on 9 August 1976, with the second prototype following on 21 October. Funding for the AMST program was deleted from the 1979 budget, though there is a possibility that it will be revived. Boeing leased its two prototypes back from the Air Force for continued testing, but they were later mothballed by the Air Force at the Air Force Logistics Command Military Aircraft Storage and Disposition Center at Davis Monthan AFB near Tucson, Arizona. One of the mothballed YC-14s was later put on display at the Pima County Air Museum just outside the Davis Monthan complex.

While the YC-14 may never fly again, much of the technology that it helped pioneer almost certainly will. The small supercritical wing and the utilization of Upper Surface Blowing to create lift are innovations which will likely be seen in both military and commercial transport aircraft of the future. Because of the need of the Military Airlift Command to support both the Rapid Deployment Force as well as regular forces in remote areas, the need for STOL aircraft is great. The commercial advantages of a STOL type aircraft in hauling freight to and from remote or short runways have not been fully explored, but the prospects are promising.

Toward this end, Boeing has become involved in NASA's Quiet Short-haul Research Aircraft (QSRA) program. The testbed is a De Havilland C-8A Buffalo light military aircraft lent to NASA by the US Army and modified by Boeing to incorporate the technology of Upper Surface Blowing. NASA testing, taking place at the Ames Research Center near San Francisco, is aimed at studying Upper Surface Blowing, and at developing criteria for certification of future transports using the technology pioneered in the YC-14.

In 1981, Boeing received a contract to apply the supersonic transport (SST) technology that they were working on to a supersonic military fighter aircraft. Boeing had won the NASA contract in four-way competition with Grumman, Rockwell and McDonnell Douglas, the latter also winning a study contract. Concepts will be developed for a European theater tactical aircraft with a 500 mile combat radius and a Middle-East theater fighter with a 1500 mile radius.

Boeing's fighter will have vectorable nozzles on its underwing pod-mounted engines. The vectorable nozzles can be moved to change the direction of thrust, improving performance of the aircraft from short landing fields, in effect giving it STOL characteristics. The new fighter would also incorporate low aspect ratio wings blended into the fuselage, with variable-camber control surfaces and vortex lift. The latter involves controlling the flow of air over the wings with special leading-edge devices, to enhance high angle of attack performance. The plane would be equipped with variable cycle engines that would be efficient under a range of operating conditions. The recessed weapon carriage would be such that it would permit supersonic operation of the aircraft with weapons attached. Furthermore the weapons could be launched when the aircraft was travelling at supersonic speed.

Boeing has indicated that these studies will be used as a point of departure in the development of a 'larger, longer-range combat airplane' (a bomber). Technology that will probably appear in both aircraft includes weight saving nonmetallic composites and specially formed and bonded titanium structures, as well as active controls (automatically responding to changing loads) and digital avionics for improved control response.

Specifications: YC-14
Advanced Medium STOL Transport
Boeing Model Number 953

Span	129 ft
Length	132 ft
Wing Area	1762 sq ft
Tail Height	48 ft 4 in
Gross Weight	216,000 pounds
Gross Weight (STOL)	170,000 pounds
Top Speed	547 mph
Cruising Speed	460 mph
Ferry Range	2990 miles
STOL Range	460 miles
Service Ceiling	45,000 ft
Powerplant	two 50,000 pound thrust General Electric CF6-50 Turbofans

THE JET AGE

The first commercial jet airplane in the world was the British De Havilland DH-106 Comet. Powered by four De Havilland Ghost turbojets which were buried deep in the wings, this advanced concept of manned flight flew first in the summer of 1946. Tests were successful, and the British Overseas Airways Corporation, BOAC, placed an order for 16.

The Ghosts provided 4450 pounds of thrust each, giving unprecedented power and speed to the Comet, a swept-wing introduction to the Jet Age. Though passenger seating was limited to 36 at first, the Comet cruised at 490mph, beating its nearest competitor, the Boeing Stratocruiser, by 190mph. Its range was only 1750 miles, but this was a limitation that could be improved,

Above: A **707-120** in Trans World Airlines markings. TWA received its first 707 on 20 January 1959 and has ordered 15 707-120s and 123 707s of all types.

Right: The **367-80 Dash Eighty** after being redesignated 707 and re-engined, on its way to being turned over to the Smithsonian Institution.

as jet engine efficiency increased with more study. On 2 May 1952, the Comet I left London Airport, making a successful flight to Johannesburg, and the world took notice.

In August 1952 the Comet I started operations between London and Ceylon, cutting flying time by 12 hours. Several months later, Comets were reaching Singapore in 25 hours, against the two and a half days it took for piston-engined aircraft. Jet aviation was on the way to solid respectability, as other European airlines, notably Air France, put Comets to work.

Then tragedy struck. In January 1954 a Comet disintegrated over the Mediterranean, killing all passengers and crew. The Comets were grounded, and extensive examinations were conducted. No lethal weaknesses were discovered. In March the jets were returned to service, but fate was aiming another blow. Two weeks later, a second Comet broke up over the Mediterranean near Rome. The flying world that had been excited about the new airplane was stunned. Again, the Comets were grounded.

Diligent searching yielded pieces of the wreckage. It was discovered that metal fatigue (a previously unknown phenomenon) around the square-cut windows resulted in a weakening of the

jets, but they had been proven. They were safe, and as for capability, Douglas's DC-6 flew coast to coast easily, and both United and American Airlines liked them. In April 1951 the company introduced the DC-6B. It seated 102 passengers, cruised at 315mph, and was thought by many to be the finest piston-engined airplane ever built. In 1951 Lockheed also introduced its L-1049 Super Constellation. Powered by four 2700hp Cyclone engines and carrying 66 passengers, this graceful airplane went into service with Eastern Air Lines in December 1951, and performed well.

Boeing's own Stratocruiser (Model 377) had evolved into a sound and comfortable airliner, but by comparison to the likes of the DC-6 and the Constellation, it was a sales failure. Boeing realized that in order to compete in the fierce and expanding world market, they would have to build a better airplane and that airplane would have to be a turbojet with sufficient range to cross the North Atlantic. The crucial decision was taken at a board of directors meeting in April 1952.

The B-47 program was underway and the Boeing engineers went to work on a design for the jet transport which would ulti-

fuselage structure that could have caused the crash. It was also possible that the engines, deep in the wings, caused problems that led to the twin deaths of the world's first jet-propelled commercial aircraft. Although the Comets' problems were solved by improvements in design and maintenance, other manufacturers had a clear opportunity to catch the Comet's lead.

Wellwood Beall had seen the first Comet himself, and alerted Boeing executives. He felt that if Boeing were to survive in the commercial field, the company must think about jets. The company had the technology, based on B-47 experience, and Beall knew that a commercial jet could be built.

In spite of the excitement caused by the Comet's appearance, jets did not immediately catch on in the US. Pan American, American Airlines and other carriers knew that pistons worked. Maybe the internal combustion engine did not get the speed of

mately be designated 707. For reasons of corporate secrecy, as we noted in the last chapter, the project was disguised as a variant of the Model 367/C-97 military transport, the military equivalent of the Model 377 Stratocruiser. Because the program designation was Model 367-80, the new jet transport prototype acquired the nickname 'Dash Eighty.'

The fuselage was longer than that of the C-97 or the Stratocruiser with a more pointed nose, and did not show the 'double bubble' of the original 367. Early drawing-board versions of the 707, including Models 367-40 to 367-70, differed in the location of engines and landing gear. Aerodynamically, the Dash Eighty was closer to the B-47 than the piston driven C-97. One of the early studies considered placing four Pratt & Whitney JT3 engines in double nacelles like those on the B-47, one pod under each wing. In the final version, though, each of the four engines

Above and below: The **Dash Eighty** as originally configured.

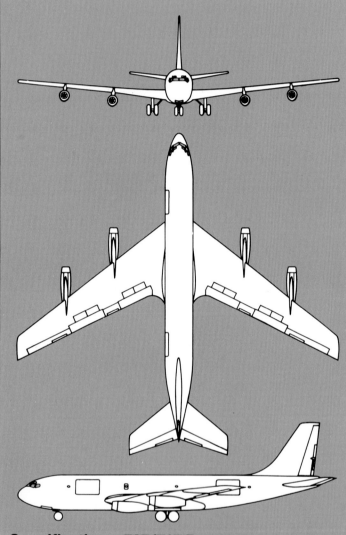

Specifications: 707/717 Prototype Boeing Model Number 367-80

Span	130 ft
Length	128 ft
Wing Area	2402 sq ft
Tail Height	38 ft 4 in
Gross Weight	160,000 pounds
Cruising Speed	600 mph
Service Ceiling	42,000 ft
Range	2000 miles
Powerplant	four 11,000 pound thrust Pratt & Whitney JT3P Turbojets

was housed in a single nacelle. Four such nacelles gave a structural advantage, through better weight distribution. An entirely new type of tricycle landing gear was adopted. The main wheels retracted inward from the center wing stub, nesting in recesses in the lower fuselage.

Boeing pumped its own money into the Dash Eighty prototype. Though Wellwood Beall and others tried to interest Pan American and United Air Lines in signing advance orders, they had no luck. Most airline executives, aware of the Comet's fate, were still wary. There were other doubts. For example, could airline pilots, schooled in piston-engined aircraft, make the transition to an airplane whose speed approached that of sound? And how about the 'little old lady in the street?' Could she adjust to that terrific increase in speed? And furthermore, an awful thought, because of the increased seating in these powerful airplanes, a crash would be catastrophic.

The work was kept secret, though William Allen admitted in a September 1952 magazine article that 'The company has for some time been engaged in a company-financed project which will enable us to demonstrate a prototype jet airplane of a new design for both armed services and commercial airlines in the summer of 1954.'

The American jet transport era began when the 367-80 first flew on 15 July 1954. With four P&W JT3 powerplants, the swept-wing prototype reached speeds of 600mph.

On 1 September 1954, the Air Force contracted with Boeing for 29 tanker versions of the Dash Eighty which were given the Boeing model number 717. Nevertheless, sales of the commercial transport version, the 707, were not immediately forthcoming and Boeing executives began to ponder the possibility that they might have a white elephant on their hands. They were also worried about Douglas's new DC-8, a jet powered transport, equipped like the 707, with P&W JT3s.

There now began what came to be known as the 'great Boeing-Douglas jet transport sales race.' Sales began to break for Boeing. Juan Trippe, president of Pan American World Airways, became interested in the 707. Always in the vanguard, he pursuaded Pan Am to invest $296,000,000 in the jet. The order was placed on 13 October 1955, and at $5,500,000 per plane, was the largest order for commercial aircraft ever placed, but Trippe had confidence in Boeing. 'People thought we were crazy,' he admitted later, but airline history was being made as the 707's success was to prove.

After Pan Am's purchase, United Air Lines announced it would buy 30 DC-8s, and Bill Allen told his staff to work harder. They did, and on 8 November 1955, American Airlines bought 30 707s.

Specifications: Boeing Model 707-120

Span	130 ft 10 in
Length	145 ft 1 in
Wing Area	2433 sq ft
Tail Height	41 ft 8 in
Gross Weight	248,000 pounds
Cruising Speed	600 mph
Service Ceiling	41,000 ft
Range	3000 miles
Powerplant	four 13,500 pound thrust Pratt & Whitney JT3C-6 Turbojets
Capacity	181 passengers

At the same time Pan Am purchased the 707s, however, the company also placed an order with Douglas for 25 DC-8s. Boeing went into production at once, and delivered the first 707-120, the production model, to Pan Am on 15 August 1958, three months ahead of schedule.

In the following months, Continental, Braniff and Sabena of Belgium ordered more 707s. Trans World Airways, Air France and Quantas also invested in the sleek turbojet. The 707's performance was impressive and helped sales. It could cross the Atlantic in six and a half hours, and could carry as many passengers as the *Queen Mary* could in the same amount of time. Even so, Eastern Airlines, KLM of Holland and Scandinavian Airways System (SAS) committed themselves to DC-8s.

The 707's advantage over the DC-8, however, was timing. It appeared nearly a year before the DC-8. This by no means undercuts the importance of the DC-8. Together, the two airplanes pointed the way to a new era in air travel. After the appearance of the DC-8 and the 707, the world of flying was forever transformed.

Airline people learned through the American transports that customers everywhere enjoyed the luxury of the skyliners. The 707's interior had been developed by Walter Dorwin Teague Associates, and was called a 'penthouse in the sky' by news people. 'It's like flying ten miles a minute in my easy chair,' said a passenger. The 707 had the longest, widest cabin ever seen on a commercial transport, measuring 12 feet 4 inches wide, and 100 feet in length. More than 100 windows studded the fuselage, allowing even aisle passengers 'windows of their own.' The many windows lent the interior a sense of spaciousness, and a feeling of freedom. Sliding shades effectively cut out light for those wishing to nap, and in some of the 707s there were as many as three lounges where restless passengers could snack, have a drink, or simply strike up a conversation. Galleys located in both forward and aft positions contributed to passenger wellbeing, for electric ovens and refrigerators made it possible to serve meals of a wide variety.

The 707 catered to owners, as well as passengers. The airplane's seating configuration could be all first class, all tourist or any combination desired. This was a point looked upon favorably by operators whose business took them to many places in the world with varied and unpredictable requirements.

Flying high and fast, the 707 soared above the weather. Even in rare disturbances, which could not be avoided, the 707's swept-back wings provided an easy, springy ride, with none of the jolts and bumps encountered in earlier aircraft.

The air conditioning was the finest and most complete ever provided in an airplane. Outside air was drawn in and auto-matically heated or cooled as needed. It was filtered, humidity-controlled, and even deodorized for passenger comfort. At 40,000 feet cruising altitude, cabin equivalent altitude was 7000 feet. Sea-level cabin pressure was maintained to an actual altitude of 22,500 feet.

Airline operators were learning, to their relief, that pilots trained in the piston-engine era could be switched to jets with additional training. Boeing and other manufacturers were equipped to provide that training. Thus skilful pilots continued their careers into the jet age, and everybody, operators and passengers alike, was better off.

Pan American began the new era with its first transatlantic 707 flight on 26 October 1958. In six weeks company 707-120s carried 12,168 passengers across the sea. At first only two 707s

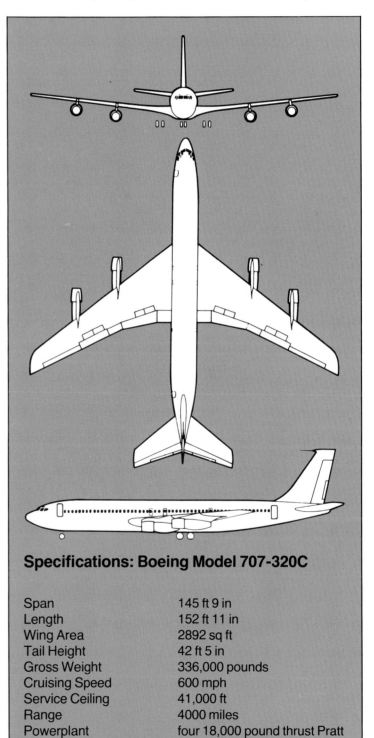

Specifications: Boeing Model 720 (707-220)

Span	130 ft 10 in
Length	136 ft 9 in
Wing Area	2433 sq ft
Tail Height	41 ft 8 in
Gross Weight	230,000 pounds
Cruising Speed	600 mph
Service Ceiling	41,000 ft
Range	3000 miles
Powerplant	four 12,500 pound thrust Pratt & Whitney JT3C-7 Turbojets
Capacity	167 passengers

Specifications: Boeing Model 707-320C

Span	145 ft 9 in
Length	152 ft 11 in
Wing Area	2892 sq ft
Tail Height	42 ft 5 in
Gross Weight	336,000 pounds
Cruising Speed	600 mph
Service Ceiling	41,000 ft
Range	4000 miles
Powerplant	four 18,000 pound thrust Pratt & Whitney JT3D Turbofans
Capacity	219 passengers or 96,800 pounds of cargo

Left: **707s** under construction on the floor of Plant 2. Note the B-52 and the *Dash Eighty* being re-engined in the far background.

Right: Kayo II, the **720-023** used by the Los Angeles Dodgers baseball club to transport the team to away-from-home games.

Below: An American Trans Air **720** preparing for takeoff.

Bottom left: The cargo door of the **707-320C** Convertible measures 7½ feet by 11 feet, is designed to accept up to 5693 cubic feet of containerized cargo or shipping pallets.

Bottom right: The Boeing **Model 707-320** Intercontinental made its maiden flight on 11 January 1959.

Above: A Pan Am **707-321B**. Pan Am was the 707's 'launch customer,' the customer that made the 707 program possible. Pan Am has ordered 128 707s since 1955.

Specifications: Boeing Model 707-320

Span	142 ft 5 in
Length	152 ft 11 in
Wing Area	2892 sq ft
Tail Height	41 ft 8 in
Gross Weight	316,000 pounds
Cruising Speed	600 mph
Service Ceiling	41,000 ft
Range	4200 miles
Powerplant	four 15,800 pound thrust Pratt & Whitney JT4A Turbojets
Capacity	189 passengers

were available, but daily service across the Atlantic was maintained. The tremendous capacity for work demonstrated by the 707s began to show. The two airplanes replaced six piston-engined aircraft that had previously carried passengers to Paris.

On 10 December 1958 Pan Am began jet service between New York and Miami, under lease to National Airlines. The cash registers rang like fire alarms, one report happily put it. Thousands purchased tickets for Florida, or to warm, overseas destinations, leaving winter behind.

The number of jet routes increased, as more airlines bought this stunning transport. American Airlines put 707-120s into transcontinental service on 25 January 1959. It was the first cross-country jet travel in the US. Continental Airlines and Western Airlines were also quick to put the 707 into action.

Transatlantic records were still being set. Flight engineers aboard 707s watched for shifts in the jet-stream, that eastward blowing, high velocity, high altitude wind. Flying toward Europe, the 707s capitalized on the added push of the jet-stream between the 29,000 and 37,000 foot altitudes. On 12 December 1959, a 707 averaged 626mph on a New York–London flight, crossing the mighty Atlantic in 5 hours and 41 minutes. Homeward bound 707s ducked under the full force of the jet stream. Though sometimes bucked by strong headwinds, the big airplane bored ahead, still remaining above the worst of lower-level storms.

The first 707s on Pan Am's transatlantic flights were fitted with 109 passenger seats, 44 first class forward, and 65 economy seats aft. Economy became a popular feature of jet travel. People could enjoy the thrill of a new adventure and visit exotic destinations at an affordable price. Passenger service soared. By 12 October 1959 1,000,000 passengers had been carried by Boeing's entry into the Jet Age.

An important factor in making profits for airline operators was cargo. A study conducted by Stanley E Brewer, Professor of Transportation at the University of Washington, was revealing. The study, sponsored by Boeing, noted that air cargo had 'a greater potential in the international market than in the domestic, because of the longer distances to cover, and the slower speed of competing forms of transportation in the international market.'

Professor Brewer's findings were on the mark. During the first 15 days of December 1958, 707s carried 117,291 pounds of mail and cargo to Paris. This averaged 7819 pounds per flight, a figure comparable to the combined capabilities of both a Stratocruiser and a DC-7. During this same period, 707s carried 85,928 pounds of cargo and mail to London, averaging 7161 pounds per flight.

Airline officials were delighted, as profits climbed. Investment in the 707s had been deep, at $5,500,000 per airplane, and corporate wisdom was at stake. Things were turning out well. Flight crews were also pleased with these maintenance-free wonders. The 707s, as a group, clocked 987 hours of scheduled service, and

280 hours of training flights during one six week period without a hitch.

However, the 707 did have problems, some of them serious. In spite of elaborate testing with passenger safety the primary goal, a Pan Am 707-120 suddenly went crazy during a trans-atlantic flight in early February 1959. Captain W Waldo Lynch, the pilot, was conversing with passengers in the cabin when the ship whipped into a downward spiral. Lynch sprawled on the deck, but managed to crawl to the cockpit. Captain S T Peters, the co-pilot, was wrestling with the wheel, which was locked in a hard right position. Between the two men, the 707 was leveled off, but not before it fell from 29,000 feet to 6000. Disaster had been averted, and the ailing 707 made a safe landing at Gander, Newfoundland. Examination showed that the autopilot had been at fault.

On 1 March 1962 an American Airlines 707-120B crashed at the New York Idlewilde International Airport. All 87 passengers and 8 crew members were killed. The CAB reported that the yaw, sideslip and roll, observed by witnesses just before the crash, probably resulted because of a malfunction of yaw damper. This was created by an exposed wire short-circuiting in the servo unit. Investigation revealed that a workman had used tweezers for positioning the eight-wire bundle within the unit. The wires were damaged by pinching, and, in time, two of them separated, resulting in tragedy.

In neither the headlong plunge of the -120, nor the fatal crash of the -120B had there been any structural failure in the air-planes. The fault lay in equipment manufactured by outside contractors.

In 1960 the Boeing jets were given a dramatic opportunity to show the world what they could do. Africa's Congo was in bloody rebellion, and thousands fled their homes. Between 9 and 28 July, Sabena Belgian World Airlines flew over 15,000 men, women and children to safety. Using its five 707 Interconti-nentals, the airline mounted a ceaseless ferrying operation be-tween the main airports of the Congo and Brussels. On one trip,

303 passengers were carried nonstop from Leopoldville, a 4000 mile flight. The airplane was in the air for more than seven hours. Altogether, the Sabena 707s made 62 round trips, carrying more than 250 passengers on each flight.

Boeing was doing well with its 707, selling to both civilian and military markets, but company executives did not linger over the triumph. The 707 was a great airplane, and everybody knew it, but it was only the beginning. The next design to come off the boards was a short-to-medium range airplane with the model number 720. It was not so heavy as the 707, having been built specifically for the less lengthy air routes of the world. A shorter body, new full-span leading-edge flaps, lighter structure, a new inboard wing profile and less fuel capacity were the principal changes over the 707. Maximum speed was raised to Mach 0.9, nine-tenths the speed of sound, but cruising speed was kept at 600mph. Field length requirements were also shortened, a boon for out-of-the-way areas where field conditions were not practical for big jets.

United Air Lines became the first customer for this new mem-ber of Boeing's jet family when the company signed a contract in November 1957. The first 720s went into service on 5 July 1960 over the Chicago–New York/Washington routes.

The most significant change in the basic 707 design arrived with the very long range 707-320 Intercontinental. It was equipped with four JT4A turbojets. The 707-420 Intercontinental, twin to the -320, except for power, was fitted with Rolls-Royce Conway Mk 508 Turbofan engines, which developed 17,500 pounds of thrust.

The -320 and -420 were also eight feet five inches longer than the -120, and had 11 feet seven inches more wingspan. Beginning in August 1959, the Intercontinentals went into service over the longest air routes in the world. The fuel capacity of 23,815 gallons gave these airplanes a range of nearly 5000 miles, with a full passenger payload – 189 for each.

An improved Intercontinental, the 707-320B, was ordered by Pan American, along with Air France and TWA. The -320Bs were to become, by a large margin, the longest range jets in com-mercial service. The main change over the -320 was in the engines and high-lift flaps. Four 18,000-pound thrust P&W JT3D turbo-fans extended the range of the -320B to 6000 miles with a maxi-mum load. As in the original 320, 189 passengers could be carried.

Because cargo had become so important, the 707-320C con-vertible cargo/passenger airplane was the next development in the 707 series. The -320C retained all the major systems and compo-nents of the -320B Intercontinental, but included a strengthened structure to allow for heavier loading. A large 7 feet by 11 feet cargo door made it easier to handle pallets as well. Although conversion of a 'C-Jet' was (and is) possible in a few hours, most airlines preferred to use the plane in a single service, converting to passenger or cargo configuration only if unusual demand called for it. Where cargo and passengers share importance, the -320C accommodates cargo pallets in the forward main deck, and passenger seating in the aft cabin. Some versions of the -320C were ordered strictly as freighters, with plugged windows and no conversion features. A complete cycle of loading and unloading a 90,000 pound palletized payload can be accomplished in less than one hour.

An additional innovation aboard the -320C Intercontinental is its ability to carry its own cargo handling equipment. It is stored in a lower deck compartment, and offers independence from outside cargo handling facilities. There are three cargo compartments: a full upper main deck, with 8000 cubic feet of space, and two lower decks totaling 1712 cubic feet.

While the 707 was making its mark as a long range carrier, Boeing had, by the late 1950s, discovered that there was a substantial market for a medium range jetliner that would be as economical on the short to medium distance routes as the 707 was on transcontinental and transoceanic routes.

When Jack Steiner was appointed project engineer for what was to become the 727 in 1958, the choice had not been haphazard. There were other competent people on Boeing's engineering staff, but Steiner's ability had been proven by front-line experience. He had contributed to the Model 314 Flying Boats, the KC-135 tankers, and the latest success, the 707.

Steiner's first problem was deciding how many engines to use. Would there be two, three or four, and should they be jets or turboprops? France's slick Caravelle was proving that twin jets, rear-mounted on the fuselage, were practical, but on the

other hand, the Vickers Viscount V-700, powered by four Rolls-Royce turboprop engines, was a successful airplane, too.

Competition was on the rise in the short-to-medium range market. Boeing had not been the only airframe builder to anticipate the need. Lockheed's solution was its Electra, powered by four Allison 501 turboprops. Douglas, Boeing's competent long-time adversary in the marketplace, was planning its DC-9.

At the start, Boeing thought a scaled down 707 with four engines would be best, but Steiner opted for an airplane with either two or three engines. There was a reason for this. After consulting with a number of airline people, he noted that inexpensive operation was the factor of prime interest. Low operating costs were the common denominator. Yet, United Air Lines wanted an airplane with four engines to provide what was considered an adequate margin of safety. If one engine malfunctioned, there were to be three left. Counter to this, American Airlines

Below: An Eastern Airlines **727-200**. Eastern was one of the first customers for the 727 and has ordered 88 727s of all types.

Bottom left: An Alaska Airlines **727-100**.

Bottom right: A **727-200**. The -200 is 20 feet longer than the 727-100.

believed two engines were enough. In the middle stood Eastern Airlines, with a very clear preference for a trijet pushing a Caravelle type fuselage.

The solution to the dilemma lay in developing a trijet. Steiner's reasoning was this: United would go for three engines if they were powerful enough, so two would provide the margin of safety expected – it would also mean considerable savings for the company by eliminating a fourth engine. American Airlines would probably go for three engines if operating costs were reasonable and Eastern, of course, had already called for three. Steiner's problem was to prove that a trijet could be inexpensive to operate. As he saw it, Boeing had to come up with an airplane that would:

1. Reduce operating costs, but retain efficiency.
2. Increase speed spread, particularly on the low speed end, to make the airplane suitable for fast service into smaller airfields.
3. Obtain a significant increase in the fatigue life of the airplane structure.
4. Gain equipment reliability compatible with short-to-medium ranges.
5. Operate with lower weather minimums.

It was a perplexing situation, one which called for more study. Developing a trijet was going to cost money, too, perhaps too much. However, Boeing was not a newcomer to spending its own money. The famed Dash Eighty, prototype for both the 707 and KC-135 (717), had been designed and built with in-house funds. To look more deeply into 727 problems, Bruce Connelly, head of the Transport Division, authorized a committee to make a study. Steiner headed the committee.

What he learned was not encouraging. Customers would have to pay up to three and one half million dollars for even a twin engine airplane. The turboprop Viscounts were selling for a little over one and one quarter million; turboprop Electras were priced at 2.1 million, and even the Boeing 720, twice the size of the projected 727, was going for three and a half.

By the spring of 1959, the idea of building a trijet was fading. Engineering opinion remained split over two or four engines. Three engines were barely in the running, though Steiner still thought they were feasible. Fortunately, he had the backing of Ed Wells, vice president of engineering. Wells believed that the 727, as envisioned by Steiner, was a sound bet. Maynard Pennell, chief engineer, also saw possibilities.

Specifications: Boeing Model 727-100

Span	108 ft
Length	133 ft 2 in
Wing Area	1650 sq ft
Tail Height	34 ft
Gross Weight	170,000 pounds
Cruising Speed	600 mph
Service Ceiling	42,000 ft
Range	2500 miles
Powerplant	three 14,000 pound thrust Pratt & Whitney JT8D-7 or 14,500 pound thrust D-9 Turbofans
Capacity	131 passengers, or 46,000 pounds cargo (727-100C/QC)

In July 1959 Steiner presented his designs to Boeing's chief executives. President William Allen was interested, but the price for a prototype with two or four engines was 130 million. The company was not yet breaking even on its 707 investment and that did not help arouse enthusiasm for a new, costly project. Taking everything into consideration, company purse strings were drawn tight.

Jack Steiner was stubborn, though, and he refused to let his 727 die. He went to England in order to look over the Rolls-Royce engines being built for the Trident. The same engine, he learned, could be used on the Boeing trijet, too. Rolls-Royce would be happy to provide them when he was ready, and Steiner returned to America.

There was bad news waiting. Boeing was in financial trouble. The 707 was yet to keep its promise, and losses were very heavy. Further, since Douglas and Convair were both building short-to-medium jets, the market place would be crowded, and Boeing was reluctant to compete. The DC-9 was the largest threat, with Boeing projections forecasting it would cut into 720 sales, and casting more doubt on the feasibility of the expensive 727. President Allen pointed out that operators were apparently happy with Lockheed's turboprop, the Electra. Would they want another jet?

In spite of financial problems and stiff competition, there was enough interest in the 727 to allow design work to go ahead. Over 150 designs were drawn for wing placement and fuselage configuration. Thousands of hours of wind tunnel tests were made on a variety of models. The venerable Dash Eighty (for it was venerable by now), was put to work testing flaps and engines. The 727 had to be designed so it could land on La Guardia Field's 4860 foot runway, an Eastern Airlines requirement. For a fast-flying jet transport, such a short landing space was considered impossible, but out of that requirement came the triple-slotted trailing edge flaps, along with the leading edge flaps and slats. These innovations created an 'umbrella,' with 25 percent more wing, enabling the 727 to land at very low speeds. In the air, the flaps and slats were retracted, streamlining the wing for the sake of speed. Because of this startling use of flaps on both leading and trailing edges, the 727 was to become known as the 'airplane whose wing comes apart.'

A unique T-shaped tail sprouted from the rear of the fuselage. To quote Steiner in regard to this: 'To achieve the difficult economic capabilities of the turboprop Electra, the 727 had to climb fast, fly fast, and descend fast. One of the advantages of the "T" tail was that it permitted deployment of wing spoilers without airplane vibration, leading to a very high useable rate of descent.'

As the aerodynamic problems of wing, tail and body were being solved, engines were still in question. Steiner had convinced the company that three engines were adequate, but now the problem was how to place them. Should there be two engines in the wing, and one aft? Or should there be three engines aft?

Steiner was for the three aft-mounted engines. He had found a way to cluster them that would actually cut down on drag. His team also showed that it would be cheaper to place them in a tight group. The engine systems would be better co-ordinated than if two were in the wing, and another far to the rear. A side benefit of rear engines would be that landing and taking off would seem quieter in the front cabin, though, once in flight, that slight edge would be lost.

The final decision on engine placement showed two aft-mounted engines, each in an individual pod, one on either side of the fuselage. The third, enclosed in a cowling, was suspended from a beam at the rear of the fuselage. An air duct led to it from the base of the vertical fin. Thrust ripped out of a nozzle in the end of the tail.

So there it was: the drawing board prototype of the 727 showed an airplane with less wing than the 707, and less sweep. It would be powered by Pratt & Whitney JT8 turbofan engines, instead of Rolls-Royce. The substitution was made at the request of Eastern Airlines, and Boeing did not quibble. Customers got what they wanted. As it happened, the JT8s were quickly designed and installed without the usual thorough testing both Pratt & Whitney and Boeing demanded. Consequently, the prototype 727 had engine problems, but they were solved during the testing period.

The 727's internal design was made with passenger comfort in mind. Six abreast seating was so arranged that there was no feeling of being crowded. Lighting and interior decor lent an air of spaciousness to the main cabin.

It was now time to meet once again with the Board of Directors. The 727's design was in hand. It was February 1960 and Steiner had been on the project for nearly two years. He had done his best. The next hour or so would tell the story.

The meeting was not an easy one. President Allen was concerned about labor costs. In France, where the Caravelle was built, labor costs were 40 percent lower than those in the United States. In Britain, home of the Trident, labor was 50 percent lower. These were significant differences. Tooling costs for the 727 would also be high, hitting the $100 million level.

The fact that the airline industry was suffering a slump was not lost on the Board either. TWA was in financial trouble, and would not be purchasing new airplanes – as far as it knew. American Airlines was holding to the Lockheed Electra. United Air Lines wished for something the company called 'Airplane X,' and nobody knew for sure if the 727 was that airplane, though discussions with United had taken place. Eastern had not made any commitments yet.

Allen, however, wanted the company to start making money. He knew that a lot of effort by a lot of good men had gone into the 727's design. It was a good airplane, a 'pilot's airplane.' So he compromised. Before any money would be appropriated for a prototype, there would have to be a guarantee of one *billion* dollars in orders! Could the 727, still on the drawing boards, sell that much? It was a mighty question, a billion dollar question. Allen set a deadline of 7 December. If the billion dollars in sales was not there, the 727 program would be shelved.

Though not all that could be hoped for, the proposition was better than nothing. The public relations and sales forces went to work – and gave a good account of themselves. By 30 November, the day before Allen's deadline, contracts had been signed for 80 Model 727s. Eastern Airlines had overcome its reserve and ordered 40. They were the first customers. Next, United Air Lines signed for 40 more, with 20 of them on option. They were apparently convinced that the 727 would meet 'Airplane X' requirements. The two contracts totaled $420 million, and though the figure was not the billion Allen had wanted, it was heartening. On the basis of two large companies buying, it was reasonable to expect that more sales would follow. The 727 program went into high gear.

Roll-out took place in Renton, on 27 November 1962, and presented the world with a breathtaking sight. The 727's high T tail was clearly unconventional with its horizontal stabilizer and elevators on top and the third engine air scoop at the base of the vertical stabilizer. Witnesses were impressed, and noted the old saying about airplanes that if they looked good they were good. The 727 looked good.

Costs for the prototype were a walloping $150 million, 20 million more than originally estimated. One of the reasons for the escalation was the intensive testing. Ed Wells and George Schairer, with typical Boeing thoroughness, had ordered an airframe solely for the purpose of loading to destruction to test the structure. A second airframe was employed in metal fatigue tests, and a third was especially equipped to measure and confirm flight loadings under every condition.

Bill Allen had not flinched because of rising costs. In a speech made in March 1964 he said, 'A substantial portion of the increased costs of the 727 were deliberate. The development programs were enlarged with greater testing – static, fatigue, flight. On the long pull, I think that was good.'

Evidently, TWA thought so too, because the company managed to scrape up $700 million despite financial difficulties. The money went for 727s even *before* the airplane's November 1962 roll-out.

The Boeing 727 took off for the first time from Renton's 5000 foot runway on 9 February 1963. It was 11.33 a.m. The prototype's test pilot was S L 'Lew' Wallick, co-pilot R L 'Dix' Loesch, and M K Shulenberger sat at the flight engineer's panel. They were all old Boeing hands. As the brand new airplane lifted, she shot up so suddenly that, as one observer put it, 'I thought somebody up there had yanked her into the sky.'

The yellow-backed airplane cruised smoothly out of sight, her silver underbelly gleaming, contrails of jet exhaust streaming behind. Two hours later, Wallick set her down at Paine Field near Everett, Washington, where Boeing had leased a flight testing facility. The sleek prototype used very little runway, an important plus. She had been designed to land and take off on short runways. Subsequent tests showed that she could brake to a stop in as little as 700 feet.

Lew Wallick's remarks as he left the cockpit were music to Boeing executive ears. 'The control systems are better than expected,' he said. 'I think they are well advanced over previous airplanes. It feels good.' Then he made a prediction. 'I think airline pilots are really going to like this one.' He was proved correct.

Dix Loesch was also enthusiastic. 'The entire period of flying was very smooth,' he told reporters.

William Allen, president of Boeing, was also at the Paine Field landing. He had bet millions of company dollars on the success of Boeing's new short-to-medium range transport, and he was happy. 'I confidently assume that our people have developed another great aircraft,' he said in a short speech. 'It should prove to be a major source of business for a number of years ahead.'

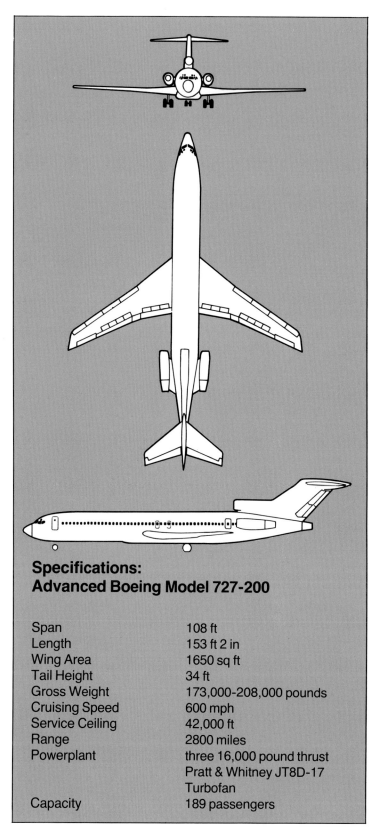

Specifications:
Advanced Boeing Model 727-200

Span	108 ft
Length	153 ft 2 in
Wing Area	1650 sq ft
Tail Height	34 ft
Gross Weight	173,000-208,000 pounds
Cruising Speed	600 mph
Service Ceiling	42,000 ft
Range	2800 miles
Powerplant	three 16,000 pound thrust Pratt & Whitney JT8D-17 Turbofan
Capacity	189 passengers

He, too, was correct. As of 1982, some 1831 727s had been sold. This was more than any other single commercial jet transport.

'I have had a few dreams in my life,' Allen said once, 'one of them was to have a large airline customer call me up, and instead of giving me hell, tell me he was really delighted with an outstanding airplane. That has happened with the 727.'

On 3 November, nearly a year after roll-out, the 727 started on a tour of the world. President Allen was aboard, along with other top executives. He wanted to fly in the airplane that had cost so much and meant so much financially to the company. Though he left the ship in Japan, the 727 continued its world flight, touching 44 cities in 26 countries. It landed at airfields not equipped for

Above: A Delta Air Lines **727-200** in flight. Atlanta-based Delta Air Lines, one of the largest and most successful domestic carriers in the United States, owns 116 727s.

Below: Trans Australia Airlines was instrumental in showing the Boeing Company the potential for the **727-200**. Shown here is the first of TAA's dozen 727-200s to be painted in the new TAA livery at the company's Tullamarine facility.

jets, and made stops within 1500 feet of touchdown, proving that its triple-slotted wings could do the job they were meant to do. The airplane was so well built that mechanics and technicians brought along for trouble-shooting had little to do but enjoy the trip – all 76,000 miles of it.

Orders rushed to the home office from all over the globe. Australia's Ansett ANA and Trans Australia became customers, seeing in the 727 an excellent medium for bush as well as inter-city flights. Japan's All-Nippon Airways dropped their Trident orders for the 727, and Japan Air Lines also signed purchase contracts. Back home in the United States, Northwest Orient Airlines and National Airlines placed orders. Allen's one billion dollar figure had been well met.

After the world tour, another 727 made a spectacular entry into the Latin American market. High altitude landing for jets was not considered feasible until the 727 landed at La Paz, Bolivia, whose airport was 13,358 feet above sea level. It was the first jet to do so.

Production was in full swing even before the world tour took place, and Boeing made deliveries without delay. United received five on 29 December 1963, Eastern received two and American Airlines one. Crew training began at once.

Eastern was first to operate a 727. On 1 February 1964, the company established services connecting Miami, Washington, and Philadelphia. United followed on 6 February on its San Francisco–Denver route. American was next, establishing the 727 on its New York–Chicago run, and TWA was fourth, starting operations with the new Boeing jet on 1 June 1964. Four major airlines had commenced 727 service within a span of four months.

More orders arrived. Lufthansa, the German airline, bought 12. The company initiated service on the Hamburg–Dusseldorf–London route on 16 April 1964. Called *Europa Jets,* these were the first 727s exported to Europe.

As sales mounted and more pilots flew the 727s, reports came back to Boeing. It was, indeed, a 'pilot's airplane,' as Lew Wallick, the test pilot, had predicted.

Among its many attributes, the 727 was the first Boeing commercial airplane to be equipped with an auxiliary power unit, APU. It is a small gas turbine capable of supplying electrical and pneumatic power, as well as air-conditioning, when the main engines are shut off. The APU, along with integral aft boarding stairs, makes the airplane essentially independent of ground power facilities. This was important to airlines operating in areas where airport services were not adequate.

The success of the convertible cargo/passenger airplane in the 707 series made itself felt in the developing 727. The basic 727, the -100 series, had maximum seating for 131, but in July 1964 the 727-100C appeared. The floor and the undercarriage had been strengthened to take additional weight. The -100C was similar to the 707-320C, and was convertible to either passenger or cargo service within a few hours.

The next modification was an outgrowth of an idea advanced by United Air Lines. It was called the 'Quick Change,' or, simply, QC. Unlike the 727C, the QC's conversion could be accomplished in a short time by using palletized seats and galleys, with a full set of pallet rollers in the floor. At the end of a passenger flight, the seats and galleys can be detached from locks, and rolled out through the cargo door into a waiting storage van. Cargo pallets can then be rolled directly into the airplane and locked into place. The entire procedure takes less than an hour. Thus passengers can be carried by day, cargo by night.

With an eye on military sales, Boeing offered the US Air Force a -100C in 1965. Designated 727M, it was so designed that it could be employed as a general transport, a paratroop carrier, an ambulance or a tanker. Though versatile, it did not attract orders. However, the 727 did find its way into military service. In 1976, the Belgian Air Force acquired Sabena's series of -100s, and converted them for military use.

By late 1964 it became apparent that certain air routes had need of a higher capacity, medium range jet transport. An obvious answer was a larger 727. It would be basically the same trijet, but with a longer body to accommodate more passengers. The 727-200 was born, a -100 with an additional 20 foot extension to the cabin. The result was a passenger capacity of 189 people and range up to 1500 miles. Northeast Airlines put the new -200 to work quickly. On 14 December 1965 the company introduced the airplane on its New York–Miami route. Air France was the first foreign buyer, putting the 727-200 into service on 15 April 1968.

The success of the 727 escalated, as more attracted the attention of domestic and world airlines. On 29 November 1973, the 1000th 727 rolled out the Renton factory doors, making this the first time any commercial airliner had reached such a production figure. Number 1000 was delivered to Delta Air Lines on 4 January 1974.

Certain specifications from Trans Australia Airlines and Ansett ANA (Australian National Airlines) led to the Advanced 727-200, though Boeing had already seen the need prior to

Above: A detail of the interior of a **727's three-man cockpit**, with its three throttles and one of each gauge for each of three engines.

receiving the requests. The Advanced 727 featured more powerful engines and structural changes, which included thicker wing skins, stronger main landing gear and heavier nose gear. Up to 2400 more gallons of fuel could be carried in extra tanks, increasing the range by more than 1000 miles.

As part of a continuing effort to reduce noise levels in all its aircraft, Boeing fitted the Advanced 727 with 'Quiet Nacelles,' making it one of the quietest jets in the air. The body was the same width as that of a 707, 12 feet 4 inches, allowing six-abreast seating. Thus, the Advanced 727-200 can haul more people over heavily traveled air routes than other aircraft with narrow fuselages. This meant increased earnings for airline executives, whose job it was to make a profit.

According to Jack Steiner, in an article appearing in *Jet Age*, the 727 had led two lives. The first began in 1963, on initial delivery. The second began in the 1970s with the Advanced model. No other jetliner had, up to then, such a capability for

changing configuration. This ability extended the 727's life, and forecasts predict sales of 1831. Once again, Boeing proved itself in the market place. What the customer wanted, the customer got. Bill Allen's billion dollar gamble was a gamble no more.

In addition to having been America's first certified commercial trijet, the 727 was the first airliner to have the now-common triple-slotted flap system for superior takeoff and landing performance. The 727 was also the first Boeing jetliner with completely powered flight controls. All flight controls are hydraulically powered with dual units, except for the horizontal stabilizer, which is trimmed electrically. It was the first commercial airplane to win a medal of honor. In late 1972 a Royal Air Maroc Airlines 727, with King Hassan aboard, was strafed by three jet fighters manned by dissident Moroccan Air Force officers. The 727 pilot radioed the attackers saying that the king had been killed in the first attacks, and the firing ceased. The king in fact was unharmed. The 727 was later decorated with the Head of the Order of the Throne, for taking severe punishment and yet landing safely. Boeing sent technicians to repair the damage caused by bullets, and the 727 continued in service.

The 727 was the first jetliner to use an engine specifically designed for it, the P&W JT8D turbofan. It was the first to use the 'jet mixing' principle for quieter operation. Because the engine had the lowest jet exit velocity of any engine when it was introduced, it also created the lowest noise level from the tailpipe. As part of now standard testing procedures the 727 was the first airplane to be subjected to Boeing's brutal fatigue testing and static airframe testing prior to flight. The $30 million test program was designed to ensure that no redesign of production models would be necessary. During fatigue testing, for instance, the airframe demonstrated a useful life of more than 20 years of normal service.

Yet another service provided by Boeing for all its airplanes is the in-field repair unit. When a 727 plowed into a moose on the Cordova, Alaska runway, there was extensive damage to the nose wheel and the undersides of the airplane. It was then that the 'diplomats with tool boxes,' as they are called, came into action.

A team of experts arrived in hours from Seattle to assess the damage. They got an idea of what was needed, then returned to Seattle, 1300 miles away. Five days later a crew of company specialists arrived in Cordova, made the repairs, then flew the 727 to Seattle for final testing. The airplane was returned to service a few days after that.

Anytime, anywhere, a Boeing customer asks for help, he gets it. Boeing repair crews have served from London to Bombay, from Tokyo to Beirut, and from Honolulu to Karachi.

This special service unit keeps detailed records of all its repair jobs, and compiles thick technical documents. It also shares what it learns. When a non-Boeing airplane overshot a San Francisco runway and was dunked in the bay, technicians were able to shorten repair time by borrowing Boeing records of a similar accident. Boeing does not play the role of a dog-in-the-manger. Though fiercely competitive in the marketplace, the company provides a helping hand where needed.

Above: An American Airlines **727-35** of the 727-100 series. American has a fleet of over 150 727s which it operates on nearly all of its short feeder routes.

Upper right: A United Air Lines **727-222A** of the 727-200 series in flight over snow-capped mountains. United was the launch customer for the 727 and now operates well over 200 of the durable trijets.

Right and far right: The **727 assembly line at Renton**, with 737s in the background. A total of 1832 727s will have been built when the assembly line closes in late 1984. The 727 could not continue in production with a three-man crew and older, less fuel-efficient engines in an era of high-bypass ratio turbofans. They are gradually being replaced on this line by 757s.

The Model 737, smallest of the Boeing jets, was conceived in 1964. Company executives had been concerned about the Douglas DC-9, and the British Aircraft Corporation's BAC-111 cutting into the short-range market. It was thought that another airplane should be developed to meet this double threat. The 727, Boeing's hope for the short-to-medium range market, was in danger of losing sales to the DC-9, which had entered service with Delta Air Lines in December 1965. Boeing wasn't a company that willingly let the competition take over, and the race was on. The old competition between Boeing and Douglas had never died. Sometimes it slept, but it was awake and kicking again.

President Allen agreed that a new airplane could be the answer to the DC-9, and BAC-111, but he wanted assurance. As he had with the 727, Allen wanted pre-construction sales figures. Sell at least eighty 737s, he said in effect, and the green light will shine. Boeing could not possibly tackle the enormous expense of designing, testing and manufacturing a new airplane without commitments.

Below: An Air California **737-200** taxis to the terminal gate at San Francisco International Airport after a flight from Los Angeles. Air Cal operates 10 daily flights between the two cities, one of the busiest air corridors in the world. Air Cal is one of two major airlines whose primary function is operating intra-California commuter flights.

With that in mind, engineers went to work. There was the problem of engines. Some thought three engines in the rear, as with the 727, would be feasible. Some of the original two-engine designs when the company was exploring 727 possibilities had been sound, however, and Joe Sutter, chief of technology, pointed out that twin engines in the wings would be enough if the engines were large. The twin engine version won.

Then a cockpit controversy divided opinion. Should the crew consist of two or three? United Air Lines and Western opted for three-man crews (pilot, co-pilot and flight engineer). Others preferred two-man cockpits, pointing out that the DC-9 and the BAC-111 carried only two. Less payroll meant more profit for the operator. Boeing decided to leave it up to the customer. While there are now 737s with three in the cockpit, the large majority are equipped for two.

It was decided to use the same upper fuselage as earlier jets in the Boeing family. This would provide for six-abreast seating. Douglas's DC-9 seated only five, a point in favor of the 737. Douglas was ahead in its design, though, and would reach buyers

Above: Lufthansa was the **737** launch customer, seeing the need for a small short-range jet to funnel passengers between its principal air hub in Frankfurt and other points within Germany and neighboring countries. Lufthansa now operates over 30 737-200s and a half dozen 737-200C Convertible passenger/cargo planes.

Near right: A **737-200C** belonging to Federal Express, a courier service that offers overnight package delivery throughout most of the United States and Canada.

Far right: British Airways operates 19 **737s** on domestic and short-distance international routes.

Below: An Angola Airlines **737-200**. The 737 has been immensely popular with smaller Third World nations because it is economical and because most of their passenger routes are relatively short and have relatively low passenger density. In addition to simply selling airplanes, Boeing offers a wide range of services. These services, which the smaller airlines often take advantage of, include pilot training, route planning, graphic design for the markings and colors of the aircraft and interior design. Boeing can also even provide designs for the flight attendants' uniforms.

Specifications: Boeing Model 737-100

Span	93 ft
Length	94 ft
Wing Area	980 sq ft
Tail Height	37 ft
Gross Weight	111,000 pounds
Cruising Speed	575 mph
Service Ceiling	35,000 ft
Range	2140 miles
Powerplant	two 14,000 pound thrust Pratt & Whitney JT8D-7 or 14,500 pound thrust JT8D-9 Turbofans
Capacity	107 passengers

first, so Boeing came up with competitive innovations to make its newest design attractive. The 737 would, for example, carry more seats, and thus earn more profit.

Competition was fierce. In order to keep an edge, Douglas brought out another version of the DC-9, while the 737 was still an untried prototype. This was the more powerful DC-9-10, with P&W JT8D-1 turbofans. Continuing improvements on the basic DC-9, Douglas next brought out its DC-9-30, 15 feet longer than the original airplane. It entered service with Eastern Air Lines on shuttle operations on 1 February 1967, when Boeing was yet to take its prototype aloft.

The sales race was hot between the two firms but because Douglas was in the sky first, it began to look as if Douglas had won. There was a positive side to an apparent set-back. As Jack Steiner said, 'The 737 was the product of competitive sources. Because of this competition, all airplanes improved.'

In February 1965, Boeing made two important announcements. First, Lufthansa had contracted to purchase 21 of the 737-100s, making it the only Boeing airliner ever sold to a foreign buyer before an American purchase was made. It was a key sale, one that would attract the attention of European operators. Boeing had beaten BAC's One-Eleven to the Lufthansa sale, much to BAC's disappointment, but Lufthansa saw only good sense in buying the 737-100. It had 'commonality' with the 707, 720 and the 727s, sharing many features of the earlier aircraft. The other announcement Boeing made was its decision to go ahead with the 737. It would be built in a new factory near Plant 2, but, warned President Allen, domestic sales were important to the airplane's success. The American market must buy, because, with its aggressive thrust, it was the most sustaining.

Boeing did not have long to wait after the Lufthansa sale. United Air Lines called for the 737, but wanted a larger airplane, so Boeing lengthened the fuselage by six feet. Passenger capacity was raised from 107 to 119. The longer version was designated 737-200, as those of original design had been designated 737-100.

United's order was for 40, but the company did not stop there. In addition, United purchased twenty 727QCs, and took an additional 25 on lease. The order, in aggregate, totaled nearly half a billion dollars, setting another record for commercial airplane negotiations. However, United did not leave Douglas out, and purchased nine DC-8s at the same time.

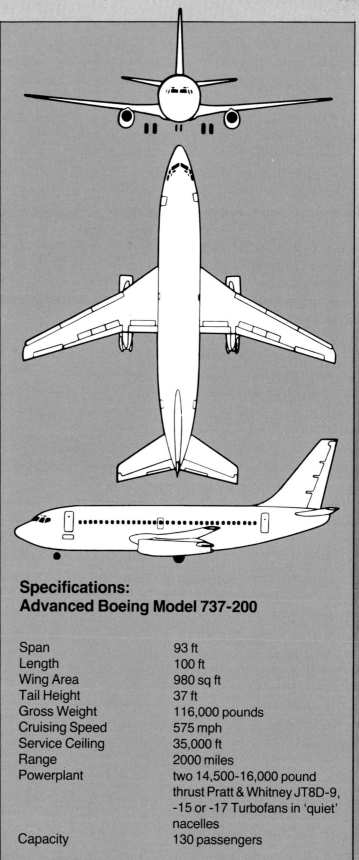

The prototype 737-100 rolled out on 9 April 1967, and the first 737-200 flew first on 8 August. There followed a period of intense testing. The 737 was encountering more drag than had been expected, and some redesign work was necessary. Despite this, Boeing promised its customers delivery on schedule. Six 737s were flown for a total of 1300 hours, and both the -100 and -200, received FAA certification in December. For the first time, certification also included approval for automatic approaches in bad weather under Category II conditions. These were defined as 100 foot ceilings and 1200 foot forward visibility.

The 737-100 entered Lufthansa service on 10 February 1968. United's inaugural flight followed with the -200s on 28 April. The Boeing Baby rapidly became a favorite with both passengers and operators, providing a smooth, comfortable ride at low costs. Both models were powered by P&W JT8D turbofan engines. Both versions were fitted with APU, auxiliary power units. High-lift flaps and leading edge devices similar to those on the 727 ensured excellent low-speed performance. The 737 was also equipped with an electronically controlled cabin pressurization system. It automatically maintained proper cabin pressure at all altitudes.

As before, Boeing offered -100C and -200C versions for cargo/passenger conversion, and the company also adopted the 'Quick Change,' QC, ability of the 727. It takes only a couple of hours to change configuration on the QC, but the C version became the choice of airline operators for mixed traffic. The first of the 727-200C convertibles was delivered to Wien Consolidated Airlines of Fairbanks, Alaska on 30 October 1968.

In May 1971 the Advanced 737 was introduced. This version came with automatic wheel brakes, more powerful engines and a

Specifications:
Advanced Boeing Model 737-200

Span	93 ft
Length	100 ft
Wing Area	980 sq ft
Tail Height	37 ft
Gross Weight	116,000 pounds
Cruising Speed	575 mph
Service Ceiling	35,000 ft
Range	2000 miles
Powerplant	two 14,500-16,000 pound thrust Pratt & Whitney JT8D-9, -15 or -17 Turbofans in 'quiet' nacelles
Capacity	130 passengers

greater fuel capacity. In all the Advanced 737 had a 15 percent improvement in payload/range over its younger brother.

Another innovation was the optional gravel field kit. This allowed the 737 to operate into more remote strips which had never before been usable by jets. Because it has the same fuselage, the 737 can handle the same cargo pallets as the 707 and 727, and such interchangeability was noted by airline operators – that, and the fact that the 737 could land in 4000 feet.

The 737 was to become a popular airplane, because of its dependability and versatile internal configuration. It became a

holiday cruise ship on weekends and a cargo-hauling workhorse during the week. In August 1976 one British Airways 737-200C flew for 19 hours out of 24, while the rest of the 14 airplane fleet flew for 14 hours. It was the kind of reliability operators loved.

In 1973 a military version of the 737-200 was ordered by the US Air Force, marking the first new Boeing fixed-wing aircraft sale to the military since the KC-135 program had ended in 1966. Designated as T-43A, the airplanes are used as navigation trainers. Nineteen were converted for the Air Force, replacing the older Convair T-29s (see page 156).

There are 19 stations inside the T-43A, 12 are for navigation students, four are for proficiency training and three are for the instructors. The student training compartment is equipped with advanced avionics gear identical to that in Air Force operational aircraft. This includes Doppler and mapping radar; LORAN (Long Range Navigation); VOR (VHF Ominirange) and TACAN (Tactical Air Navigation) radio systems. There are facilities for inertial navigation training, as well as radar altimeter and all basic communications equipment. Five periscope sextants are spaced along the length of the training compartment for use in celestial navigation studies.

Most of the T-43A trainers were based at Mather Air Force Base, California, where the Air Force also trains Navy and Marine navigators. Several have now been turned over to the Air National Guard. The airplane is powered by two 16,000-pound thrust P&W JT8D-9 turbofans, with a range of about 3000 miles. Fuel capacity is 5961 gallons. Some changes appear from the basic 737, including strengthening of the floor to support the heavy consoles, and some windows and two fuselage doors were also removed. Other than those, the T-43A retains the original 737-200 configuration.

An additional eight 737s have been ordered by various world governments from Brazil to Thailand for use as VIP and military transports and three are in service with Indonesia's Air Force in a maritime surveillance role.

On 26 March 1981 the go-ahead was given for the 737-300, a re-engined, lengthened version of the basic 737. Designed for the newly available high bypass CFM56-3 engine with a 20,000-pound thrust (developed by CFM International), the -300 will be more efficient and quieter. The -300 is lengthened 104 inches to accommodate up to 21 more passengers, with a fuel burner per seat significantly reduced over the -200, with lower direct operating costs. On a typical 500-mile trip, the -300 will burn from 18 to 20 percent less fuel per seat, putting it in the same class as Boeing's 757 jetliners.

The 737-300 retains 70 percent commonality with the -200, and was integrated into the same production line in Renton. Changes included: strengthened wing to accommodate more engine weight; heavier wheels, tires and brakes; revised wing leading-edge slats and tailoring of the aft flaps in the area of the engine exhaust for improved performance.

Roll-out of the 737-300 took place on 17 January 1984, with the first

Specifications: Boeing Model 737-300

Span	94 ft 10 in
Length	109 ft 7 in
Tail Height	37 ft
Gross Weight	130,000 pounds
Cruising Speed	575 mph
Service Ceiling	35,000 ft
Range	1322 miles
Powerplant	two 20,000 pound thrust CFM International CFM56-3 Turbofans
Capacity	121-149 passengers

flight coming on 24 February and FAA certification on 14 November. Both USAir and Southwest Airlines took delivery of their first 737-300s immediately after certification and began revenue service in December 1984. By January 1989, orders for the 737-300 had reached 785, and nearly 500 were already in service with more than a dozen airlines worldwide. This made it the third most successful subvariant in the Boeing jetliner history after the 727-200 (1245 units sold) and the 737-200 (991 units sold) neither of which were in production after mid-1988.

Meanwhile, in June 1986 and May 1987, Boeing announced development of the 737-400 and 737-500 subvariants, both of which were seen as follow-ons to the revolutionary turbofan-powered 737-300. These two new birds–also powered by CFM56 turbofans–made their respective first flights in February 1988 and July 1989, and the first 737-400 saw service with Piedmont in October 1988. By January 1989, 283 of these two subvariants had been ordered. With 1649 total 737s delivered and another 615 of all 737 types on the order books by that time, the 737 was on its way to surpassing the 727 as the most successful jetliner in history.

Above, from left: Second generation 737s on their maiden flights: the **737-400** (1988), the **737-300** (1984), and **737-500** (1989). Note their high-bypass CFM56 turbofan engines. These powerplants served to make the second generation much more economical and reliable for airlines to operate.

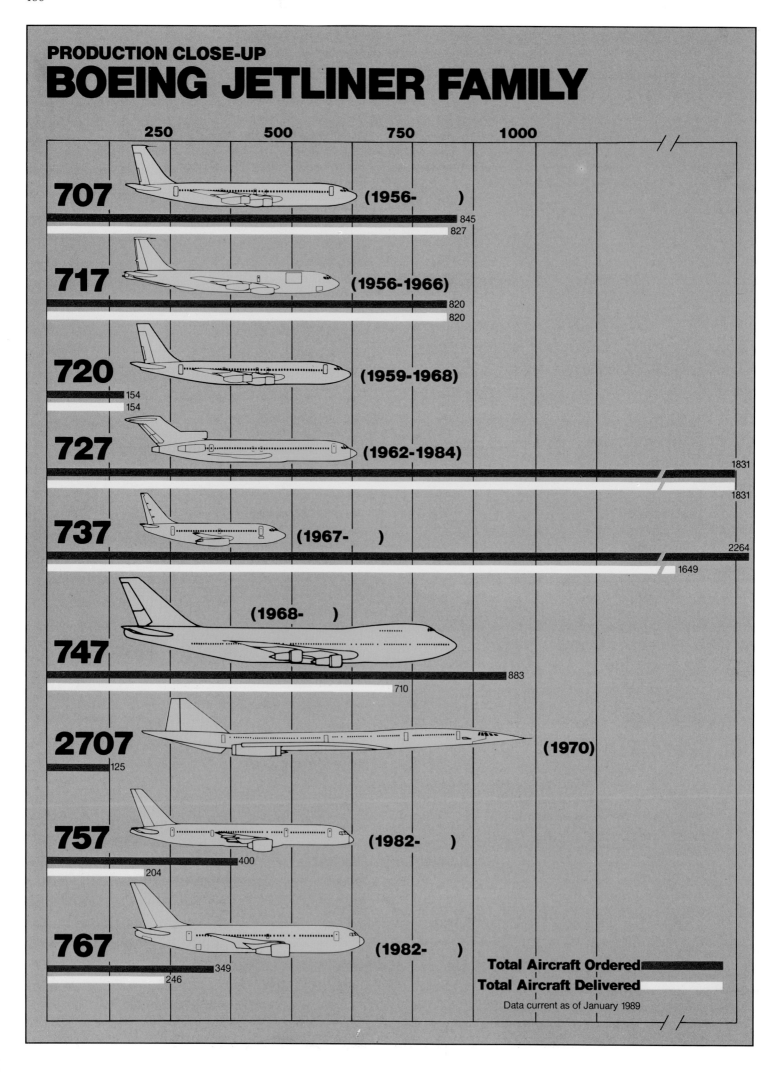

PRODUCTION CLOSE-UP
BOEING JETLINER FAMILY

250   500   750   1000

707 (1956-)
845
827

717 (1956-1966)
820
820

720 (1959-1968)
154
154

727 (1962-1984)
1831
1831

737 (1967-)
2264
1649

747 (1968-)
883
710

2707 (1970)
125

757 (1982-)
400
204

767 (1982-)
349
246

Total Aircraft Ordered
Total Aircraft Delivered

Data current as of January 1989

In November 1955, Boeing and North American Aviation were awarded study contracts by the Department of Defense for Weapons System 110-A. It was to be a supersonic bomber with the Air Force designation B-70. It would be capable of Mach 3 speeds, or over 2000mph. Artists' impressions of the design show a tapered body, a long gooseneck and Delta wings. As one observer put it, the airplane had the appearance of being 'supersonic just sitting still.'

Designs submitted by both Boeing and North American were not satisfactory, and the Air Force requested both companies to continue the study. Though Boeing worked hard, North American won the contest. However, the B-70 program was cut back by the DOD in 1960, and eventually cancelled when a change in weapons policy took place, as we have seen.

Though Boeing lost the B-70 contract, the company once again came out ahead in experience. Lessons learned designing the B-70 were applied to something already under consideration, a supersonic transport, the SST.

Before the SST, however, came the TFX (Tactical Fighter Experimental). During the summer of 1961, the Department of Defense let it be known that designs would be accepted for the new airplane, which was to be designated F-111.

Boeing went after the contract. The Bomarc missile program was nearing completion, and it was important to acquire the additional income the TFX would bring.

In December 1961 six leading aircraft manufacturers submitted proposals to the DOD. After evaluation, the DOD narrowed the competition down to Boeing and General Dynamics (together with the Grumman Aircraft Engineering Corporation). Though it was rumored for a time that Boeing had won the contract, it was finally awarded to General Dynamics. After some serious teething problems the F-111 has come to be a successful airplane, and General Dynamics has rolled out over 500 of them.

As with the B-70, Boeing took the loss financially, but chalked up a gain in the experience department. Lessons learned in designing the TFX served Boeing's next project, the SST, called SCAT by NASA, for Supersonic Commercial Air Transport.

Boeing had set up an SST study group in 1958. The company had already had several years of preliminary investigation, including design work on the B-70 and TFX, by the time it was ready to enter the project in earnest.

In June 1963, President John F Kennedy, recognizing the implications of Pan American's expressed intention to purchase the British-French Concorde SST, advocated that the United States enter the SST program. In August the FAA issued requests for proposals from major industry firms. In January 1964 Boeing submitted its ideas, amid some stiff competition. Lockheed and North American were also bidding, and were respected as tough adversaries. In May North American was eliminated, and Lockheed and Boeing were left in the running, but they were asked to design larger versions of the SST with lower seat-mile costs.

Boeing and Lockheed were given separate NASA contracts to evaluate four types of supersonic aircraft: the four were called SCAT 14, 15, 16, and 17. SCAT 16 would be an airplane with a variable-sweep arrow wing, and SCAT 17's design showed a delta wing with small, finlike canard control surfaces well forward of the wing.

After consideration, Boeing submitted plans for SCAT 16, the variable wing design. By now, the company had spent $20 million on the SST, and nothing was certain yet. However, there was something new in financing. The federal government assumed participation on a fund-sharing basis, not a normal policy, but the SST was important enough to warrant partnership. The Soviet government had spent money building its SST, the Tu-144, and both the British and French governments had invested in the Concorde. Such an airplane was too expensive for private financing.

The SST program continued on a month-to-month basis until July 1965, when President Lyndon Johnson announced an 18 month competitive phase. A year later, Boeing submitted plans for a mock-up, and was granted a contract to go ahead. General Electric was awarded a contract to develop the powerplants.

In May 1967 Boeing was given the green light to build two prototypes. However, Boeing did not feel quite ready, and asked

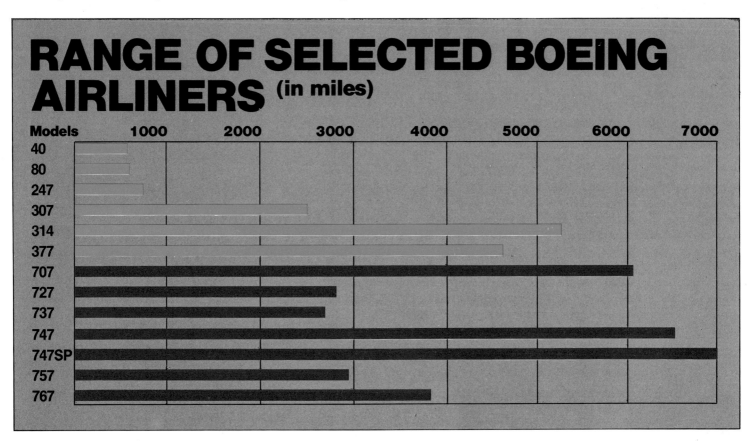

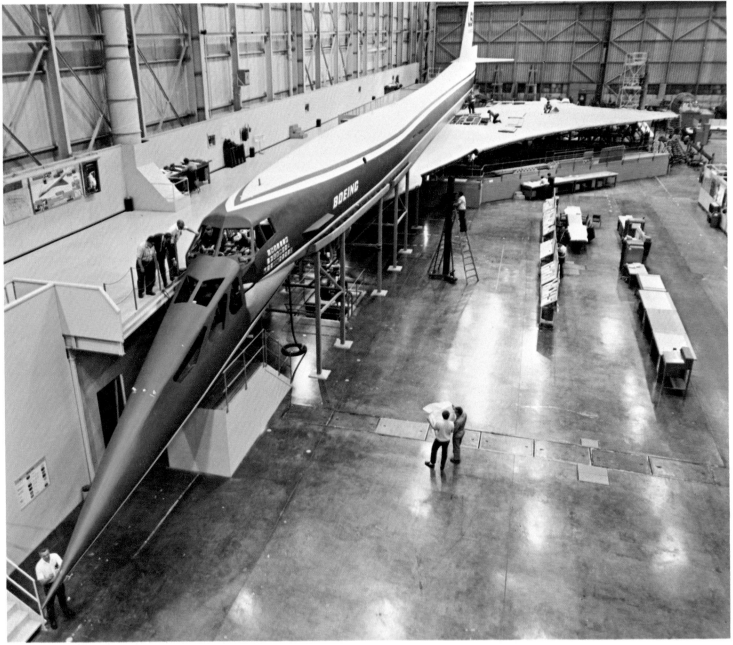

for an extension for further configuration development. By January 1969 the company had completed its design changes, and was ready to begin the prototype. Governmental approval had to come first, however. In September 1969 President Richard Nixon granted that approval, thus becoming the third US President involved in the SST program.

The prototype SST was to be 286 feet long, 50 feet tall, and have a wingspan of over 141 feet. The leading edge of the wing would be swept back 50 degrees. The airplane would be constructed of titanium and weigh 635,000 pounds fully loaded. For power, there would be four GE4 engines of more than 60,000 pounds thrust each. The airplane was to cruise at altitudes above 60,000 feet and would travel at Mach 2.7, or more than 1800mph.

Boeing had by now contacted airlines throughout the world about its SST, now designated Model 2707. Many were interested in buying. Pan Am opted for 15, TWA 12, United Air Lines 6, Japan Air Lines 5. Altogether, 26 operators ordered 122 of the supersonic transports. It was considered the way future air travel would turn, and airlines caught short would fall behind.

But problems arose. By 1970 such questions from the public as to why the government was subsidizing what was essentially a private venture with taxpayers' money were being asked. Who needed an SST? Subsonic jets were fast enough. The government replied that its spending of taxpayers' money was not a grant, it

Above: The full-scale mockup of Boeing's **Model 2707-300** supersonic transport inside the Boeing developmental center in the Plant 2 complex. The mockup was complete with interior detail including all of the passenger seats in the five-abreast seating arrangement.

would be paid back. Indeed, as soon as the 500th SST was sold, the government would net a one-billion dollar profit. As to who needed it, the government responded by saying that those who flew wanted it, because of time saved in long-distance travel. SSTs, it was argued, were inevitable. The Russians and the French and British would have them.

The Anglo-French prototype, 001, flew on 2 March 1969. Both British Airways and Air France put commercial models to work simultaneously in January 1976. The Russian Tupolev version, which paralleled the Concorde so closely that espionage was suspected, did not fare so well. It flew first on 31 December 1968, but suffered problems. A second Tu-144 was built, but this crashed at the Paris Air Show in 1973. After some changes, the Tu-144 was reintroduced, but it was withdrawn after the completion of over a hundred operational flights. A fatal crash was thought to be the cause of withdrawal.

Public controversy in the United States continued. There were doubts that the SST was the wave of the future, and would not the SST create high sound levels disturbing millions of people?

PASSENGER CAPACITY OF SELECTED BOEING AIRLINERS

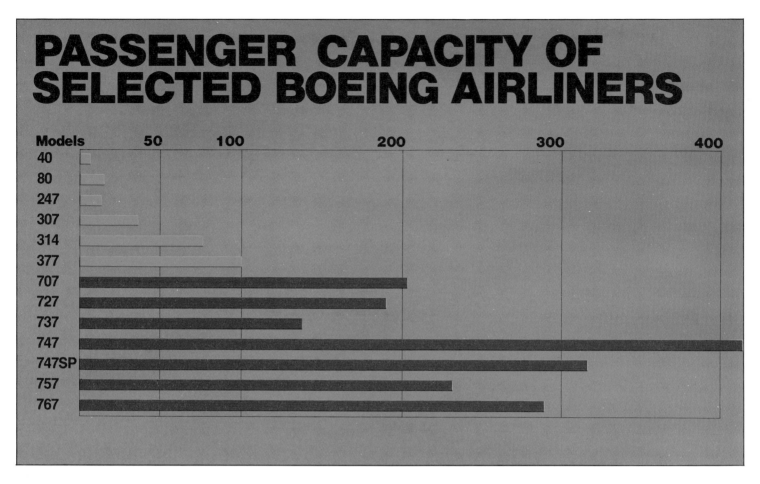

By March 1971 engineering on the Boeing Model 2707 prototype was virtually completed. The program was proceeding on schedule and within costs, the major problems were well in hand, metal was being cut and 15 percent of the first airframe had been completed. Political forces, however, were coming into play back in Washington, and on 24 March the government voted to terminate the program. As provided in the contract, Boeing's share of program costs was refunded, but thousands of Boeing workers were laid off and the American hopes for a supersonic transport were dashed.

It was a serious blow to Boeing, coming as it did at the same time as the serious early difficulties of the 747 program. The airplane market had collapsed during the 1969 recession. Boeing's earnings dropped 73 billion dollars in one year.

Specifications: Boeing Model 2707-300

Span	141 ft 8 in
Length	268 ft 8 in (296 ft*)
Wing Area	8497 sq ft
Tail Height	50 ft 1 in
Gross Weight	635,000 pounds
Cruising Speed	1890 mph
Service Ceiling	60,000 ft
Range	5000 miles
Powerplant	four 60,000 pound thrust General Electric GE4/J5P Turbojets
Capacity	250-321* passengers

*A 'stretched' version of the 2707 Supersonic Transport was already being planned when the program was cancelled

In 1968 Thornton Arnold Wilson (today known universally as 'T' Wilson) had succeeded Bill Allen as company president. Wilson was an engineer and saw the solutions to the company's problems in engineering terms. The only way to save Boeing was to reduce costs drastically, and that meant layoffs. Boeing's work force of 105,000 was cut to 38,000. Engineers were seen pumping gas. Former Boeing employees spread across the Northwest like spilled ink, trickling into and seriously affecting job markets as far away as Montana.

Wilson's painful surgery saved the company, and the dreadful loss of the SST program turned out to be a blessing in disguise. With the dramatic increase in oil prices as a result of the Arab oil embargo of 1973, cost per mile formulae for all aircraft, especially the thirsty SSTs, were rendered obsolete. Though a functional design, the Anglo French Concorde would never be commercially successful. It would continue to see service with British Airways and Air France, the national airlines of the two countries whose governments bankrolled it, but it would never prove to be anything but a lossmaker for them. Interest on the part of various airlines such as Pan Am, Iran Air, Singapore Airlines and the now defunct Braniff, waned for various reasons, and the two original operators remain the sole users of the Concorde.

Boeing's 2707, while larger, faster by over 400mph and of greater range than the Concorde, probably would have shared a fate similar to the Concorde, but without the resources of a national airline available to keep it flying for purely prestige reasons. The supersonic transport is, however, like many aircraft that have gone before it, an idea ahead of its time. It is entirely likely that a commercially viable SST will fly before the end of the century. It will benefit by the mistakes of the Concorde and it will benefit from advances in engine technology unknown during the development of the Concorde and the 2707 in the late 1960s. Boeing, while scrapping the project, never burned all the files, so it is indeed possible that the first commercially viable SST will be a Boeing.

Above: A United Air Lines **747-100** at San Francisco International Airport. United, itself once part of Boeing, operates nearly 400 Boeing aircraft, more than any other airline. However, it flies fewer than 20 747s, most of them on transcontinental flights and flights connecting Hawaii with the US mainland.

n the early summer of 1964, the US Air Force invited Lockheed, Douglas, and Boeing to submit designs for a large military transport. It would carry up to 750 troops over very long ranges. Called at first the CX-HLS, the designation was later changed to C-5A. Boeing's president, William Allen, felt that the company should go after the contract. Boeing had two other major projects on the boards already, the SST and, in the Aerospace Division, a manned orbital laboratory, MOL. The latter two were Boeing probes into the latest challenges, supersonic travel and deep space, but a contract for the C-5A was pragmatic, a foot-on-the-ground venture. Boeing could build transports. It had become famous because of them.

While the design of the C-5A was taking shape, Boeing investigators went abroad to examine the airline industry. Experience was telling the company that the time was coming for another new airplane, perhaps a superjet. The investigating team went to Europe, Japan and Australia, finding that experience had not led them astray. The world market would be ready for a

Above: With its pilot grinning from the cockpit, the Canadian Pacific Air **747-200B** *Empress of Asia* crosses the Canadian Rockies en route to the Far East.

superjet by the mid-1970s, if not sooner. Traffic was increasing by 15 percent a year, and the studies found that future airliners would have to seat up to 375 passengers if the congestion was to be relieved. The time for designing the new airplane was at hand because Boeing knew airplanes designed to fit a market should be ready at least four years ahead of time.

The C-5A plans were submitted to the Air Force, and Boeing waited. Rumors floated back to the company. Boeing was high on the technical side, Lockheed low on price by 250 million. Tense days followed. Boeing was deeply involved in the 737 program and money was scarce. A military contract would mean money in the bank.

When the news came that Lockheed had won the C-5A contract, the news was not greeted with cheers. To further the gloom, the International Association of Machinists had gone on strike at Boeing. It had always been company policy to base promotions on a merit rating system. The union wanted seniority to be the primary criterion. The longer a man or woman worked for the

company, the better the chance for promotion in spite of ability. The company and the Union locked horns over the issue. The matter was finally resolved when a joint resolution was reached in which the employee merit system would continue as policy for an additional six months while the matter was given more study. In the meantime, work on money-earning projects went begging, not a boon to the company treasury.

There were grumbles in the industry about Lockheed's winning the C-5A contract with such an enormous underbid. Two hundred and fifty million dollars pretty well knocked out any competition. Could Lockheed really build a super transport for the price? As we have seen, Lockheed's C-5A Galaxy, while eventually a good airplane, was wracked with serious development problems and huge cost overruns.

Though Boeing had been hurt by the loss, the company did not brood. Sales for the 707, 720, 727 and the new 737 were picking up, and it was easy to regain the old enthusiasm. Now that the company was freed of the C-5A responsibility, thoughts turned to a giant commercial transport in earnest. If the one failed, perhaps the other would be successful.

At first a stretched 707 was considered, but the idea was abandoned in favor of an all-new concept. Joe Sutter, chief of technology, an engineer who had helped develop the 737, was asked to design such a plane. Using the advantage gained in designing the big C-5A, some startling results appeared: using the engines that were to have powered the C-5A, the superjet could promise a 25 percent reduction in fuel consumption. Improved leading edge and trailing edge flaps, coupled with further high-lift studies employed in the C-5A research, would enable the giant to land at existing world airports, an important feature if the aircraft were to reach for big sales.

In October 1965, Sutter was made chief engineer on the 747 Project. In consultation with Pan American World Airways it was decided to build an airplane for fast service, reaching speeds over 600mph. In that case, there would be more sweep to the wings, and there would have to be very powerful engines, the most powerful ever developed.

Both Pratt & Whitney and General Electric had competed for the C-5A power plants. General Electric had won. Its TF39, with 41,100 pounds of thrust, is considered to be the first turbofan suitable for wide-body jets. P&W's loss, however, was actually to become a gain. Boeing asked that the P&W JT9D engines be perfected for the 747.

Altogether, P&W had spent six years on the JT9D bypass turbofan. The company built a special factory just to assemble it because all new tools and methods of fitting the parts together were necessary. Its eight-foot diameter inlet was twice the size of 707 long range turbofans. However, it was only 128 inches in length. The engine weighed 8470 pounds and was capable of generating from 43,500 to 53,000 pounds of thrust. That's about 87,000 horsepower at the lower end of the scale.

In order to test the engine in actual use, P&W leased a B-52 from the Air Force. After extensive modification to reinforce the wing, the huge engine was mounted in the place of two J57s. In the trials that followed, the TJ9D took the B-52 nine miles up into the sky, much more altitude than expected.

There was debate on the fuselage design. It was thought that the developing SST would capture most of the passenger traffic, so planning the 747 fuselage required careful study. Maritime container shipping had proved successful, and Boeing designers felt that the basic 747 would be a freighter with container capability. In line with this thinking, a body was developed that would comfortably hold two 8 foot by 8 foot containers side by side. This was the origin of the 'wide body,' which at first had little to do with passengers or their comfort.

The airplane that came off the drawing boards had a configuration, however, that would take either passengers or freight, or a combination. Of course the SST would be cancelled and there was accordingly no intrusion by it into the passenger market. The final version of the 747 fuselage had three decks. The flight deck, on a level above the main deck, permitted straight-in loading through a hinged nose door in freighter and convertible models. Behind the flight deck on some passenger models there is a luxurious lounge, reached by a stairway from the main deck. The main deck allowed ten-abreast seating. It could also be used for freight or a combination of freight and passengers. Below the main deck was space for 26 containers, capable of holding $16\frac{1}{2}$ tons of baggage, mail, and cargo.

The first-class passenger cabin was forward in the nose. The 747-100s, as the first production Superjets were designated, seated 58 first-class passengers, and 304 economy class. There were three galleys aboard, and food caterers had to think big in order to serve the large number of passengers. The average crew on a 747 consists of the captain, the first officer, flight engineer, a steward, and ten hostesses.

While the planning was going ahead, the then chief executive of Boeing, Bill Allen, and Pan Am's Juan Trippe were negotiating. Trippe was looking for a big airplane that would save from 30–35 percent per seat-mile. This meant lower fares and cargo rates, giving Pan Am a considerable edge over the competition. Trippe was a man of action. He was aware that Boeing was chary of the development costs of such an airliner – at least 500 million dollars. So on 13 April 1966 he signed a contract for $525 million. This was for 25 airplanes, two freighters, and the others to carry from 350 to 400 passengers. On the basis of another record order, Boeing's financial worries vanished. William Allen gave the go-ahead to build the largest commercial airplane ever.

In June 1966, three months after the 747 program was launched, 780 acres of land were purchased next to Paine Field, Everett, Washington. For such a huge airplane, a special manufacturing complex was needed. It included the world's largest building by volume. Originally measured at 200 million cubic feet, the building has recently been enlarged to 285 million cubic feet in order to accommodate production of Boeing's new 767 airliner. As a result, major portions of manufacturing, subassembly and final assembly functions for both aircraft are housed under one roof.

Also at the site is an area for cleaning, sealing and painting the airplane sections before they go into final assembly. The structural static test area is inside the huge complex, too, but the structural fatigue-test area lies outside the factory.

In addition, there are warehouses, a service building, several office buildings and a cafeteria. Paint hangars and a field-support building are located on the preflight apron adjoining Paine Field.

The site also includes a 15 million gallon holding basin to catch surface runoff water. A five mile railroad spur, the second steepest standard gauge section in the USA, was built to bring in construction steel for the buildings and production parts and subassemblies for fabricating the aircraft.

Before production actually began, Boeing devoted 14,000 hours of wind tunnel testing to a variety of models. It spent 10 million engineering man hours on the project. Everything about the 747 was big from the very beginning. Four years of continuous testing in areas ranging from metals selection to systems operation preceded the first superjet. It was not born overnight.

The 747 Division of the Boeing Commercial Airplane Company (a wing of the corporate Boeing Company) was established. John Steiner was made vice president in charge of production development. The new division was made directly responsible for designing, developing, and manufacturing the 747, a formidable responsibility.

The first production operations at the new Everett plant began in January 1967. The buildings were occupied in stages throughout the year as each was completed. Activation of the mammoth assembly plant began on 1 May 1967, just over a year after the 747 program was announced. Actual assembly of the first airplane started in September of the same year. Later that year, components for the first nose section arrived at Everett from Boeing's Wichita, Kansas division. Because the job was so big, Boeing signed contracts with other industry-related firms to make a variety of parts. Without outside help, the 747 production would have suffered. Concurrently with the nose section, other components manufactured by major contractors arrived, and the job was under way.

While parts for the 747 were taking shape, another aspect of the project reached a satisfactory conclusion. This was the 'selling'

Below: Scandinavian Airlines 747-200B *Dan Viking* was the fifth of the jumbo jets to be built for SAS but had the distinction of being the **500th Boeing 747** to be built. The *Dan Viking* is a 'Combi' model able to carry mixed loads of passengers and freight on the main deck. SAS received its first 747 on 27 February 1971 and now operates a half dozen of the big jets, that number equally divided between the 200B model and the 200B 'Combi.'

of the Class III 747 mock-up on 12 January 1968. The mock-up was a full-scale airplane, minus engines, seats and one wing. Its purpose was to verify engineering drawings, determine assembly crew sizes and the tooling needed, set instruments for flight testing and check out specific airline cabin and cockpit arrangements. The 'buyers' were two Boeing men, the chief of the Model 747 mock-up engineering, and the chief of mock-up quality control. Their acceptance meant that crews could start on non-structural items such as wiring, panel-making, tubing and pumps. The wing and body sections were already under construction.

The first wing assembly was removed from the assembly jig in March 1968. The wing weighed 28,000 pounds, or ten times the gross weight of Boeing's first plane, the B&W.

Production moved ahead swiftly, and on 30 September 1968 the first 747 Superjet made its world debut in a roll out ceremony at the Everett plant. By January 1969 the prototype 747's major systems had been activated, and its landing gear and flight controls operationally tested. Compass calibration, fueling and engine tests came next. After that, there was nothing to keep the 747 from its big moment, the first flight.

According to *Boeing Magazine* for March 1969, this is what happened. It was 9 February, and the weather was not great,

somewhere between bad and uncertain. Shortly after 11.00 a m, however, the overcast thinned and lifted. Three men were in the 747's cockpit. They were pilot Jack Waddell, co-pilot Brien Wygle and flight engineer Jess Wallick. One of them mentioned it would be nice if there were less people on the runway. Large crowds of newspeople and photographers, company executives and employees were present to see the largest transport in the world make its maiden flight. 'Like flying in Africa,' observed another of the cockpit crew, 'you have to chase the wildlife off the runway first.'

The people moved back, though, and pilot Jack Waddell eased the throttles forward. Co-pilot Brien Wygle called out speeds as this giant of the air began to gather momentum. Flight engineer Jess Wallick kept his eyes glued to the gauges. The Boeing Model 747 superjet gained speed. The nose lifted. After 4300 feet, less than half the Paine Field runway, the main gear left the concrete. The take-off speed was 164mph. At 11.34 a m, quietly and almost serenely, the age of spacious jets began.

'The engines,' reported one witness, 'made no more noise than a stiff breeze through a forest.' Pratt & Whitney had developed the JT9D high bypass turbofan with community noise concerns in mind. A giant step toward quieter airliners had been taken.

Above: To manufacture the world's largest jetliner, the 747, Boeing built near **Everett, Washington**, the largest building in the world. The building, enlarged in 1980 to 291 million cubic feet, encloses all major portions of manufacturing and final assembly for the 747, and recently for the 767. The four large colored doors seen here are each seven stories high. In the foreground, the new 747s are prepared for final delivery. Boeing began building the 747 at the Everett plant in 1967 and the first 767 was rolled out in 1981.

Left: The flight line at **Paine Field**, adjacent to the big Everett complex. The Everett flight line is like a United Nations of airlines, with dozens of carriers from every continent having been represented here.

Below: A **747 forward fuselage section** is joined to the rest of the fuselage.

Waddell accelerated the airplane to 184mph, and climbed nearer to the overcast at 2000ft. He then circled back over the airport and began his climb to the 15,500 feet test altitude. Snuggled close to the big airplane, and appearing, to one man, 'Like a flea about to jump on the 747's back,' was a North American F-86 chase plane. Its pilot's job was to conduct external studies of the superjet's operation.

After putting the 747 through a series of sideslips and other tests, including one simulating a loss of hydraulic systems, Waddell headed for home. At 12.50 p.m. the superjet touched down at Paine Field in a perfect landing. Waddell used light braking and thrust reversers to bring the plane to a stop, again using about half the runway. He then rolled on to make way for the chase plane coming down behind him. The 747's landing speed was 150mph, without full flaps.

Led by a string of official cars and buses, the 747 taxied into the Boeing ramp, and the engines were shut down. A few minutes later, the crew, their business suits still unwrinkled, emerged from the forward passenger door to be greeted by well-wishers. 'Look at 'em' said an East Coast newsman, 'they just flew the world's largest commercial jetliner, and they seem about as ruffled as my stockbroker.'

That may have been true, but Jack Waddell was all pilot. He had learned to fly PBYs during World War II, and after the war he earned a master's degree in aeronautical engineering at Cornell University. After five years as an engineering test pilot for North American Aviation, he joined Boeing in 1957.

Shortly before taking the world's largest commercial airplane up, he was interviewed. The interviewer caught him laid up with a badly swollen ankle. 'How do you feel about flying an untried aircraft?' he was asked. 'Safer than staying at home,' replied Waddell, with a nod at his ankle. 'How did that happen?' 'Jogging,' replied Waddell with a grin.

He made no secret about his enthusiasm for the 747, after the flight. 'It's a pilot's dream,' he said. 'I'd call it a two-finger airplane.' He curled his forefinger and thumb as if gripping a control

Above: The company-owned **747-100 prototype** dubbed *City of Everett*, in the colors representative of Boeing-owned aircraft of 1969, and sporting the insignia of all those airlines which had placed orders for the big jet.

Below: A Middle East Airlines (Lebanon) 747-200B lifts off from **Paine Field**.

wheel. 'The plane,' he said, 'has a very light, responsive touch: two fingers.'

The business of testing the prototype now began. After ten hours of flying time, the 747 was taken to Seattle for more trials. Not long after, a second 747 joined it. The 747 testing program was to be the most extensive ever undertaken in commercial aviation history. In addition to laboratory tests of parts and components, the program included the assignment of five Superjets to a $28 million, year-long Boeing and Federal Aviation Administration flight testing program. By the end of the year, the five jets had logged more than 1400 hours of flight time in 1013 trips aloft. Finally satisfied that the 747 was a reliable aircraft, the FAA gave certification on 30 December 1969.

Yet, there had been problems. One of these was the 'ovalizing' of the large JT9D engines. They changed shape after running under loads. Pratt & Whitney studied the problem and engineered a structure that held its shape under the terrific stresses. In the meantime, airframes were lining up waiting for re-designed engines. By mid-October 1969, 22 airframes were idle at the Everett plant, 17 of these without engines. Subcontractors were so efficient that, regardless of a lack of engines, components arrived and airframes were completed.

Because of the engine problem, Pan Am was worried about delivery schedules. The company had millions tied up in the 747. Boeing, proud of its record of delivery-on-time, did not let Pan Am down. The company received its first superjet on time. Boeing people fully realized the importance of getting their products to customers when they said they would, and they were committed to delivery schedules.

When Boeing delivered two 747s to Pan Am for pilot training, Pan Am's new president, Najeeb Halaby (Juan Trippe had retired), took one up for a test of his own. Halaby was a jet pilot, qualified for transports. Aboard were Pan Am and Boeing officials, who were in for the ride of their lives. In the words of Robert Daly, who wrote *An American Saga*, a history of Pan Am, Halaby 'Wrung the 747 out like a fighter plane: dives, stalls, violent pull-ups that made the whole plane shudder and shake, the huge wings flapping 12 feet up and down. His conclusion: this was the safest, most comfortable, most magnificently-built plane in history.'

His findings were not mere chance. As with the 727 before it, the 747 had endured severe tests to destruction. Static testing, using one of the non-flying airframes, verified the strength of the entire frame. In one test, the 747 wing tips were deflected upward 26 feet before structural failure occurred.

Fatigue testing made use of the other non-flying airframe, and duplicated the stresses experienced in day-to-day airline flying. It was a task for which Boeing was well qualified. The fatigue-test program took the airframe through the equivalent of 20,000 airline flights, or 60,000 hours. Following this, fail-safe testing with the structure cracked or sawed through in 28 critical places, put the equivalent of 12,000 additional hours in airline flights on the structure. Boeing wanted to make certain that the 747 would continue to operate safely, even after damage. As always, it was safety first with Boeing.

After the five 747s completed their tests with the FAA and Boeing, four of them were refurbished and delivered to waiting airlines for service. The fifth 747, the first one to fly, remains in flight-test status with Boeing. It is used for checking out modifications which lead to production improvements.

On 3 June 1969, the prototype flew 5160 miles across the Atlantic for the Paris Air Show. The flight proved that the giant airliner was capable of world-wide travel. There was no distance too great for the 747 to cover. Airlines took notice.

On 21 January 1970, Pan Am inaugurated its first transatlantic flight with the Superjet. It was a grand occasion, with many people attending. The pilot started the JT9Ds for the New York–London flight, then chopped them off. One of the engines was overheating. There was a 24 hour delay, but on 22 January, the 747 taxied out once more. Again, the engine overheated, and the flight was delayed. Despite the embarrassment Pan Am was not to be thwarted and the company substituted another 747. This one took off, and the age of the 'jumbo jet' arrived.

The 747 rose swiftly in public esteem. Airlines were buying them as fast as they came off the assembly line, peaking out at seven airplanes a month. But the 1973 oil crisis brought soaring fuel prices, rising fares and a decline in airline traffic. Airline

Above: **Boeing's jumbo jets** have proven extremely popular for national airlines such as Alitalia who fly long-distance routes, particularly the North America – Europe run. Alitalia flies 14 747s of various types.

operators were hesitant about purchasing jumbo jets. Boeing survived another lean time, by introducing new models of its superjet, and by mid-1979 production had risen again to seven per month. It remained at seven throughout 1980, leveling off at five per month for 1981. One a month was forecast for 1983. It may be that three, five, or even seven superjets roll out each month, but it actually takes two years to assemble each one.

Each member of the Boeing 747 family of airliners takes years to build because much goes into them, and big is the watchword. There are three decks, and the main deck is 20 feet wide. This permits, in addition to the seats, two 20-inch aisles to extend for the entire 185 foot length of the cabin. Side walls of the cabin are nearly vertical, and the 8-foot 4-inch high ceiling is flat. Center-line galley and washroom installations divide the cabin into five separate compartments. The 747 has 10 double-width doors, five on each side of the cabin. Several are used for passenger boarding, others for airplane servicing, but all can be used for emergency evacuation if necessary.

To carry all of this safely, the airplane has a 16-wheel main landing gear, four units of four wheels each, and a two-wheel nose gear. These allow even distribution of loads on airport aprons and runways. The airplane can be landed with only one main gear unit on each side extended.

The 747-100 has led to a variety of commercial versions, with all but the 747SP having the same external dimensions.

The 747-100B carries a typical load of 452 passengers and baggage a distance of more than 4500 miles. First versions used four P&W JT9D-3 engines with 43,500 pounds of thrust each, though there was an option available for the JT9D-3W engines with 45,000 pounds thrust. Later versions employed the JT9D-7 series, providing up to 50,000 pounds thrust, or GE's CF6-50 engines.

Above: The configuration of the **inboard landing lights** on the 747 is visible here as the big bird touches down.

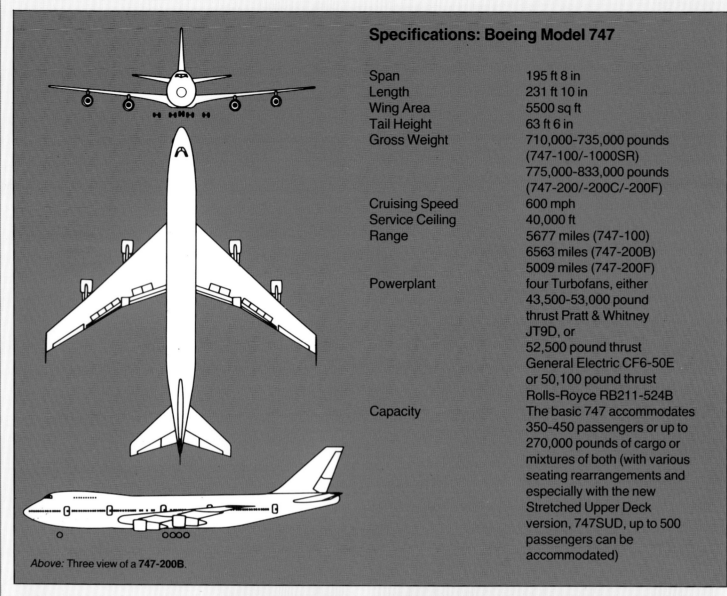

Specifications: Boeing Model 747

Span	195 ft 8 in
Length	231 ft 10 in
Wing Area	5500 sq ft
Tail Height	63 ft 6 in
Gross Weight	710,000-735,000 pounds (747-100/-1000SR)
	775,000-833,000 pounds (747-200/-200C/-200F)
Cruising Speed	600 mph
Service Ceiling	40,000 ft
Range	5677 miles (747-100)
	6563 miles (747-200B)
	5009 miles (747-200F)
Powerplant	four Turbofans, either 43,500-53,000 pound thrust Pratt & Whitney JT9D, or 52,500 pound thrust General Electric CF6-50E or 50,100 pound thrust Rolls-Royce RB211-524B
Capacity	The basic 747 accommodates 350-450 passengers or up to 270,000 pounds of cargo or mixtures of both (with various seating rearrangements and especially with the new Stretched Upper Deck version, 747SUD, up to 500 passengers can be accommodated)

Above: Three view of a **747-200B**.

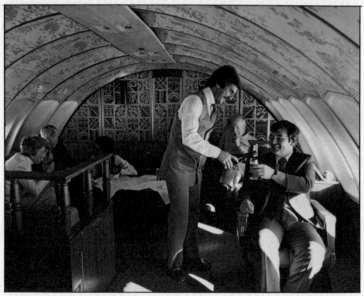

Above: A passenger enjoys a glass of champagne in the **upper-deck lounge** of a Hawaii-bound United Air Lines 747. Many airlines opt to install additional seating in the upper deck.

Left: The **staircase** which connects the first-class galley with the upper-deck lounge. In some aircraft it is a spiral staircase.

Right: The typical **747 flight deck**.

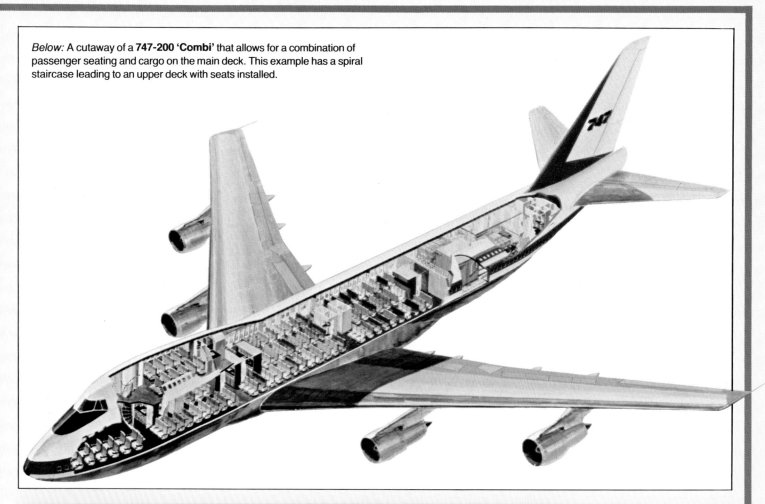

Below: A cutaway of a **747-200 'Combi'** that allows for a combination of passenger seating and cargo on the main deck. This example has a spiral staircase leading to an upper deck with seats installed.

The 747SR (Short Range option on the 747-100) was designed specifically to fill the need for high-capacity transports on routes as short as 200 miles. The 747SR was structurally strengthened to permit it to make twice as many landings in 20 years of short-range flights, yet retain its long-range capability. Components of the 747SR and the basic 747 have 99 percent commonality, and flight characteristics are identical. Gross weight can vary from 520,000 pounds at take-off on short-range flights, to 750,000 pounds for long-range flights.

The 747-200B is an 833,000 pound gross weight passenger plane that can carry a standard 452 passenger load more than 5000 miles non-stop. It is powered by Pratt & Whitney, General Electric or Rolls-Royce engines delivering up to 54,000 pounds of thrust. The 747 Combi, an option on the 747-200B, can be operated in either all-passenger or combination passenger/cargo configurations. It offers airlines an economical means of adapting to the variations in seasonal markets and charter flights. It is equipped with a side cargo door on the main deck, permitting cargo loading in the aft section, while passengers board in the forward section. Main deck cargo capability in this combination arrangement can be either six or 12 pallets.

The 747-200C, convertible, was first ordered in 1972 by World Airways, which was once one of the largest charter air carriers in the world. The -200C is capable of transporting 500 passengers in 10-abreast economy seating, or a cargo payload of up to 250,000 pounds. A typical all-passenger flight would carry 380 persons in a mixed-class configuration 5800 miles. (A typical North Atlantic non-stop cargo load would be 180,000 pounds.) The '747C', as the airplane is commonly called, has a swing-up nose for cargo loading. It also carries integral mechanical cargo loading and handling machinery.

Also in service since 1972, the 747-200F freighter can carry a maximum payload of about 250,000 pounds for more than 3000 miles.

It will carry more than 200,000 pounds over 4000 miles, or well beyond the transatlantic range. Maximum gross take-off weight is 833,000 pounds. Like the 747C, the 747-200F has a mechanized cargo handling system on the main deck. The nose swings up (as in the 747C) so pallets or eight-by-eight-foot containers can be loaded straight in on the power-driven cargo system. Two men, one at the nose and one in the interior of the airplane, can complete the unloading and loading cycle in 60 minutes.

The seventh 747 derivative was the 747SP (Special Performance), which was designed to fly higher, faster and farther than any other airplane in its class. It is 47 feet shorter than the standard model, and is suited for air routes where passenger traffic requires an airliner with a capacity between that of a 707 and a full-size 747.

The first 747SP was rolled out of the Boeing 747 Division factory in Everett, on 19 May 1975. It first flew on 4 July in a test flight that was described as the most ambitious test series ever attempted on the first flight of a Boeing jetliner. The fourth 747SP, and the first to be fitted with a full passenger interior, went on a world demonstration tour in late 1975. The first four airplanes made up the test group for certification, and then became part of the Pan American World Airways fleet. Certification for commercial service came on 4 February 1976.

Pan Am received its first 747SP on 5 March 1976, and put it into non-stop service between Los Angeles and Tokyo, and New York and Tokyo. Later it was put into service on the world's longest scheduled non-stop, between San Francisco and Sydney, Australia. This service, started in December 1976, covers 7197 miles. Proving its long-range ability even more, a 747SP being delivered to South African Airways flew non-stop from Paine Field to Capetown, covering 10,290 miles in 17 hours 22 minutes.

Although the 747SP is shorter than the standard 747, it has the same

cabin width, and the usual three decks. The upper deck has a capacity of 32 passengers, but because the 747SP is shorter, overall seating capacity is reduced by 110.

The 747SP differs from earlier 747s in several other respects. It has a lighter weight structure in parts of the wing, fuselage and landing gear. It also has a taller tail, with double-hinged rudder for control equalling that of the other 747s. It has a horizontal stabilizer wider than those on the earlier models, and it carries new trailing-edge flaps. Cruising altitude is from 4000 to 6000 feet higher than any other wide-body jetliner, providing passengers with a smoother ride. A welcome feature to operators and pilots alike is the 747SP's ability to overfly slower air traffic on congested routes. Its speed has reached Mach 0.97 in tests, without experiencing flutter. It normally cruises at over 600mph.

As we have seen, the 747 has been pressed into duty in special applications for the US Air Force. The E-4 Airborne Command Post, a modified Boeing 747 aircraft equipped with extensive electronics, would be the critical communication link in the event of an attack on the United States (see pages 156-157).

In 1989, the Air Force took delivery of the first of two 747-200s that were specially configured as VIP transports for the president of the United States. Designated VC-25A, these aircraft are better known under the call sign 'Air Force One' which they carry while transporting the president. The VC-25As will serve with the 89th Military Airlift Wing based at Andrews AFB near Washington, DC and will replace

Below: First delivered in 1972, the **747-200F** freighter featured both side and front loading, as well as the largest payload capacity commercially available. Northwest is one of the world's largest users of 747s in this all-freight configuration. *Above right*: One of three **747SP** aircraft ordered by the People's Republic of China.

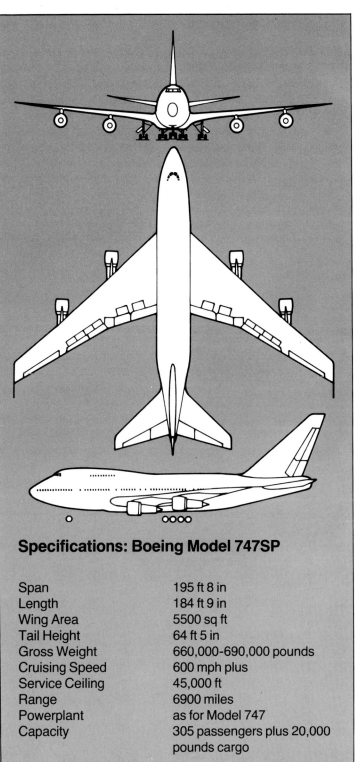

Specifications: Boeing Model 747SP

Span	195 ft 8 in
Length	184 ft 9 in
Wing Area	5500 sq ft
Tail Height	64 ft 5 in
Gross Weight	660,000-690,000 pounds
Cruising Speed	600 mph plus
Service Ceiling	45,000 ft
Range	6900 miles
Powerplant	as for Model 747
Capacity	305 passengers plus 20,000 pounds cargo

the two Boeing VC-173s (Model 707) that served in the 'Air Force One' role since the Kennedy Administration nearly three decades before.

Another 747 was acquired by NASA for use as a carrier for the Space Shuttle. While more like an airplane than any spacecraft before it, the Space Shuttle Orbiter does not have the air-breathing engines necessary for powered flight within the atmosphere. It glides to a landing, and must be transported back to its launch pad for reuse. NASA bought a 747-100 from American Airlines on 18 July 1974, and Boeing modified it for its piggyback role. The shuttle-carrier is used to ferrying the Orbiter from its landing site at Edwards Air Force Base in California back to Kennedy Space Center in Florida.

The modified 747-100 is equipped to carry the Orbiter atop its fuselage attached by struts at three points on the Orbiter. One is forward, two are aft. The attach points match socket fittings built into the Orbiter for attachment to its external take-off fuel tank. Among the modifications needed to fit the 747 for its new duty was the addition of horizontal stabilizer tip fins, each measuring 10 feet by 20 feet. These fixed-position fins give the air raft added aerodynamic stability when it is carrying the Orbiter. The aircraft's longitudinal trim system was also modified to counteract a nose-up tendency caused by downwash off the Orbiter wing onto the 747's horizontal stabilizer. Modifications were also made in the cockpit for controls and displays necessary for air-launching and ferry missions. Under a separate contract the 747's P&W JT9D-3A engines were converted to the JT9D-7AH, increasing take-off thrust from 43,500 pounds to 46,950 pounds. In all, the modifications added 11,500 pounds to the plane's weight, but as the world has seen, the conversion was a great success.

On 12 June 1980, more than a decade after the 747 program was born, Boeing announced a 'second generation' of 747s. The first of the

At left: NASA utilizes a **specially configured 747** to transport Space Shuttle Orbiters which cannot takeoff from runways. This aircraft carried the Orbiter *Enterprise* during glide tests in 1977, and since 1981 it has been used to carry Orbiters back to the Kennedy Space Center after their orbital missions.

Above: The **747-300**, with its distinctive extended upper deck, first flew in 1982. Compare the **flight deck** of the **747-300** of 1982 *(below left)* to the **747-400 flight deck** of 1988 *(below)*. The latter's high-tech, two-crew deck (which is similar to that of the 757/767) is literally worlds apart.

new series were similar to the standard 747-100/747-200 configuration but were immediately recognizable by the configuration of their upper decks by 23-feet, 4-inches. This translated into an increase in upper deck passenger capability from 32 to 91 in an all-economy configuration or 26 seats in a first class sleeper configuration.

Originally designated as 747-EUD for 'extended upper deck', the new bird went into service as 747-300. The first flight of the 747-300 came on 5 October 1982 with initial deliveries to Swissair and UTA of France coming on 28 March and 1 April 1983 respectively. Both 'SR' and 'Combi' versions of the 747-300 were also available. By January 1989, a total of 80 of the big aircraft had been put into service.

In May 1985, Boeing announced a second extended upper deck 747 to be built as 747-400. This aircraft differed from the 747-300 by its advanced two-crew flight deck and the use of new materials and alloys to lighten its airframe weight, improve fuel efficiency and permit greater payload capacity. The first customer for the 747-400 was Northwest Airlines which placed an order for 10 aircraft in October 1985. Less than a year later, in March 1986, Singapore Airlines placed the largest dollar-value order in history by putting down $3.3 billion for 14 747-400s.

The first 747-400 rolled out in January 1988 and made its first flight on 29 April. By the time that Northwest took delivery of this aircraft at the end of the year, Boeing had orders for 166 747-400s, including 16 combis.

The 747-400's most noticeable aerodynamic improvement are its wings, which are six feet longer *and* tipped with six-foot-high winglets *(see photos)*. The winglets are designed to reduce fuel burn by three percent and extend the big airplane's range. The 747-400 is equipped with a customer's choice of three engine types: the Rolls-Royce RB211-524D4D, Pratt & Whitney PW4000 or General Electric CF6-80C2. All of these engines are rated at 56,000 pounds of thrust, giving the 747-400 a 28 percent increase in total thrust over the heavier 747-100, while the new wings and winglets gave it a 25 percent improvement in fuel efficiency over the earlier 747s and a 15 percent better fuel consumption rate than the 747-300!

The aggregate effect of these new improvements was to make the 747-400 not only the largest, but the most modern jetliner in the world.

At right: Boeing's first **747-400** during her early flight tests in 1988.

Specifications: Boeing Model 747-400

Span	213 ft
Length	231 ft
Tail Height	63 ft 4 in
Gross Weight	870,000 pounds
Cruising Speed	600mph
Service Ceiling	45,000 ft
Range	8000 miles +
Powerplant	four turbofans: customer choice of Pratt & Whitney PW 4000, Rolls-Royce RB211-524D4D, or General Electric CF6-80C2 (all rated at 56,000 lb thrust)
Capacity	400 +

BOEING VERTOL

About the year 1500 the great artist and engineer Leonardo da Vinci planned a helicopter. His drawing shows an airscrew type machine with a helical wing. When rotated, the wing would have lifted the machine – in theory, at least. However, Leonardo never followed through on his concept, and the idea remained a dream.

Man tinkered with the idea of vertical lift throughout the years. In 1809, Englishman George Cayley published a design for a model helicopter. It worked on the principle of two contra-rotating air screws, and was the subject of much popular attention in Great Britain, for a time. Cayley's model has been the prototype for subsequent experiments in helicopter invention.

In the early 1930s, another inventor, Igor Sikorsky, started design work on helicopters. By 1938 he had produced the Vought-Sikorsky VS-300. Fitted with cyclic pitch control, his machine used a single rotor for lift, the torque being counteracted by two small tail rotors. Tethered to the ground, the VS-300 made a tentative ascent on 14 September 1939. Its first free flight came on 13 May 1940, and it was this flight that ushered the first practical single-rotor helicopter into the airways of the world.

Helicopter development continued under such names as Sikorsky, Bell, Hughes, Hiller, Piasecki and Kaman. Frank Piasecki and a group of young engineers, formed the P-V Engineering Forum in the early 1940s. This organization designed and built the PV-2, which flew first on 11 April 1943. It was the second US helicopter to be flown publicly. The P-V Engineering Forum also developed the PV-3 for the Navy in 1944. It flew on 6 March 1945 and became known as the 'Dog Ship.' Only one PV-3 was manufactured.

In 1946, the company changed its name to the Piasecki Helicopter Corporation. As such, the company designed and built the world's first tandem-rotor helicopter, the XHRP-1. It flew first on 3 November 1946, and two more were sold to the Navy. It was promptly dubbed the 'Banana,' because of its shape. In spite of this shape the XHRP-1 was a success, and the Navy ordered 20 more. Officially called the 'Rescuer,' the less-formal nickname stuck, and is still applied to helicopters with long bodies.

In the late 1950s Piasecki and other helicopter manufacturers were breaking away from piston-driven powerplants and experimenting with turbine engines. The Kaman Aircraft Corporation made its first experiments with a Boeing 520 gas turbine while Piasecki developed the turbine powered YH-16 for the USAF in 1955 and in 1957 delivered the H-21, each with two turbines to the Army. A new era was beginning. During this period also the

Piasecki company became the Vertol Corporation. In 1960 Boeing purchased the business and it became the Vertol Division of the Boeing Company.

On taking over Boeing enlarged the main plant and manufacturing facilities which were located on a 300 acre site in Delaware County, just outside of Philadelphia, Pennsylvania. The complex, today known as Boeing Center, is situated about three miles from the Philadelphia International Airport. Over 2,000,000 square feet of covered area are devoted to the manufacture of helicopters and aircraft assemblies. This huge area includes a 1,250,000-square-foot manufacturing room, engineering and office complexes, and a whirl tower for testing rotor blades. Boeing Vertol has one of the largest wind tunnels in the United States. The company's Flight Test Center is located at the Greater Wilmington Delaware Airport, 25 miles south of Boeing Center. It is situated on an 8.4 acre site, and consists of two buildings, which house computers and automatic data acquisition equipment to monitor helicopter flights. The Test Center is designed to handle the simultaneous flight testing of four helicopters.

In 1972 Boeing's Vertol Division became the Boeing Vertol Company. Since that time, the company has delivered over 2500 tandem-rotor helicopters (in which the company specializes) to the US military services and many foreign nations.

In April 1958 the turbine powered Model 107 made its appearance, and has reached a wide market throughout the world. The first of the 25 passenger Vertol 107-II helicopters was completed for commercial service by New York Airways, in 1961. It replaced the older Vertol 44s, which had gone into service under the Piasecki name in 1956. By 1965, two 107-IIs were transporting a record 44,000 passengers monthly. Also in 1965, Kawasaki

Specifications: CH-46E Sea Knight
Boeing Vertol Model Number 107

Rotor Diameter (each)	51 ft
Fuselage Length	44 ft 10 in
Maximum Weight	23,300 pounds
Top Speed	166 mph
Cruising Speed	150 mph
Range	230 miles plus
Powerplant	two 1870 shp General Electric T58-16

Specifications: CH-113
Boeing Vertol Model Number 107-II

Rotor Diameter (each)	50 ft
Fuselage Length	44 ft 7 in
Maximum Weight	22,000 pounds
Top Speed	168 mph
Cruising Speed	153 mph
Range	750 miles
Powerplant	two 1400 shp General Electric GECT-58-140

Below and opposite: Exterior and interior views of a USMC **CH-46E Sea Knight** helicopter aboard a helicopter carrier.

Above: A US Army **CH-47 Chinook** of the 1st Air Cavalry Division dumps drums of riot-control gas on suspected Vietcong positions during Operation Pershing near Binh Dinh, Vietnam, in July 1967.

Below: A US Army **CH-47** landing to pick up troops in Vietnam.

Heavy Industries of Japan acquired worldwide marketing rights (except for military versions in North America) and continues to produce these helicopters under the designation KV-107/II.

The US Army ordered ten Model 107s in July 1958 under the designation YCH-1A. The first one flew 13 months later, but by that time the Army was more interested in the Vertol Model 114, and the original order was reduced to three.

In 1961, a special version of the Model 107 won a US Navy design competition for a Marine Corps assault transport helicopter. With the primary mission of deploying large numbers of combat-equipped Marines to remote areas, the Sea Knight became operational with squadrons of the Fleet Marine Corps in early 1965. It was originally designated HRB-1 but this was changed to CH-46A.

The CH-46D, a later version, carried a crew of three and up to 25 troops. It could fly 4000 pounds of equipment over a radius of 115 miles at 150mph. This ability was more than twice that of the helicopters it replaced. The CH-46D is essentially similar to the CH-46A, but incorporates 1400shp (shaft horsepower) General Electric T58-GE-10 turboshaft engines. A later version for the Marines added a more advanced avionics package and was designated CH-46F. Some 273 of the USMC Sea Knights are being retrofitted with 1870shp T58-GE-16 turboshafts, and will be redesignated CH-46E. Other CH-46E improvements will

Specifications: CH-47A Chinook
Boeing Vertol Model Number 114

Main Rotor Diameter (each)	59 ft 1¼ in
Fuselage Length	51 ft
Maximum Weight	33,000 pounds
Top Speed	175 mph
Cruising Speed	155 mph
Range	962 miles
Powerplant	two 2200 shp Avco Lycoming T55-L-5

Specifications: CH-47C Chinook
Boeing Vertol Model Number 234

Main Rotor Diameter (each)	60 ft
Fuselage Length	51 ft
Maximum Weight	50,000 pounds
Top Speed	195 mph
Cruising Speed	170 mph
Range	250 miles
Powerplant	two 3750 shp Avco Lycoming T55-L-11A

Specifications: International Military Chinook
Boeing Vertol Model Number 414

Main Rotor Diameter (each)	60 ft
Fuselage Length	51 ft
Maximum Weight	50,000 pounds
Powerplant	two 4500 shp Avco Lycoming T55-L-712

include pilot and co-pilot crash attenuating seats, crash and combat-resistant fuel systems and an improved rescue system. The program is scheduled for completion in 1983.

Another program was launched in 1975 to replace metal rotor blades in the entire US Navy/Marine H-46 helicopter fleet. The more structurally reliable fiberglass blades are to be used. Approximately 2600 fiberglass blades will be replaced during a ten year period.

The Safety, Reliability and Maintainability (SR&M) Program commenced in December 1980. This program will extend the life of another 368 H-46 helicopters. The program includes 29 individual changes, the major changes being complete aircraft rewiring to the current state-of-the-art technology, and an advanced flight control system.

In January 1964 the US Navy ordered another series of Sea Knights, which it designated UH-46A. Its primary duty was in replenishment of combat ships. Since 1964 additional orders for the Model 107 have been placed by the Royal Canadian Air Force, where it is known as the CH-113 Labrador. It is also employed by the Canadian Army as the CH-113 Voyager. The Royal Swedish Navy and Air Force both ordered the 107 using the designation HKP-4, for both services.

The Boeing Vertol Model 114 is a larger, more powerful version of the Model 107. It was originally evaluated by the US

Army under the designation YHC-1B in September 1961. It was selected as the Army's Battlefield Mobility helicopter and deliveries began in May 1967 under the designation CH-47A Chinook. Since then the Army has received 354 CH-47As, 108 CH-47Bs and 270 CH-47Cs.

During the Vietnam War, the helicopter matured as a gunship and deployment vessel for combat troops. Wartime exigencies brought out the good and bad points of helicopter transports, but the lessons learned were learned the hard way. Some 5000 helicopters of all types were lost during counter-insurgency (COIN) campaigns. Despite the losses helicopters proved their value and the US military forces are now the largest users of rotor aircraft in the world, with some 9000 machines. This compares to the Soviet Union with 6000 machines.

Because helicopters are often vulnerable to ground fire, a version of the Chinook was built in 1965 with improved protection. Called the Armed/Armored Chinook, it carried a heavy arsenal and enough armor to protect the crew and vital parts against ground fire. A grenade launcher was placed in the nose, and was turret mounted, controlled by the pilot. The flanks were protected by four gunners, two on each side of the cabin, using either 7.62mm or .50 caliber machine guns on flexible mounts. Another gunner was stationed aft on the rear loading ramp. A new type of steel armor plate was built into crew seats and other steel plates were positioned to deflect hostile bullets from different vital areas of the aircraft. Over a ton of steel plate was installed, assuring a high degree of survivability. This version served in Vietnam.

More recently a CH-47 Modernization Program has begun which will result in 436 of the earlier version CH-47A/B/Cs being upgraded and redesignated CH-47D. This new version will extend the life, increase the operational capabilities and lower the operating costs of the Army's medium-lift helicopter fleet. The CH-47 Modernization Program meets these goals at the lowest possible cost. At present, 28 aircraft have been contracted for with the Army, with 24 in the DOD FY 1983 budget request. Production is planned to continue into the early 1990s.

Modernization of the first CH-47D aircraft has been completed with the initial flight taking place on 26 February 1982, 13 days ahead of schedule. Before undergoing the modernization process, this aircraft had compiled a 2600 flight hour record as a CH-47A. As a completely modernized aircraft, the new CH-47D was delivered to the US Army on 20 May 1982, 11 days ahead of schedule.

The Modernization Program began in 1976 when, after four years of extensive study and review, the Army signed a research and development contract to build three CH-47D model prototypes. These aircraft have since successfully completed an extensive 1500-hour flight test program. During this program, they demonstrated that the CH-47D met or exceeded all of its reliability, availability and maintainability characteristics, as well as providing improved operational capabilities.

These improved operational capabilities were brought about by several new components and systems which have been incorporated into the D model, including improved transmissions with 7500shp rating; redundant and improved electrical systems; fiberglass rotor blades; Avco-Lycoming T55-L-712 engines with emergency power; modularized hydraulic systems; triple cargo hook suspension system; advanced flight control system; improved avionics; aircraft survivability equipment; single point pressure refueling; night vision goggle compatibility and a T62-T-2B auxiliary power unit.

The CH-47 Modernization Program involves more than just the installation of new components and systems. Each aircraft

Specifications:
Model 234 Commercial Chinook
Boeing Vertol Model Number 234

Main Rotor Diameter (each)	60 ft
Fuselage Length	52 ft 1 in
Maximum Weight	51,000 pounds
Top Speed	195 mph
Cruising Speed	170 mph
Range	852 miles
Powerplant	two 3750 shp Avco Lycoming T55-L-11C

Above: Boeing's **Model 234 Commercial Chinook** helicopter began service with British Airways Helicopters during 1981, supporting oil exploration and development activities in the North Sea. Currently, BAH operates five daily round-trip flights to the Shell/Esso Brent platform (seen here), 270 nautical miles offshore. Six of the 44-seat helicopters are used to transport oil workers to offshore platforms from Aberdeen, Scotland. The 234, the helicopter of choice for North Sea oilmen, is now also in service with Norway's Helikopter Service A/S, operating out of Stavanger, Norway. Helikopter Service will shuttle oil-company personnel between their Forus heliport, near Stavanger, and the offshore oil platforms in the Ekofisk and Valhall fields some 170 nautical miles offshore.

Upon entering the Boeing 234, the passenger steps into a comfortable interior whose standup head room, seating, overhead baggage bins, galley service and stereo headphones make it strikingly similar to the interior found on many contemporary jetliners.

Above: The **Chinook HC Mk 1** used by Britain's Royal Air Force is similar to the US Army CH-47C. Several Chinooks were sent to the Falklands in 1982 but only one saw service. The others went down with the container ship *Atlantic Conveyor* which was sunk before they were deployed.

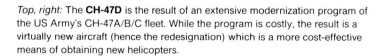

Top, right: The **CH-47D** is the result of an extensive modernization program of the US Army's CH-47A/B/C fleet. While the program is costly, the result is a virtually new aircraft (hence the redesignation) which is a more cost-effective means of obtaining new helicopters.

Second from top, right: The Boeing Vertol **Model 347** first flown in 1970 was a CH-47A which was experimentally retrofitted with 340-square-foot wings.

Right: Developed in partnership with Bell Helicopter Textron, the **V-22 Osprey** tilt-rotor made its first flight on 23 March 1989 at Arlington, Texas. Designed to take off like a helicopter and fly like an airplane, the V-22 has a great deal of potential for both the military and commercial market.

Marine Corps Brig Gen Harry Blot, program manager for the Osprey for Naval Air Systems Command said it 'looked steady as a rock' on its first flight.

At the time of the first flight shown here, procurement plans called for delivery of 552 for the US Marine Corps, 55 for the Air Force and 50 for the Navy. However, within a month, the program had been stricken from the Defense Budget.

is cleaned, stripped to its frame and then separated into sections. When finished, a new aircraft will be available for the Army's use, regardless of its prior history. Each of the three prototypes had logged over 2500 flight hours and was involved in combat operations in Vietnam leading to varying degrees of fuselage damage.

The D model has a maximum gross weight rating of 50,000 pounds, with an empty weight of 23,189 pounds. It can also be used for external load lifting with its center cargo hook rated at 26,000 pounds, while both its forward and aft cargo hooks can move loads as large as 25,000 pounds. This leads to improved operational flexibility which supports the Army field commander's ability to conduct combat operations.

Examples abound of the types of missions only the CH-47D can perform. It can transport the M198 howitzer, the Army's new 155mm artillery piece. It is capable of lifting, with its center cargo hoist, a D5 Caterpillar bulldozer (gross weight 24,750 pounds). It enhances the Army's resupply capability by being able to lift Milvans (Army supply containers) at speeds up to 138 knots, two or three times current capability. It can also carry up to seven fuel blivets (each weighing 3500 pounds when fully loaded) in a single mission.

When compared to the model A Chinook, the CH-47D offers more than a 100 percent increase in performance when operated in a standard European climate. It also offers a 68 percent increase in performance capability when compared to both A and B models when operated in a hot climate.

By modernizing the Chinook fleet the Army will meet its medium-lift helicopter requirements, while saving over $1 billion in development and operating costs. Fleet modernization, rather than designing and developing a new helicopter, has cut the time to field an advanced medium lift helicopter.

Since Boeing Chinook helicopters were introduced in the early 1960s, almost 1000 have been sold in 14 countries. During this period, they have logged more than 1.6 million hours of flight time. While the majority have gone to the US Army as CH-47s, a number have been acquired by the armed services of Canada, Spain, Italy, Iran, Libya, Morocco, Australia, Thailand, Argentina, Tanzania, Greece, Austria, Germany, South Korea, Turkey, Egypt, South Vietnam (before it became part of reunified Vietnam) and the United Kingdom.

Currently production is under way on an order for 33 military Chinooks for the Royal Air Force. First going into service in August 1980 under the RAF designation HCMk I, it incorporates such features as fiberglass blades, triple cargo hooks and an advanced flight control system, all of which will be standard on the US Army CH-47D. A single British Chinook saw action in the Falklands in 1982. The similar international military Chinook, Vertol Model 414, is also going into service with the Spanish Army's Transport Battalion, BHELTRA-V. The first of the Spanish 414s, powered by Avco-Lycoming T55-L-712 engines, was delivered in June 1982.

The Chinook has a combat-proven record of achieving rapid deployment of men and materiel. It can transport up to 44 combat personnel to new positions in minutes, carry up to 14 tons with its three-hook system or accommodate up to 24 litters for medevac operations.

In addition to its combat service, the Chinook has been an important vehicle in rescue and relief missions. Chinooks have proven especially valuable in moving people and goods to and from remote areas made even more inaccessible by the ravages of natural disasters. In the early 1970s US Army CH-47Cs rescued people stranded on a mountainside in Huaraz, Peru after a disastrous earthquake made the town inaccessible. A few years later, US Army Chinooks were again put into service in the after-

Above: The fuselage of Vertol's **Heavy-Lift Helicopter (HLH)** (Boeing Vertol Model 301). The prototype, designated XCH-62A, was powered by three 8079shp XT701 turboshaft engines.

math of earthquakes in Guatemala and Nicaragua. Spanish Army Chinooks were also used during the mid-70s for disaster relief, rescuing thousands of people that had been stranded by flood waters in rural areas. The US Army used some of its CH-47Bs to lift cars and trucks stranded by the eruption of Mount St Helens in May 1980. When President Jimmy Carter made an inspection of the disaster site, he and his entourage were aboard Army Chinooks.

Just as Kawasaki in Japan obtained a manufacturing license for the Model 107, so has the Agusta Group of Cascina Costa, Italy been licensed by Vertol to manufacture the Chinook. The Agusta Group has Chinook sales and service contracts throughout the world as well as in Italy. While Boeing Vertol has licensed foreign firms to manufacture its products abroad, it has itself obtained a license to market the German Messerschmitt-Bölkow-Blohm Bo-105 executive and utility helicopter in Canada, Mexico and the United States.

In November 1978 the Boeing Vertol Company introduced its first commercial Model 234 Chinook, which was ordered by British Airways Helicopters, Ltd. BAH ordered three and has since placed orders for three more.

There are two versions of the 234. The 234LR (Long Range) is a passenger carrier and the other, the 234UT (Utility), is a cargo carrier. The 44-seat 234LR features the most restful and attractive helicopter interior ever developed. Major features

for external lift missions, giving it an external lift capacity of 14 tons for altitudes up to 12,000 feet. It is particularly useful in logging operations and in mining efforts far from the beaten path in high mountains or deep jungles. The 234 Utility is powered with the same Lycoming engines as the passenger ship.

In response to a US Army competition aimed at producing a successor to the ubiquitous Bell UH-1 Huey assault/transport helicopter, Boeing Vertol developed the YUH-61A which was flown in competition with Sikorsky's YUH-60A. The competition and flight testing concluded in December 1976, with Sikorsky being declared the winner. The YUH-61A was a twin engined advanced technology helicopter with a unique hingeless rotor system with a lightweight titanium hub and four fiberglass rotor blades. The prototype could accommodate up to 20 troops or mixtures of troops and materiel.

Vertol's parallel development of the commercial version, Model 179, ended at the same time with again a single prototype. This machine remains in company service and can carry 14–20 passengers.

For the future, Boeing Vertol has plans for a BV-234-68, which is a stretched version of the 234. If British Airways Helicopters gives the green light, the machine could be ready by 1985. The BV-234-68 would have two 5000shp T64/T5A engines, and a gross weight of 51,500 pounds. At a cruising speed of 160mph, with 68 passengers, its range is calculated at 345 miles.

The BV-234-68 will be an improvement insofar as passenger and cargo capacity are concerned, but Boeing Vertol plans to beat even that. The company's proposed BV-307, seating 225, makes its older brothers seem small. The BV-307 would be operational by 1989.

The company was recently awarded a contract to continue such heavy lift helicopter (HLH) studies. Forging ahead on all fronts, commercial and military, Boeing Vertol is following in its parent company's footsteps. Where the latest developments are, there, too, is Boeing Vertol. When better helicopters are in the sky, Boeing will have representatives among them.

include stand-up headroom, a refreshment galley, a lavatory and in-flight music. There are large jumbo-jet type overhead baggage bins, and 727 style windows. The lighting is soft and there is carpeting on the deck.

The 234 was certified for passenger operations by the FAA on 19 June 1981. It was certified to a maximum gross take-off weight of 48,500 pounds, and for full day/night IFR (bad weather) operations. Approval for British passenger service was received when the Civil Aviation Authority issued its Airworthiness Approval Note on 26 June 1981.

The 234 began scheduled passenger service with BAH on 1 July 1981, and is currently used in transporting workers to off-shore oil platforms in the North Sea. Nearly 41,500 passengers were carried during its first seven months of service, such service made possible by its bad-weather capabilities, substantial fuel reserves and a cruising speed of 135 knots. It has a 574 nautical mile flight range. It is powered by twin Avco Lycoming AL5512 engines, each delivering a continuous rating of 2975shp. Should one of the powerplants fail, its twin can be boosted to an emergency rating of 4355shp to bring the 234 safely home. For flights over the stormy North Sea, passengers would not have it any other way. The engines are podded and are easily accessible for maintenance.

The Utility 234 was certified by the FAA on 2 October 1981. It was approved for a maximum gross weight of 51,000 pounds

Specifications: YUH-61A
Boeing Vertol Model Number 179

Main Rotor Diameter	49 ft
Fuselage Length	51 ft 9 in
Maximum Weight	18,700 pounds
Top Speed	195 mph
Cruising Speed	190 mph
Range	300 miles plus
Powerplant	two 1500 shp General Electric T700-GE-700

Specifications: Commercial Model 179
Boeing Vertol Model Number 179

Main Rotor Diameter	49 ft
Fuselage Length	51 ft 9 in
Maximum Weight	18,700 pounds
Top Speed	220 mph
Cruising Speed	200 mph
Range	475 miles
Powerplant	two General Electric GE-CT7-1

THE OTHER BOEING

The Boeing Company has passed through many changes since it began in 1916, but its primary aim has been to build airplanes. This is now closely partnered with the manufacture of missiles for national defense, and with inventing spaceships for probing the universe. There is another Boeing, though, one that investigates such terrestrial activities as computer technology, automated transit systems, agriculture, and even ships that fly.

As early as 1910, Bill Boeing showed his interest in boats when he purchased the E W Heath Shipyard in Seattle. Though his primary interest in the yard was to build a yacht for himself, the shipyard became a part of the Boeing airplane factory and Boeing's interest in boats remained.

In 1919 three years after the first flight of Boeing's first airplane, he became involved in developing the Hickham Sea Sled. The venture failed, but Boeing in the meantime became acquainted with Professor Frederick Kirsten of the University of Washington. Kirsten was interested in designing a cycloidal propeller and joined Boeing to form a company, K-B Engineering, to develop the idea. A sports boat, the M-879, was constructed to test the propeller, and it was launched in August 1922. According to eyewitnesses, the M-879 was provided 'substantial forward propul-

Right: The US Navy **PHM-2 Hydrofoil Missileship** built by Boeing Marine Systems at Renton was delivered to the Navy in 1972. The PHM-2 and her four sister ships are nearly 133 feet long, 28 feet wide and are powered by two Mercedes-Benz 8V331 diesels driving two Aerojet waterjets when hullborne and one GE LM2500 gas turbine with one waterjet when foilborne. The PHMs have a speed in excess of 40 knots when foilborne and a range of over 1200 nautical miles if hullborne. (The range is cut in half if the foils are deployed for the entire distance.) They carry a 21-man crew and are armed with eight Harpoon missiles and a 76mm rapid-fire gun.

Below: The *Bima Samudera* is a **Model 929 Jetfoil** built for the government of the Republic of Indonesia and delivered in 1982.

sion,' by its cycloidal propeller. The propeller also enabled the boat to turn on its own axis. The boat moved easily in shallow water, a forerunner of today's marine jet engines.

However, the project proved too costly for it to go into commercial production. Boat and prop would also be too expensive to maintain, and after sinking $150,000 into the venture, Boeing wrote off the K-B experiment in 1927.

Several Boeing officials were enthusiastic about the cyclodial propeller idea, though, and tinkered with the idea of using them instead of wings in a modified PW-9 pursuit aircraft. The propeller, it was believed, would give the airplane the ability to take off and land vertically. In effect, they were thinking 'vertol.' The company contracted Army and Navy engineers with their radical idea, but there was no money for such a project, and the matter was shelved. Had experiments taken place, Sikorsky, the helicopter pioneer, might have come in second.

In 1959 the Boeing company's interest in boats was renewed, when hydrofoil research began. Research culminated in 1960, with the completion of a hydroplane test craft. Constructed mainly of mahogony plywood, the boat was nicknamed 'Aquajet.' From above it looked like a giant lobster, with two prows reaching forward, each with a cockpit and instrument compartment. The open center was used like a wind tunnel for preliminary hydrodynamic testing.

Specifications: Jetfoil
Boeing Model Number 929

Cruising speed	42-45 knots
Weight	115 long tons
Length	90 ft
Beam	30 ft
Powerplant	two Allison 501-KF turbines, with two Rockedyne PJ-20 waterjet pumps. Engines rated at 3800 hp each
Crew	Two-six, depending on need

In 1962 Boeing Marine Systems (BMS), built another experimental boat, the *Little Squirt*. It was a company-financed vessel, built to prove the feasibility of waterjet propulsion, a system later used on all Boeing hydrofoils. *Little Squirt* demonstrated that hydrofoils have a 50 knot capability, an important quality. Speed was one of the requisites if hydrofoils were to compete with boats of conventional and proven capabilities.

It is generally agreed that airplanes belong in the air, boats on water, but it is different with hydrofoils. They seem to fly over the waves on waterborne wing-like structures. Attached to the hull by a system of struts, the foils lift the boat several feet above the surface, using water in the same way as airplane wings generate lift, allowing the boat to travel with its main bulk unaffected by water resistance.

There are two basic types of hydrofoil boats. On one, the foils ride on or near the surface of the water, following its contours, rising and dipping with the waves. At times this can let passengers in for a rough ride. A number of vessels using this type of foil are currently in use, mainly in Europe and Asia.

The other hydrofoil operates with its foils fully submerged. Being completely under water, this hydrofoil is unaffected by waves and other surface turbulence. The result is a smooth ride, even in rough water. BMS builds several different types of vessels with completely submerged foils.

Working on Navy contracts, BMS has experimented with a variety of hydrofoils. In 1965 the Navy awarded a contract to Boeing to build a hydrofoil gunboat. Named *Tucumcari* after the city in New Mexico, it was the first of its kind in naval history.

Designated PGH-2, for Patrol Gunboat Hydrofoil-2, the *Tucumcari* was launched in July 1967, and 'flew' first in October. The vessel did not have a conventional propeller, but used Boeing's waterjet system of propulsion. Water was drawn through the craft's rear foil struts into a pump, then jetted through nozzles under the stern. There were no lubrication problems and no complicated transmission system as is required on propeller craft. A 3100shp gas turbine supplied the foil-borne power, while a second waterjet pump, powered by a 150bhp diesel, drove the ship during slower hull-borne operations.

The *Tucumcari* was 74.6 feet long, with a 19.5 foot beam, and was capable of speeds over 50 knots. It displaced approximately 60 tons, and the hull and superstructure were aluminum. The foils and struts were of corrosion-resistant steel. This swift little ship, a relative of the World War II PT-Boats, was manned by one officer and 12 crewmen. She had a short, but noble, history. After serving in the coastal waters off Vietnam, she was assigned to the Navy's Amphibious Force at Little Creek, Virginia. She became the prototype for the Patrol Hydrofoil Missileship (PHM). In the fall of 1972, the *Tucumcari* ran aground in the Caribbean and was decommissioned.

In November 1971 BMS was awarded a contract to design the Patrol Hydrofoil Missileship. With years of experience to draw on, BMS produced a satisfactory plan, and the company was awarded a construction contract.

On 9 November 1974, the first missileship, *Pegasus*, was launched. Designated PHM-1 by the Navy, she made her first 'flight' on 25 February 1975. In October that year, *Pegasus* made a record sailing from Seattle to San Diego in 31 hours and 21 minutes, averaging 37 knots. As the ship was 131.2 feet long, with a beam of 28.2 feet, and a displacement of 239.6 long tons, such speed was to be noted. It was, and a contract for five more PHMs was granted. Named after the constellations, as was the first, they are the *Hercules*, PHM-2, *Taurus*, PHM-3; *Aquila*, PHM-4; *Aries*, PHM-5 and *Gemini*, PHM-6.

Fully submerged foils and advanced automatic control systems give PHM the missile platform stability and ride comfort in heavy seas usually found only in large ships. A powerful offensive armament makes the PHM an effective weapons system for strike, patrol and surveillance missions. Waterjet systems, pioneered by Boeing, speed the craft along, when flying on its foils, or when traveling on its hull. The foil-borne system consists of a single Aerojet Liquid Rocket Company waterjet capable of pumping approximately 90,000 gallons per minute.

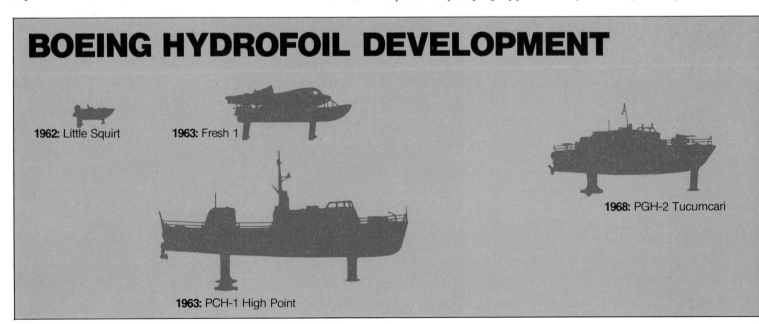

BOEING HYDROFOIL DEVELOPMENT

1962: Little Squirt

1963: Fresh 1

1963: PCH-1 High Point

1968: PGH-2 Tucumcari

It is driven by a General Electric LM 2500 marine gas turbine. When hull borne the ship is powered by two 30,000gpm Aerojet waterjets. Each is driven by a Mercedes-Benz 8V331 diesel engine. Foil-borne cruising speed is in excess of 40 knots. The ship can be operated by as few as six officers and men on any watch, but berthing is provided for 24. The normal crew is 21, four officers and 17 enlisted personnel.

Boeing is not excluding the commercial possibilities of hydrofoils, and BMS has developed the *Jetfoil*. Hailed as a new dimension in marine transportation, the *Jetfoil* hydrofoil for commercial passenger use was announced in October 1972. The first one, Model 929-100, was launched 29 March 1974. Jetfoil service was initiated on 25 April 1975 by Far East Hydrofoil Ltd between Hong Kong and Macao.

The Jetfoil combines fully submerged, computer-controlled steel foils on an all-aluminum hull. Ride quality is unmatched by any other marine craft, assuring all passengers an unobstructed view, smooth and serene, even in rough seas. Environmentally, the Jetfoil claims kudos, too. Because only narrow struts pierce the water when foil borne, there is almost no wake. The Jetfoil is so well constructed that it had no problem finding certification in such diverse countries as the US, China, Venezuela, Belgium, Japan and Britain.

The ship has a 30-foot wide cabin, which allows for two decks with large seats. The standard configuration Jetfoil, the Model 929-100, can carry up to 250 passengers and provide space for luggage and galleys. Design flexibility permits variations according to what the customer needs, and as many as 350 seats can be provided.

Jetfoils are now in use throughout the world, from China to the Republic of Indonesia, making a total fleet of 18 vessels. A derivative, HMS *Speedy* (Model 929-115) was built for the British Royal Navy for North Sea patrols. Though the US has not used this remarkable design yet, it seems likely that the foreign market will expand.

In the spring of 1950, Lloyd Hull tested a Kenworth truck using a Model 502 175hp Boeing-developed gas turbine. Truckers who saw the twin-stacked vehicle were curious. They liked the engine, because the 502 weighed only 200 pounds. A standard diesel engine could weigh up to 2500 pounds. By any trucker's definition, that difference meant profits in the payload cargo. Development of the 502 continued, but *Boeing Magazine* for July 1951 revealed that the gas turbine seemed destined for a military rather than a commercial career. Pinpointing it further, the 502 was being tested on Navy boats in Lake Washington, adjacent to Seattle.

Improved 502s in the 240–330hp range were tested on everything military from tanks to helicopters to hydrofoils to pumps. A 520 series was developed by Boeing's Industrial Products Division, producing up to 600hp. Still another model was able to net 550hp. It might be pointed out here that Boeing had reserved model numbers 500–599 for industrial non-aircraft products. Models 502, 520, 540, 551 and 553 were gas turbine engines.

There were many firsts for Boeing gas turbines. They included the world's first turbine and twin turbine helicopters, first turbine highway truck, first turbine locomotive, commercial boat, earthmoving tractor, racing car, minesweeper and landing craft.

The market for the Boeing turbine seemed assured, but in 1969 the business was phased out. Competitors were making good products, and Boeing decided not to compete. The company decided that the money used on gas turbine development could be better employed on new airplanes and aerospace research. So Boeing bowed out.

With the swift proliferation of computers throughout the world, Boeing set up the Boeing Computer Service, BCS, in 1970. Its purpose was twofold: to fulfill the data processing requirements of The Boeing Company and to offer advanced information processing services to commercial and government markets. It currently services more than 2500 customers in the US, Canada, and Britain. To transmit data reliably and economically, BCS operates one of the largest privately managed telecommunications networks in the world. Major data centers are located in Philadelphia, Wichita, Vienna (Virginia) near Washington, DC, and two in the Seattle metropolitan area at Bellevue and Kent.

The people of BCS provide computer support services for business, scientific, engineering, industrial and government uses, as well as nationwide consulting, educational and other training services.

Ten years after its inception, the number of BCS commercial customers had risen to over 2500, including a substantial number of very large corporations. Because of increased demand for commercial data processing services in the fields of financial management and design engineering, BCS is emphasizing products relevant to these activities. Under one such contract, electronic funds transfer services are being provided to a con-

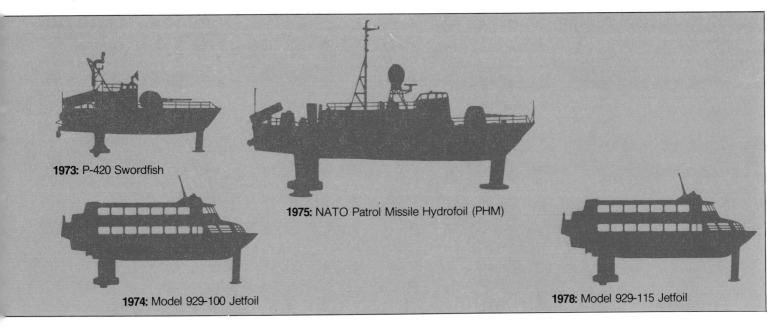

1973: P-420 Swordfish

1975: NATO Patrol Missile Hydrofoil (PHM)

1974: Model 929-100 Jetfoil

1978: Model 929-115 Jetfoil

Above: A **Model 929** jetfoil in service with Sealink on the English Channel.

Above right: The US Navy's **PHM-3** during trials on Puget Sound in 1982.

sortium of 22 mutual savings banks in New York City. Under another contract, BCS provides computer software and large scale data processing to 41 banks in the midwest.

In addition to its many major corporate customers, ranging from IBM's Federal Systems Division to the Exxon Product Research Company, BCS provides computer support for the Federal Energy Center in Richland, Washington and NASA's Marshall Space Flight Center in Huntsville, Alabama. The US General Accounting Office selected BCS to design and operate a consolidated computer system for use in managing assignments, finance and personnel.

BCS computers are now integrated into nearly every step of aircraft design and production at Boeing's aircraft divisions. They aided in the design and production of the new 757 and 767

aircraft, and then went on to provide computer support for the flight certification programs. Such certification can be accomplished quickly, because of new computing programs developed by BCS software engineers. The system verifies the validity of test conditions inflight.

In 1974, the Boeing Engineering and Construction organization was formed. The purpose was to use Boeing's engineering experience in exploring the tasks of producing energy and improving the environment.

Today, BEC is working with government agencies, utility composites and other companies on a variety of assignments. Projects include the development of wind, nuclear and solar power generating systems; energy control systems; the recovery of energy from waste; off-shore oil production and water systems management. In addition to all this BEC has become involved in construction and design.

The accomplishments of BEC have been many. The company manufactures centrifuge machines for nuclear fuel enrichment.

Below: Boeing's **Standard Light Rail Vehicle** in service with the Municipal Railway in San Francisco.

The design and construction of a fuel-enrichment facility for the Department of Energy in Oak Ridge, Tennessee was undertaken by BEC and two other contractors.

BEC has also taken a world lead in the design and development of large wind energy systems. In August 1977 the company was awarded a contract to design a wind turbine system, specifically tailored for unattended, remote operation. The contract called for the construction, installation and testing of three machines. The MOD-2 wind turbine is the largest ever built. Power production starts at a wind speed of 14mph with an automatic shutdown at 45mph. The MOD-2 utilizes a two-blade steel rotor that measures 300 feet from tip to tip. The rotor is mounted to the nacelle, a 37 foot long boxcar-shaped structure that houses the drive train, turbine-generator, electronics and other equipment. The nacelle is rotated by a mechanism that always keeps the rotor pointing into the wind. The whole arrangement is perched atop a 200-foot tall tubular steel tower.

The first three MOD-2 units, located near Goldendale, Washington, are part of the Bonneville Power Administration's power network. Ground was broken in May 1980, and all three units were synchronized with BPA a year later.

With the MOD-2 in successful operation, the future seems assured for megawatt-size wind machines as an important factor in the world's energy mix. Others are interested in the system and among them is the Pacific Gas and Electric Company of San Francisco. Boeing made its first commercial sale to PG&E in 1980. Another MOD-2 had been installed in Medicine Bow, Wyoming, under a program funded by the Federal Department of the Interior.

BOECON, a Boeing general construction subsidiary which has focused in part on nuclear power plants, is gradually expanding into the areas of water pumping stations and coal-fired electric power plants.

Solar energy projects have included the conceptual design of a commercial size plant that will utilize the sun's rays to generate power which would operate an evaporator to clean polluted water and make it potable for a small Texas town. Two advanced heliostats (sun-tracking mirrors) have been completed and successfully tested at a New Mexico test site.

Near Colorado Springs BEC has constructed a pair of Brine Concentrators that process 576,000 gallons of water daily, returning 98 percent of it for reuse in a coal-fired power plant. Work is now underway on similar projects in New Mexico, Nevada and Texas.

Boeing Services International (BSI), Incorporated provides services that benefit a variety of customers and programs. BSI was formed in 1972 as a wholly owned subsidiary of The Boeing Company to devote its total skill and resources to facilities operations and maintenance and technical support activities. BSI was a natural outgrowth of The Boeing Company's Field Operations and Support Division, which managed large government programs and supported launch operations for the nation's manned and unmanned space programs.

From this experience, the company developed a large manpower pool whose skills range through such diverse catagories as facilities operations and maintenance, spares support, systems installation and checkout, test operations, heavy equipment and vehicle maintenance, fire protection, supply, transport, aerospace ground systems operations and administration.

Below: The US Department of Energy's **Solar Test Facility** at Albuquerque, New Mexico. The spot of light on the tower is a 13-foot diameter cavity receiver designed and built by BEC and tested here at the Albuquerque facility. During the three months of testing, an increasing number of computer-controlled reflectors called heliostats was focused on the receiver. The receiver is designed to transfer the intense heat of the concentrated sunlight to a working fluid (in this case air) which in turn drives a turbine to produce electricity. Power levels reached the design condition of one megawatt, with a gas outlet temperature of 1500 degrees Fahrenheit.

Specifications: MOD-2 Wind Turbine

Rotor Diameter	300 ft
Tower Height	200 ft
Tower Diameter	21 ft (base)
	10 ft (main shaft)
Rotor Orientation	Upwind
Rotor Airfoil	NACA 230XX
Rotor Tip Speed	275 ft/second
Rotor Speed	17.5 rpm
Rotor Tip Length (controllable)	45 ft
Rated Power	2.5 Megawatts
Average Annual Output	7.4 million kilowatt hrs
Generator Type	Synchronous
Pitch and Yaw Control	Hydraulic
Electronic Control	Microprocessor

Below: The Boeing **MOD-2** wind farm. Three giant wind turbines at the Goodnoe Hills near the Columbia River Gorge (upper left) in Washington State are now working together for the first time in the only multi-megawatt wind-turbine cluster in the US. To date they have produced more than two million kilowatt hours of electricity. The 2500 kilowatt MOD-2 wind turbines were designed and built by BEC under a program sponsored by the US Department of Energy and managed by NASA's Lewis Research Center. The output of the three machines, enough to provide electricity to 2000 average homes, is being fed into the Northwest power grid operated by the Bonneville Power Administration. The 350-foot-tall machines (from ground to tip of vertically extended blade), about one-third of a mile apart, are designed to begin producing power in winds of 14mph. They reach rated output in winds of 28mph, and when the wind exceeds 45mph, the blades automatically feather, shutting down the system.

The **MOD-5**, now in the detail design phase, represents the third generation of multi-megawatt machines. Analysis indicates that this machine will offer up to a 25 percent reduction in the cost of electricity compared to the MOD-2 under similar conditions.

Overseas, BSI provides support services ranging from traffic management and food services to communications and vehicle maintenance for eight major US military installations in Turkey and at USAF bases in Spain.

In October 1979 BSI was awarded a third European base maintenance contract at Hellenikon Air Base at Athens, and Iraklion on the island of Crete, together with five smaller sites in Greece. Boeing sells its support services by demonstrating that a private contractor can save money for the government. At a typical military installation, for example, turning over service functions to BSI can reduce manpower costs by as much as 25 percent. This also permits uniformed personnel to devote more of their time to combat-related duties.

Early in 1971 diversification was a watchword among many American corporations. Boeing was no different and in that year the company moved into the surface transportation field. Boeing Vertol was selected as systems manager for the Federal Government's Urban Rapid Rail Vehicle and Systems Program. One type was designed using traditional technology, whereas the other was an Advanced Concept Train (ACT) car for demonstrating the next generation of rapid transit cars. The 'current technology' train, designated SOAC, and consisting of two cars, was demonstrated on transit systems in New York, Boston, Cleveland, Chicago and Philadelphia.

Boeing Vertol also received contracts to build Light Rail Vehicles (LRV) for Boston and San Francisco. In both instances they were designed to replace existing streetcars on established routes. Vertol, the maker of helicopters, found itself blessed with the distinction of building the first streetcars to have been built in the United States in 20 years.

The two LRV contracts called for 175 cars to be delivered to the Massachusetts Bay Transportation Authority (MBTA), and 100 cars for the San Francisco Municipal Railway (MUNI). San Francisco, the city where the century-old cable cars 'climb half way to the stars,' was in the midst of a sort of transit revolution. The Bay Area Rapid Transit (BART) subway system was, after

years of bickering and delay, finally nearing completion and it was time to upgrade the city's streetcar system. BART is, in reality, more of a commuter railroad than a city transit system. With most of its stations located outside of the city limits and only one line actually running through the city, BART's primary function is to bring commuters to their jobs in downtown San Francisco. MUNI is San Francisco's real transit system, operating streetcars, buses and cable cars on hundreds of lines throughout the city. The excavation of Market Street, the city's transit hub, for installation of BART, provided MUNI with an opportunity to do something that they had wanted to do for many years. This was to put their streetcars underground along congested Market Street. The process was haunted by problems, not the least of which being that Market Street was a construction site for ten years, with many of the businesses located there abandoning it for adjacent streets. BART's problems could fill volumes, but MUNI's Vertol LRV had its share, among the most embarrassing of which were that initially the LRV's wheels were the wrong size for the tracks.

MBTA had problems too, but in November 1979 a settlement was reached resolving all outstanding disputes, claims and counter claims. In April 1980 the final MUNI LRVs were delivered, and after many teething troubles, the MUNI Metro, as the MUNI LRV system is called, is functioning according to plan and Market Street is slowly being revitalized.

Though the Boeing Vertol Company has withdrawn from the manufacturing of surface transportation vehicles after the costly experiments in Boston and San Francisco, in 1980 it received subcontracts from Kawasaki Heavy Industries to install equipment on LRVs and other rail transit cars for use in Philadelphia.

The Boeing Aerospace Company also became involved in ground transportation. A number of cities are looking for entirely new methods of transportation. Many major metropolitan governments are preparing to install a form of automated transit called Downtown People Movers in their central business districts. The project is being funded by the US Department of Transportation.

At present, there is only one automated transit system in operation in an urban setting. This is the People Mover at Morgantown, West Virginia. It was developed by BAC for the Department of Transportation's Urban Mass Transportation Administration (UMTA) and West Virginia University. It emerged from a long development and testing program to enter passenger service in October 1975. By 1979 expansion of the Morgantown People Mover's system was completed. It is 3.3 miles long, with a total of 8.7 miles of single-lane guideway, five passenger stations, and 73 vehicles.

The MPM system employs driverless vehicles which operate entirely under computer control. The cars cruise at up to 30mph, and being rubber-tired, they are virtually noiseless. They carry 21 passengers each, and can function in both good and bad weather. Though not yet perfected, the Downtown People Mover's program has attracted the attention of Los Angeles, Detroit, Miami, and St Paul. Such transportation seems to be the answer to smog problems, because it is electrically powered.

By 1977 the system was operating at an availability (reliability) rate of close to 100 percent and university students were being whisked from campus to campus in less than 10 minutes. Carrying some 17,000 passengers a day, it has demonstrated that automated guideway systems are now ready to serve cities much larger than Morgantown. The expanded MPM system is expected to have a ridership of six million passengers a year.

Operating statistics compiled at Morgantown indicate that such a system can achieve a lower cost per passenger-mile than

Specifications: Standard Light Rail Vehicle

Length	73 ft
Seating Capacity	68 persons
Peak Capacity	190 persons
Car Weight	69,000 pounds
Max Acceleration Rate	3.1 mph per second
Max Deceleration Rate	6 mph per second
Propulsion System	D/C traction motors at 230 hp

today's urban bus systems. Its vehicles operate under the control of computers rather than drivers, and their movement is dictated strictly by passenger needs. This eliminates one of the principal causes of today's mounting transit deficits: manned buses traveling their routes nearly empty during off-peak hours. In the US the average load factor for buses is 18 percent; that is, the average bus runs 82 percent empty. Present load factor for the expanded Morgantown system is 33 percent.

Though Morgantown is generally viewed as the prototype for the coming forms of urban automated transit, it was preceded into public service by a similar system developed by Boeing and Kobe Steel of Japan for the International Ocean Exposition on the Japanese island of Okinawa, the 1975 World's Fair.

The Okinawa system, derived from Morgantown technology, linked major exhibits at the exposition with the main entrances to the site. During the fair's six-month run, the system's 16 vehicles carried more than four million riders. For its final six weeks of operation, the system maintained an availability of 99.5 percent.

Though future roles of the automated transit function will be determined by the nation's major cities, the idea has been proven in Morgantown. If People Movers succeed, they will owe their existence to this first successful experiment.

Turning its attention even farther from the sky than transit systems, the Boeing Aerospace Company leased 100,000 acres of land near Boardman, Oregon in the early 1960s. Until BAC came to the scene, the land was considered fit only for sagebrush and jackrabbits. The vast deserts of eastern Oregon and Washington State surprise tourists since both states are known more for mountains and evergreen forests.

Though the land was leased for testing rockets and jet engines, Boeing engineers did some thinking. A pump was installed to bring water from the Columbia River to a small section of the 100,000 acre site. Beginning in 1972 potatoes were harvested. By 1975, 8300 acres were considered prime farmland, proving that the Oregon desert could successfully be made to bloom.

Other companies, following Boeing's lead, have moved into the Boardman area, and have placed nearly ten times as much land under irrigation as the area which Boeing developed. Costs were high, about $1.5 million per 1200 acres, the minimum size for an economically feasible farming venture, and only larger combines can afford it.

By the end of 1975, Boeing had met its initial objective in demonstrating desert farming was feasible. An agricultural industry had been started. BAC decided to withdraw from direct involvement in farming, but not from its commitment to developing the region. The Boeing Agri-Industrial Company was formed to handle the business, and it sub-leases to qualified farmers and to agriculturally related industries. About one percent of the nation's potato crop is raised in the region. When potatoes are rotated with wheat, most of the wheat is shipped to the Orient where it is made into noodles.

BOEING AEROSPACE

The Boeing Aerospace Company (BAC) is an operating organization of The Boeing Company, responsible for much of Boeing's military and space efforts. It was created in December 1972 by 'T' Wilson, Boeing's chairman and chief executive officer, and was an outgrowth of the Boeing Aerospace Group. When formed in 1972, BAC employed about 20,000 persons who worked on such programs as Minuteman, Short Range Attack Missile (SRAM), the Subsonic Cruise Armed Decoy (SCAD) and various military applications of commercial airplanes, such as the Airborne Warning and Control Systems (AWACS) and Advanced Airborne Military Command Post aircraft. In the space segment of the organization, BAC was engaged in construction of the S-1C, the first stage of the Apollo Saturn V moonrocket, and the Lunar Rover, the buglike surface vehicle used on the moon by the Apollo astronauts. Much of the diversification effort of The Boeing Company was also originally placed within BAC. This included advanced surface transportation systems such as the Morgantown Personal Rapid Transit

(PRT) program; the Jetfoil and Patrol Hydrofoil Missileship (PHM) ventures and the land irrigation program on the rocket and engine testing site near Boardman, Oregon. In addition to these Washington-based projects, BAC also performs work at the Kennedy Space Center in Florida, and Houston.

In its brief history, BAC has completed such successful work as the Mariner 10 spacecraft which explored Venus and Mercury; a number of small scientific satellites; Burner II and IIA booster programs; the Compass Cope remotely piloted vehicles; Apollo and Skylab related work and the 747 Space Shuttle Carrier Aircraft. Much of the firm's diversification efforts have been spun-off to other newly formed company organizations such as Boeing Marine Systems and Boeing Engineering and Construction. Some, such as advanced surface transportation and the Boardman project, still remain within the aerospace company.

BAC now has its headquarters at the Boeing Space Center built in February 1964 in Kent, south of Seattle, Washington. This 432-acre center also houses BAC's system of highly sophisti-

Below: The **Boeing Space Center** in Kent, Washington, 15 miles south of downtown Seattle, is the headquarters of the Boeing Aerospace Company.

cated laboratories and many of its spacecraft manufacturing facilities.

Minuteman, AWACS, the Airborne Command Post, the Morgantown PRT and SRAM still are part of BAC's product line. Additionally, the company has gained new customers and developed new products with the creation of such equipment as the Roland surface-to-air missile for the Army, and the Applications Explorer Missions' Heat Capacity Mapping Mission (HCMM) and Stratospheric Aerosol Gas Experiment (SAGE) base modules. It is also marketing a mobile asphalt plant under a subsidiary, the Boeing Construction and Equipment Corporation. BAC is engaged in development work for the MX Intercontinental Ballistic Missile system, Air Launched Cruise Missile, space shuttle Inertial Upper Stage, Multiple Launch Rocket System (MLRS) and solar power satellites. It also conducts logistics and support operations throughout the world.

In the late 1950s a visible change had taken place within the airplane industry. Airframe and engine manufacturers continued to astonish the world with improved technology, but there was an exciting newcomer to the field, and that was space. According to John Rae in his study, *Climb to Greatness*, *The American Aircraft Industry 1920–1960*, 'Aerospace was not just a fancy word for airplane, this was the age of missiles and space craft.'

In June 1945 Boeing entered the space age when the company commenced work on their model series 600–602, the Air Force's GAPA (Ground-to-Air-Pilotless Aircraft.) They were remotely controlled supersonic missiles, designed to intercept aircraft flying up to 700mph at altitudes from 6000 to 80,000 feet. GAPA could reach speeds of 1500mph with ramjet engines, and were equipped with a beam-riding guidance system. In November 1949

Above: The **IM-99 Bomarc** Interceptor Missile was designed and deployed at a time when attacks on the US by manned bombers were still a perceived threat.

Specifications:
IM-99B Bomarc Interceptor Missile
Boeing Model Number 631

Wingspan	18 ft 2 in
Overall Length	45 ft
Height	10 ft 2 in
Fuselage Diameter	35 in
Width of Horizontal Tailplane	10 ft 6 in
Powerplants	solid fuel rocket takeoff (Thiokol), 50,000 pounds thrust. Two ramjet engines for cruise (Marquardt), 12,000 pound thrust each
Armament	nuclear warhead
Speed	Mach 2 plus
Operating Altitude	sea-level to 80,000 ft
Range	more than 400 miles
Reaction time	from alert to launch, less than one minute

a GAPA reached an altitude of 59,000 feet, the highest flight for supersonic ramjet propulsion up to then.

After 100 experimental flights, the GAPA program was cancelled, however, but in the meantime Boeing had gained valuable experience in missile technology. When the company was awarded a contract in 1949 to develop its Model 621, the F-99 (later redesignated IM-99) Bomarc interceptor missile, it was ready. The name Bomarc derived from the first two letters in Boeing, and the initials of the Michigan Aeronautical Research Center, which contributed research data for the new missile. In 1951 the development contract was extended by the Air Force, and Boeing's mission was to manufacture a weapon capable of finding and destroying high-speed enemy bombers and missiles. Contact was to take place far from Bomarc's launch sites.

A primitive Bomarc was test-fired in September 1952, and on 24 February 1955, a completely instrumented test version demonstrated operational capabilities. Its two ramjet engines gave it a 200 mile range, far enough from the launch site to satisfy the Air Force.

The first production Bomarc, the IM-99A (Boeing Model 624), was rolled out on 30 December 1957. As production increased the Bomarcs were housed on a constant combat-readiness basis. Upon receiving an alert signal, the shelter roof slid back and the Bomarc was raised on its erector arm to the vertical launching position. The erector then descended, and the missile was fired. The entire process was carried out automatically in 30 seconds.

During practice firings, direct hits were scored on supersonic Regulus II drones, and a radio controlled, pilotless QB-47E jet bomber. On 3 March 1961 an IM-99B (Boeing Model 631), an improved Bomarc, made its first full-range flight, winging over the Gulf of Mexico for more than 400 miles, a considerable improvement over the IM-99A's range. On this test, the IM-99B intercepted a target at an altitude of more than 80,000 feet. The IM-99B used a solid fuel rocket engine, enabling more space to be given to ramjet fuel, which contributed significantly to the increased range.

The Bomarc IM-99A was phased out of operation during 1964, and the last Model B was produced in 1962. The IM-99Bs were eventually retired from service as technology moved beyond them, and more sophisticated missiles appeared. All Bomarc bases were closed in the early 1970s, bringing to an end an important era in missile evolution.

The Bomarc, which was able to deliver effective defense coverage to about 500,000 square miles, was guided by radio command from land-based air defense control centers. In all 570 Bomarcs were produced, including 269 IM-99As with liquid fuel and 301 IM-99Bs with solid fuel.

The Short Range Attack Missile (SRAM), another Boeing product, was developed under a contract awarded in October 1966. After a series of tests, during which a SRAM was fired from the B-52G and B-52H as well as General Dynamics' FB-111, a production contract was issued on 12 January 1971.

The SRAM has two functions: it can attack defensive installations, allowing its parent aircraft, the B-52 or FB-111, to penetrate primary targets. SRAM can on the other hand strike primary targets inside enemy lines. The missile provides the Strategic Air Command a capability never attained before. It can be launched from high or low altitudes, at subsonic or supersonic speed. It can hit targets ahead of the launching aircraft, or can turn in flight to strike objectives to the side or even behind the aircraft.

This versatile missile is 14 feet long, with a diameter of 17.5 inches. It is powered by a Lockheed LPC-415 two-stage solid fuel rocket, with another as a cruising engine. It carries a W-69 nuclear warhead, with an explosive yield of 200 kilotons. Its performance is remarkable in that it reaches speeds of Mach 3, with a hundred mile range. It was designed to destroy last-ditch enemy defenses, especially surface-to-air missile sites. A B-52 can carry eight internally, and 12 under its wings in clusters of six. The F-111 carries two internally and four under its wings.

On 30 July 1975 Boeing delivered its 1500th, and final, SRAM. By the end of the program, the missile had exceeded contract requirements in range, accuracy and reliability. Many people were involved in manufacturing SRAM. There were seven major companies among the 60 primary subcontractors.

In July 1960 Boeing signed a $247 million contract with the Air Force to continue the development of the silo-based Minuteman ICBM (named after the heroes of the Revolutionary War). Boeing had already completed two years of research on this missile for which the company received high praise. Brigadier General Don Coupland, commander of the AF Ballistic Missiles Center said, 'The company's on-schedule efforts have been important factors in the success of the Minuteman development program.'

The general also commented on the success of the first silo-launch tests at Edwards AFB. The tests, he said, saved the taxpayer some $20 million dollars. Eight Minuteman missiles were launched without a hitch.

Since 1962, the Minuteman ICBM system has been America's primary deterrent to nuclear aggression. It was nicknamed 'the instant missile,' because it is constantly ready for immediate firing. Supporting those missiles is a US Air Force/Industry team dedicated to maintaining Minuteman as an effective preventative to large scale conflict. The Boeing Company assists the Air Force in training Minuteman crews, though the missile is so designed as to eliminate the need for skilled manpower in the field. Boeing also keeps the Minuteman up-to-date as strategic requirements demand. They can be upgraded readily and at a comparatively low cost.

Deployment of the Minuteman is mainly in the midwest. Less than three years after production began, 800 Minuteman I missiles nested in underground silos were on the alert with SAC wings located in Montana, South Dakota, North Dakota, Missouri and a three-state complex centered at Warren AFB, Wyoming.

An improvement program called 'Force Modernization,' was started in 1964. It called for replacing Minuteman I missiles with Minuteman II and III. The missile silos were also upgraded.

Another wing, centered at Grand Forks, North Dakota, and armed with the larger and more powerful Minuteman II, became operational in December 1965. Minuteman II is also deployed in another 50 missile squadron near Malmstrom AFB, Montana. When this squadron installation was completed during the first half of 1967, the Minuteman force had achieved its goal of 1000 missiles.

The improvements in Minuteman II are greater range and accuracy and an upgraded guidance system. It can deliver a heavier payload over greater distances. Minuteman III incorporates all the II improvements, and carries three independently targeted warheads, a very important advance. The Minuteman missile uses a special truck-tractor for transporting it between various Air Force bases, and the last of these, also built by Boeing, went to the Air Force in February 1982. In addition to its instant readiness, great efficiency and accuracy, the Minuteman missile was attractive to the Air Force because it was cheaper to build than its predecessors, the Atlas and Titan.

The Minuteman system is a vital part of the US strategic triad. This is a combination of land-based ICBMs, submarine-launched missiles, and the manned strategic bomber. An aggressor seeking to overcome this force must be able to mobilize enormous resources in both offensive and defensive weapons. This triad forms America's deterrent to nuclear attack. With the Minuteman and B-52, Boeing has made a significant contribution to that triad.

One of the most dramatic and deadly of the Boeing missiles is the ALCM, the Air Launched Cruise Missile. Conceived as a weapon to be carried by the B-52 and the Rockwell International B-1 supersonic bomber, the first test flight took place in 1976, from a B-52. The Boeing Aerospace Company was responsible for the ALCM on which development began in 1974, after the SCAD (Subsonic Cruise Armed Decoy)

Specifications: Minuteman ICBM Series

Diameter	6 ft (at widest point)
Length	Minuteman I (LGM-30A) 54 ft
	Minuteman I (LGM-30B) 55.9 ft
	Minuteman II (LGM-30F) 59.8 ft
	Minuteman III (LGM-30G) 59.8 ft
Gross Weight	Minuteman I 65,000 pounds
	Minuteman II 70,000 pounds
	Minuteman III 78,000 pounds
Speed	15,000 mph
Range	6000 miles
Powerplant	three solid-fuel rocket engines
Reaction Time	instantaneous
Armament	nuclear warhead

Right: A Boeing **Minuteman ICBM** hurtles skyward.

Specifications: AGM-86B ALCM
Boeing Model Number 641

Length	20 ft 9 in
Height (fin deployed)	4 ft
Wingspan (deployed)	12 ft
Weight	3000 pounds
Range	more than 1500 miles
Speed	subsonic (about Mach 0.7)
Propulsion	one Williams International F-107-WR-100, 600 pound thrust turbofan
Guidance	inertial guidance, plus terrain contour matching
Armament	nuclear or conventional warhead

Left: **Air Launched Cruise Missiles** are mounted on the external weapons pylons of B-52s with their wings folded. The wings are deployed when the missile is released from the aircraft.

Below: **ALCMs** under construction on the Boeing Aerospace Company assembly line.

was cancelled. The new missile retained SCAD's shape but assumed a different responsibility: it was stripped of its electronic decoys to become a stealthy attack weapon.

The first ALCM, designated AGM-86A by the Air Force, was about 14 feet long and had a range of about 700 miles. Seven AGM-86As were built during the development and testing phase. Six were launched in 1976 from a B-52 over New Mexico's White Sands desert. The tests demonstrated successfully that the missiles were capable of doing their job. However, the AGM-86A was not put into production, and the seventh was presented to the Smithsonian Air and Space Museum.

Boeing Aerospace Company engineers next produced their Model 641, (Air Force designation AGM-86B). It is six feet longer than its brother, and is capable of traveling up to 1500

Below: A Boeing **AGM-86B** Air Launched Cruise Missile with its wings extended in flight over the Utah Test and Training Range.

it hung on the B-52's pylon. The result was a coating of ice three-quarters of an inch thick, simulating a condition that could occur on certain kinds of flights. The ALCM was released. It spread its wings and tail surfaces, and streaked through four hours of complex maneuvers before being recovered by helicopter.

Although Boeing makes the ALCM, the go-ahead didn't come by chance, but by competition. The Department of Defense's Joint Cruise Missiles Project Office included General Dynamics in the competition. Each company conducted 10 flights of its missile system. The testing began on 1 August 1979, and ended on 22 January 1980. In their 10 flights, Boeing missiles logged a total of 32 hours of free-flight time, and covered more than 12,000 miles over mountains, deserts, and oceans. All flights were launched from a B-52G. On 25 March 1980, Air Force Secretary Hans Mark announced that Boeing was the winner. It was the biggest single USAF contract since the Vietnam War.

Amid much glitter, the first AGM-86B roll-out was similar to those roll-outs undertaken for Boeing's commercial aircraft, with notables present from both the civilian and military sides. Among the military men present was Lieutenant General Lawrence A Skantze. He praised Boeing for a job well done, and noted that the Air Force would need more than 4000 ALCMs with a price tag of one million each. Boeing's efforts to stay afloat in the highly competitive aerospace business had been successful once again.

miles, a considerable range improvement. It has been designed as an extremely versatile, unmanned, self-guided airplane and is capable of electronically reading the terrain over which it flies. It continuously compares these readings with maps stored in an on-board computer and corrects any deviation from its planned course. Thus, it can guide itself through the enemy defense systems to predetermined targets.

During a test in January 1982, an ALCM was launched from a B-52 over the Pacific Ocean, off California. The missile's inertial navigation system then guided it to the coast, where its contour matching system came into operation. The ALCM continued on a preplanned route across California, Nevada and finally Utah, where it reached its target. The missile, which weighs 3000 pounds, was then recovered by helicopter in mid-air. The ALCM is so accurate that if one were turned loose over Cleveland, it could hit a target between the goal posts in the Pasadena Rose Bowl.

The AGM-86B is an all-weather weapon, as one particularly severe test proved. An AGM-86B was taken up over the Utah Test and Training Range by a B-52. Before launching, a KC-135 Stratotanker drew close and sprayed water on the ALCM where

In May 1964 Boeing signed a contract with NASA to design five flight test, and three ground test models of a moon-photographing spacecraft called the Lunar Orbiter. Orbiter's task was to obtain detailed photographs of selected areas near the moon's equator to help scientists choose the safest sites for a manned landing. The photos would be of particular significance to the Apollo program.

When completed, the Lunar Orbiter was an 850-pound, open-truss structure, with a 145-pound photographic subsystem, flight programmer, inertial reference unit, transponder and batteries on the lower deck. The upper deck held the 100-pound thrust velocity control engine, fuel, and oxidizer tanks. Not counting solar panels and antennae, the spacecraft was 5 feet wide, and 5

Below: Twelve **ALCMs** can be mounted on the external pylons of the B-52G and H. B-52Gs based at Griffiss AFB in New York were the first to become operational with the ALCM.

Above: An artist's conception of **Lunar Orbiter I**, NASA's first spacecraft to orbit the moon. Launched on 10 August 1966 aboard an Atlas Agena rocket, this spacecraft surveyed nine primary and seven potential Apollo landing sites and the Surveyor I site. Readout from Orbiter I was completed on 13 September and the Orbiter was intentionally impacted to avoid interference with the second mission. Four paddle-shaped solar panels with photo-voltaic sails faced the sun. Internal parts of the Orbiter were protected from temperature extremes by a thermal barrier of aluminized Mylar. In this rendering most of the insulating shroud has been deleted to show the camera system and electronic equipment in the lower module. Oxidizer and fuel tanks are visible on the upper module just below the rocket engine nozzle.

Facing page: An artist's conception of the **Boeing X-20 Dyna-Soar** entering the Earth's atmosphere after an orbital mission. Designed to give the Air Force a manned space flight capability, the X-20 was engineered before *anyone* had flown in space and would have gone into service in 1965, but the program was cancelled in 1963. The X-20 was much smaller than the Space Shuttle, but its size and configuration was adapted during the 1990s by both Japan and France.

Specifications: Lunar Orbiter
Boeing Model Number 939

Span (across antenna booms)	18 ft 6 in
Length (across the panels)	12 ft 2 in
Weight*	850 pounds
Photographic Subsystem Weight*	145 pounds
Cruising Speed	2666.66 mph
Range	800 days
Min/Max Orbital Distance from Lunar Surface	Orbiter I-III: 28-1150 miles
	Orbiter IV: 1650-3800 miles
	Orbiter V: 125-3700 miles

*weights given are for earth gravity

feet 6 inches tall. With the panels and antennae extended, the maximum span was 18 feet. It measured six inches across the antenna booms, and 12 feet 2 inches across the panels.

From August 1966 through August 1967, five Lunar Orbiters photographed nearly all of the moon's surface, more than 14,000,000 square miles. As a result of the Orbiter and Surveyor missions (Surveyor made the first unmanned soft landing on the moon) photographs of eight landing sites were selected from a list of about 30 along the moon's equator. This was the zone of interest for the Apollo landings. Each of the sites was an oval measuring about three by five miles, with an approach path 30 miles long for the Lunar Module.

In addition to their primary photographic missions, the Orbiters were designed to monitor the strength of radiation and the density of meteoroids in the moon's vicinity. During 800 days in lunar orbit, the Orbiter spacecraft reported 18 meteoroid hits. Radiation levels near the moon were generally low. Data from Orbiter findings were correlated with radiation readings from other spacecraft, such as Pioneer.

All five flights of the Lunar Orbiter were successful. Under the terms of NASA's contract, however, penalties could be assessed for late delivery, and a bonus could be granted for outstanding technical performances. Here, a modern irony occurs: Boeing received $6,809,053 in incentive awards for the five flights, but was penalized $130,000 for late delivery of the first two spacecraft. The first launch was made on 10 August 1966, and the last left Cape Kennedy's pad Number 13, the launch pad for all Orbiters, on 1 August 1967.

The Lunar Orbiter program chalked up an impressive list of firsts. The Orbiter was the first US spacecraft to orbit the moon and provided the first photograph of Earth from the moon. The first detailed photographs were taken of the moon's far side, giving complete coverage and better detail than that available of the near side from earth. The first complete coverage of the moon's near side was also made with resolution 10 times better than possible from Earth-based telescopes. Orbiter also produced the first close-up photos of major lunar features, providing details which scientists could use to determine how the moon was formed. The first definitive information about the moon's gravitational field was made available as were the first vertical views of the moon's North and South Poles, and the eastern and western edges (right and left edges as seen from earth).

The entire highly successful program was completed in about 40 months.

In September 1965 the Air Force had awarded Boeing Aerospace a contract for the development of an upper stage rocket called Burner II (Boeing model number 946). The object was to create a highly reliable, low-cost 'kick' stage for placing small and medium payloads into precise orbit. The Burner II was also used as the main retromotor for the Surveyor spacecraft, the vehicle that made the first unmanned soft landing on the moon.

The basic Burner II upper stage had a diameter of 65 inches, a height of 68 inches without the nose shroud. It weighed approximately 1780 pounds at ignition, and approximately 315 pounds after payload separation. The motor generated 10,000 pounds of thrust.

Boeing's designers created Burner II so that it could be easily maintained and launched. Components could be serviced, adjusted and even replaced while the vehicle was on the pad. Its guidance system could accurately position the vehicle in high Earth orbit, transfer orbit or parking orbit with its altitude limited only by the power of the lower stage. It was applicable to wide varieties of payloads including scientific experiments,

weather, navigation or communications satellites. It could be used as an upper stage on almost the entire range of standard launch vehicles. Included were Thor, Atlas and various configurations of Titan.

In August 1969 the Air Force's Space and Missile Systems Organization awarded Boeing another contract to develop and manufacture a two-stage version of Burner II. The modified upper stage was known as Burner IIA. A second stage solid fuel motor with 524 pounds of propellant, furnishing 8800 pounds of thrust, was added to Burner II's 10,000 pound thrust. As with Burner II, Burner IIA had the ability to be used with virtually the entire family of Air Force boosters.

In all, Boeing built 14 basic Burner IIs, and eight Burner IIAs for the Air Force. None of them failed, though two of the overall missions were unsuccessful. In one, a shroud failed to separate from the booster, and in the other the first-stage launch vehicle failed to achieve the desired orbit.

Boeing was delivering Space Shuttle concepts long before *Columbia*'s first launch in 1981. 'The choice of flight paths available to the Dyna-Soar pilot will be almost infinite,' said George H Stoner, Boeing Dyna-Soar program manager on 22 September 1963, at the Air Force Association convention in San Francisco. The Air Force was letting the public know about X-20, its designation for the new spaceship.

The name Dyna-Soar was derived from a combination of 'dynamic' and 'soaring.' It was to be a manned, boost-glide spacecraft, a winged vehicle, designed for maneuverable re-entry through the atmosphere. It would be boosted into space by a Titan III rocket. After entry into space, Dyna-Soar would orbit Earth, then re-enter when its task had been completed.

The project began not long after that fateful day in the fall of 1957, when Russia launched Sputnik I. By March the following year, the Air Force had issued directives to the aerospace industry about Dyna-Soar, inviting response. In June the Air Force selected two major teams to prepare competitive studies. Boeing headed one team, and the Martin Company, combined with Bell Aircraft, headed the other.

The unknowns that faced Boeing in 1958 were typical of those facing all members of the fledgling space industry. Dyna-Soar, for example, would be required to fly at high Mach numbers, and there were few people in the country who had much knowledge of hypersonic flight. Boeing had experience in supersonic flight and related fields, but hypersonic was something else.

One of the first steps Boeing took toward the solutions to those problems was to select preliminary design engineers from its own staff. Among them were people who had worked on an earlier 'paper study' for ROBO, a rocket bomber design. ROBO was designed to shoot high above earth by rocket power and once in space, the bomber would attain hypersonic speed in a glide. Because of its speed, it would generate great heat once it re-entered the atmosphere. To cool off, ROBO would skip in and out of the atmosphere, like a flat rock thrown across the surface of a pond.

The 'skip-glide' concept had been advanced by a University of Vienna professor, Dr Eugen Saenger, in 1933. However, Dyna-Soar's designers set Dr Saenger's ideas aside. They would make Dyna-Soar a 'boost glide' spacecraft. Heat resistant materials

Above: The ill-fated Apollo 13 spacecraft aboard the **Saturn V** with Boeing first stage during rollout on 15 December 1969.

Opposite: James Irwin, Apollo 15 lunar-module pilot, with Boeing's **Lunar Rover** parked near Hadley Rille on 26 July 1971. Apollo 15 was the third from last moon mission and the first to be accompanied by the Rover.

Specifications: Saturn V First Stage Boeing Model Number S-1C

Diameter	33 ft
Length	138 ft
Gross Weight	5,000,000 pounds (fuelled)
Velocity	6000 mph at burnout
Altitude at Burnout	38 miles
Powerplant	five 1,500,000 pound thrust F-1 rocket engines

were tested, and it was felt that Dyna-Soar could effect re-entry in a lengthy glide, instead of skipping in and out of the atmosphere. Though temperatures would reach a mighty 4000 degrees Fahrenheit, the heat-resistant metal sheath would protect both pilot and craft. Though Dyna-Soar's surface would look like 'An old-fashioned wood stove,' on landing, 'It would be no major project to prepare this glider for relaunch,' claimed George Stoner.

There was every reason to believe that Dyna-Soar would succeed. The booster had been chosen and technical problems were finding solutions. Confidence in the outcome of the program was such that gliders, let loose from the wings of B-52s at high altitudes, were showing pilots the special techniques needed for landing this type of aircraft. A wooden mock-up of the Dyna-Soar configuration had been built for study and by 1963, $400 million had been spent on its development. That was a breathtaking figure in 1963, one that even government spendthrifts regarded with respect.

In spite of technological advances and the huge amount of money spent, Secretary of Defense Robert McNamara announced on 10 December 1963, that the Dyna-Soar project had been cancelled. There had been a change in the space program plans. The cancellation brought gloom to Boeing. Good men would have to be laid off, people with special skills. It was a sad end for a noble project.

But there were rays of light in this darkened vale. The Apollo space program was under way, and Boeing was at the center of it. Boeing's knowledge of what it took to conquer space had been considerably enriched by the Dyna-Soar project.

The Saturn/Apollo program of NASA was one of the largest peacetime industrial engineering and scientific efforts of modern times. Everything about the Saturn/Apollo undertaking could be described as big. At its peak in the mid-1960s, more than 250,000 people were directly involved including almost 10,000 Boeing management, engineering, manufacturing and administrative personnel.

NASA made the announcement on 15 December 1961 that Boeing would build the first stage (S-1C) booster for the Saturn V launch vehicle. The three-stage Saturn V, which weighed more than six million pounds at liftoff, could put a 120-ton payload into Earth orbit, or a 45-ton payload in the vicinity of the moon. It was being produced under the direction of NASA's Marshall Space Flight Center, Alabama. The Saturn's three rocket stages were put together at one of the nation's largest buildings at the John F Kennedy Space Center, Florida. Boeing produced 13 flight stages and two test stages under this contract, which ran over one billion dollars by the time it expired in September 1973.

The Saturn V with all three stages and with Apollo command, service and lunar modules on top was 363 feet tall. The first stage, Boeing's S-1C, the largest rocket booster ever produced in the US, stood 138 feet tall and was 33 feet in diameter. It had a dry weight of approximately 300,000 pounds, and a fueled weight of about five million pounds. Five engines were mounted at the base of the S-1C, four in a square, with a fifth in the center. They burned 331,000 gallons of liquid oxygen (LOX), and 203,000 gallons of refined kerosene. The combination produced a prodigious 7.5 million pounds of thrust, which took $2\frac{1}{2}$ minutes to reach burnout. By then Saturn V would be at an altitude of 38 miles and have attained a speed of 6000mph.

The second stage of Saturn V (S-II) was produced by Space and Information Systems of North American Rockwell. It provided one million pounds of thrust, and was 81.5 feet tall, 33 feet in diameter. It also was powered by five engines. The third stage,

Above: The **Saturn V** rocket with the Boeing-built first stage boosts Apollo 11 skyward from launchpad 39A at Cape Kennedy, carrying the first manned lunar mission in 1969.

Opposite: A **Saturn V** first stage under construction.

Saturn S-1C Program

Flight	Date	Vehicle	Seconds fired
Apollo 4([1])	9 November 1967	S-1C-1([2])	140.9
Apollo 6([1])	4 April 1968	S-1C-2([2])	148.0
Apollo 8	21 December 1968	S-1C-3	153.8
Apollo 9	3 March 1969	S-1C-4	162.7
Apollo 10	18 May 1969	S-1C-5	161.6
Apollo 11	16 July 1969	S-1C-6	161.6
Apollo 12	14 November 1969	S-1C-7	161.1
Apollo 13	11 April 1970	S-1C-8	163.8
Apollo 14	31 January 1971	S-1C-9	164.1
Apollo 15	26 July 1971	S-1C-10	158.8
Apollo 16	16 April 1972	S-1C-11	161.8
Apollo 17	7 December 1972	S-1C-12	160.9
Skylab 1	14 May 1973	S-1C-13	158.2
		Total	2067.3

([1]) Unmanned
([2]) Assembled by the NASA Space Flight Center. Remainder built by Boeing.

(S-IVB), was built by the McDonnell Douglas Corporation. It was 58.7 feet tall and 21.7 feet in diameter. It carried only one engine which produced 200,000 pounds of thrust.

Twelve of the 15 S-1C stages were flown on Saturn V/Apollo missions. Each performed in nearly flawless fashion during its $2\frac{1}{2}$ minute flight, and each lifted more than 3000 tons of Saturn V rocket off the launch pad and pushed it toward earth orbit.

The Boeing-built S-1C-3 launched Apollo 8 on 21 December 1968, the first flight around the moon. Apollo 11, launched by S-1C-6 on 16 July 1969, carried Neil Armstrong, the first man to set foot on the moon. And S-1C-10, launched Apollo 15, which carried the first of three Boeing Lunar Roving Vehicles (LRV), or moon cars. These moon cars were to expand the astronauts' range of exploration on the moon dramatically. The final moon mission, Apollo 17, was launched by S-1C-12. However, one of the most daring events was still to come, the launching of Skylab.

The Saturn V rocket that carried Skylab into space looked familiar, but it was a new model specially designed for a scientific role. The Boeing S-1C-13 first stage thrusters carried a very different bird into the sky. Much of the difference was apparent only to an engineer's eyes. The S-4B upper stage no longer contained the more than 100 tons of fuel and rocketry needed to boost the vehicle out of the earth's gravitational pull. Instead, it contained a lighter and more spacious workshop in which astronauts conducted experiments.

Skylab was unmanned, so the command and service modules which previously perched atop the S-4B were not used. In their

place was an aerodynamic shroud which housed a solar telescope, an airlock and an adapter to which astronauts docked their spacecraft after rendezvous in Earth orbit.

The changes shortened the Saturn V to 346 feet, and when completely fueled for takeoff it was 219,929 pounds lighter than the Saturn V which sent Apollo 17 to the moon.

This loss of weight gave Skylab added speed. The S-1C-13 was a bit hotter than its brothers, producing 7.8 million pounds of thrust, rather than the usual 7.5 or 7.6 million pounds. After blastoff on 14 May 1973 it took just 160 seconds for the S-1C-13 thrusters to burn their fuel. Skylab had attained an altitude of 45 miles, and was 46.6 miles downrange. This compares to the 35 mile height and 50 mile range attained by Apollo 17 in the same flying time with the same 4,721,000 pound fuel load.

The S-1C was a faithful workhorse, which served well, but its day has come and gone. Thirteen of them saw service, but two were not used. One of these, S-1C-14, is on display at NASA's Michoud Assembly Facility in New Orleans. The last one, S-1C-15, can be seen at the Kennedy Space Center.

In order to give Apollo astronauts more flexibility while on the moon, NASA invited competition from the aerospace industry, leading to a practical Lunar Roving Vehicle (LRV), also known as a moon buggy. Boeing and the Bendix Corporation were finalists, and Boeing was eventually awarded the contract.

Both companies had already conducted studies on several types of vehicles for traveling on the moon's surface. The most important Boeing studies were MOLAB (Mobile Lunar Labora-

tory), conducted in 1964–65, and LSSM (Local Scientific Survey Module), 1966–67. The MOLAB study yielded a fat-wheeled vehicle, a traveling laboratory, complete with atmosphere, food and equipment. Each of its six wheels was individually powered, and top speed was 10mph. It was electrically powered, and could support two men for trips of up to two weeks, with a total of 250 miles of running.

LSSM was an open spacecraft designed from the standpoint of weight saving and dependability. Also electrically powered, it was little more than a frame seat, tucked between six wheels with woven-wire tires (which eventually appeared on the LRV's final design). It also could travel at 10mph, but was designed to carry only one astronaut (two in emergency) on exploration trips. It weighed 985 pounds, and could range over 200 miles of the moon's surface.

Eight test units in all were developed leading to the manufacture of the first LRV flight model. Program management and engineering work was performed at the Boeing Company's Space Center, Kent, Washington, and at Boeing's facilities in Huntsville, Alabama. The first flight-model LRV was delivered to NASA on 15 March 1971, less than 17 months from the formal signing of the contract. This was the shortest development, design, qualification and manufacture cycle of any major item of equipment for the Apollo program.

The LRV was deceptive in appearance. It looked like a simple, familiar vehicle, perhaps a dune buggy. In reality, it was a specialized spacecraft that had been designed to function safely in the space conditions of vacuum, temperatures ranging from

234

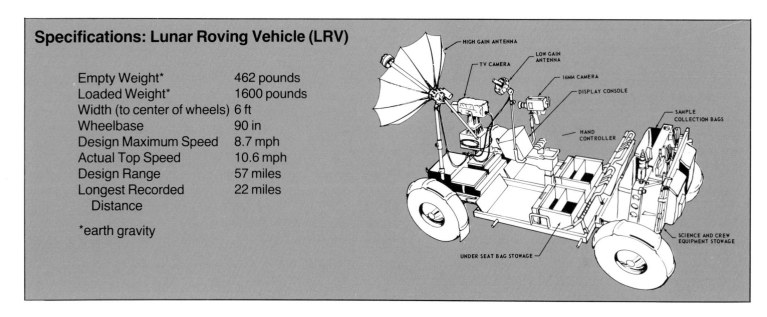

Specifications: Lunar Roving Vehicle (LRV)

Empty Weight*	462 pounds
Loaded Weight*	1600 pounds
Width (to center of wheels)	6 ft
Wheelbase	90 in
Design Maximum Speed	8.7 mph
Actual Top Speed	10.6 mph
Design Range	57 miles
Longest Recorded Distance	22 miles

*earth gravity

plus 200 degrees Fahrenheit to 200 degrees below, and to venture over rough terrain. Among its unique features were wheels specially designed for moon use. Delco Electronics, after studying reports from Apollo 11 and 12, designed a wheel with a spun aluminum hub and a titanium bump stop inside a woven tire. The tire was woven of zinc-coated piano-wire. Each wheel weighed 12 pounds on Earth, two on the moon. Their design saved well over 100 pounds over conventional wheels and rubber tires in a venture where every ounce saved was important.

The vehicles were powered by two 36 volt silver-zinc batteries, developed by Eagle Picher Industries of Joplin, Missouri. They were non-rechargeable batteries of plexiglass monoblock construction. Silver-zinc plates operating in potassium hydroxide electrolyte were used. Each battery was designed for a capacity of 121 ampere hours, and contained 25 cells. The case material was magnesium.

Each vehicle weighed 462 pounds, and the total loaded weight was 1600 pounds. They were 122 inches long, 6 feet wide to the center of the wheels. Maximum speed was 8.7mph, and they had a range of 57 miles.

Use of the first LRV took place on the Apollo 15 trip in July and August 1971. Astronauts Dave Scott and John Irwin more than doubled the amount of work accomplished by previous moon-landings. The ability to carry heavy loads and a television camera greatly expanded the scientific effectiveness of the mission. Ground controllers became part of the exploration team and participated with directions and assistance. The weight of Lunar samples returned with LRV assistance on Apollo 15 was 170 pounds, nearly double the 94 pound record of Apollo 14.

The Boeing-built navigation system on Rover 1 proved to be accurate and reliable. Astronaut Irwin reported the explorers did not hesitate to vary from their planned route, since they had confidence the system would guide them home. Accuracy was within 0.06 miles, which would enable the Rover to return to within 320 feet of its starting point. The Apollo crew found they could precisely locate their landing site by reporting the distance to the lunar module from known lunar craters as calculated by the navigation system.

On 21–23 April 1972 astronauts John Young and Charles Duke of Apollo 16 explored areas near Descartes Crater aboard Lunar Rover 2. They gathered samples of moon rocks, some of them of a different kind than seen before. More and better data was received as a result of this mission than any before it, including Apollo 15. As the astronauts grew more accustomed to their missions in space, they were able to utilize the equipment more

Below: The inflight configuration of the Boeing-built **Mariner X** spacecraft with its paddle-like solar panels deployed. The spacecraft was launched on 3 November 1973 on NASA's first dual-planet mission and the first to explore Mercury (see diagram, page 238).

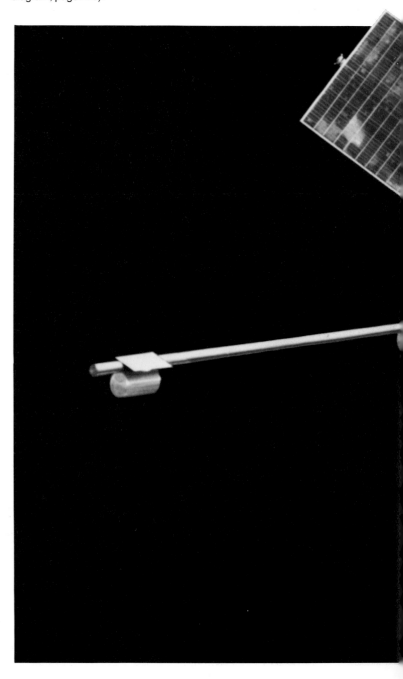

fully. Astronauts Young and Duke reported they set a 'new lunar speed record,' when their moon buggy hit 10.6mph going downhill. Rover 1 had averaged a speed of 5.7mph.

When Apollo 17 reached the moon, after a spectacular night launch on 7 December 1972, Lunar Rover 3 was unloaded from the Lunar Module near Taurus-Littrow. From start to finish, this last Apollo expedition was nearly flawless. Astronauts Gene Cernan and Jack Schmidt, who operated Rover 3, were enthusiastic about their moon buggy. Mission Commander Cernan radioed to earth, after parking Rover 3 for the last time, 'It was the finest machine I've ever had the pleasure to drive.'

On the three Apollo missions on which it was carried, the LRV went everywhere it was programmed to go. It accomplished everything expected of it. Boeing was rightfully proud of its record: three missions, three successes. By now, Boeing was well into the space programs of the United States. The Boeing experience in the technology was invaluable, and growing.

On 29 April 1971, Jet Propulsion Laboratory (JPL), at Pasadena, California, announced the selection of the Boeing Aerospace Company to design a variant of the standard Mariner spacecraft. Boeing would also build the spacecraft and test it at their Space Center in Kent, Washington. JPL had been the prime contractor for moon probe space vehicles such as Lunik, Pioneer, Prospector and Ranger. Unlike its fellows, Mariner was called a 'planet probe.'

The vehicle that Boeing contracted to manufacture was called Mariner 10. Its mission included a flyby of the planet Venus, using the gravity pull of that body to provide energy to continue on to the solar system's innermost planet, Mercury. The spacecraft had to withstand the terrific temperatures predicted at Mercury, and was to be ready for launch in the last quarter of 1973. This was the only time there would be such a launch opportunity for many years because of the changing positions of the planets and the trajectory planned.

The 1160 pound spacecraft that evolved carried a 170 pound science package that included two television cameras, an X-band radio transmitter, a scanning electron spectrometer and a scanning electrostatic analyzer. In addition, Mariner 10 carried two magnetometers, an infra-red radiometer, a charged particle telescope and two ultraviolet spectrometers. To accomplish this, the standard Mariner spacecraft design was modified by Boeing to fit the demands of the mission. Two solar panels were utilized instead of the four which Mariner 9 carried when it photographed Mars in November 1971. The two panels were mounted so they could be rotated into an off-Sun position to protect them from the

Below: Boeing's conception of an initial **Space Operations Center (SOC)** which would be used for servicing satellites and vehicles based in outer space. This space port is being studied by Boeing Aerospace for NASA's Johnson Space Center in Houston. The initial station would include a living and command control module for a crew of four; a logistics module containing food, water and other supplies; a service module containing batteries, oxygen and nitrogen with solar arrays to provide power for the center. SOC is designed to be transported and assembled in low-earth orbit by the space shuttle.

JOHN J OLSON 81

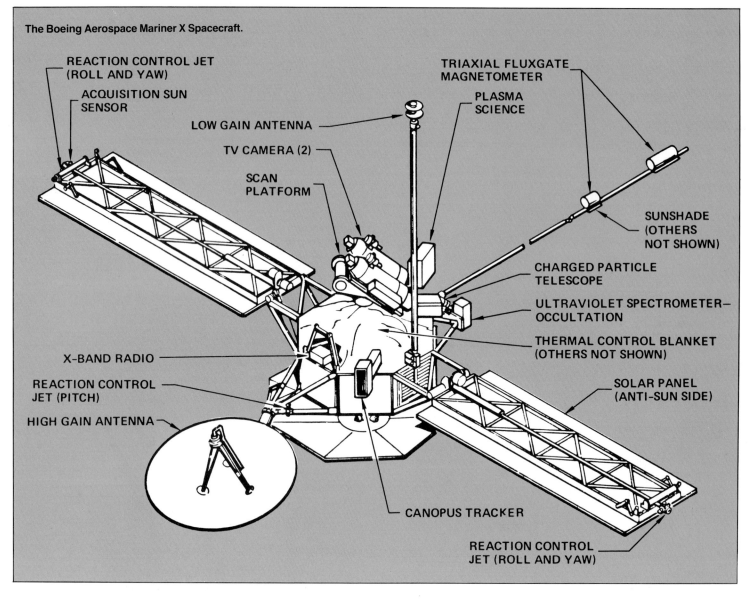

The Boeing Aerospace Mariner X Spacecraft.

REACTION CONTROL JET (ROLL AND YAW)

ACQUISITION SUN SENSOR

LOW GAIN ANTENNA

TV CAMERA (2)

SCAN PLATFORM

TRIAXIAL FLUXGATE MAGNETOMETER

PLASMA SCIENCE

SUNSHADE (OTHERS NOT SHOWN)

CHARGED PARTICLE TELESCOPE

ULTRAVIOLET SPECTROMETER– OCCULTATION

THERMAL CONTROL BLANKET (OTHERS NOT SHOWN)

SOLAR PANEL (ANTI-SUN SIDE)

X-BAND RADIO

REACTION CONTROL JET (PITCH)

HIGH GAIN ANTENNA

CANOPUS TRACKER

REACTION CONTROL JET (ROLL AND YAW)

Sun's heat. A passive thermal protection system was developed, utilizing state-of-the-art techniques and materials to provide protection from the high temperatures expected during the Mercury flyby.

Shortly after launch on 3 November 1973, Mariner 10's television cameras were activated, and a series of photos was returned of both Earth and Moon.

On 5 February 1974 Mariner 10 swung by Venus returning the first space photos of the planet. Then on 29 March the Mariner 10 cameras were turned on Mercury. On 29 March the craft passed within about 450 miles of Mercury's surface, and the photos revealed incredibly rough terrain. Temperatures ranging from 370 degrees Fahrenheit on the day side to minus 280 degrees on the night side of the planet were reported. Thermal data obtained with the infra-red equipment indicated a total temperature range of 1000 degrees Fahrenheit. There was evidence of helium, argon, neon and, possibly, xenon.

Following what was called Encounter I, the craft swung back into an orbit around the Sun. This brought it back to Mercury in six months. Through the use of a technique of solar sailing, spacecraft controllers at the Jet Propulsion Laboratory were able to conserve control gas supplies aboard. This enabled it to remain operative for subsequent flybys. In solar sailing, the twin solar panels were moved to provide a slight push from the solar wind. This was enough to guide the spacecraft. Rotation of the high gain antenna was also used to impart energy to the craft to keep it stabilized.

Over a six day period, Mariner 10 returned over 500 pictures of the surface of Mercury. The closest approach occured on 21 September 1974 at an altitude of 30,000 miles. Nearly 17 months after Earth launch, and after logging close to a billion miles of spaceflight, Mariner 10 completed its third and final flyby of Mercury in 1975. Following the third encounter, JPL engineers started a series of tests of the spacecraft to diagnose its condition after so long a time in space. On 24 March 1975, controllers estimated stabilization gases were nearly exhausted, and signals were sent to Mariner 10 turning off all equipment and silencing its radios. The spacecraft is now in permanent Sun orbit, and will remain there indefinitely.

As another credit in Boeing's long list, Mariner 10 was selected by the US National Society of Professional Engineers as one of the engineering achievements of 1974. The Society high commended the accomplishment as 'an outstanding example of systems engineering.'

Though The Boeing Company's practical experience and engineering skill have kept it in the front lines of space technology, the company has also become involved in other aspects. Its subsidiary, Boeing Services International, was formed in 1972, and employs thousands of people worldwide.

BSI's involvement with the Space Shuttle program began in 1977. Skilled technicians have been busy at the Kennedy Space Center, providing NASA with a variety of ground systems operations and maintenance service. BSI also installs and modifies launch systems ground support equipment for space flights. Its responsibilities range from operations management through institutional maintenance, including carpentry, plumbing, sandblasting, floor and ceiling care and even bridge repair. The company's people also operate cranes, forklifts and elevators. BSI employees operate the mobile launcher platform on which the Shuttle is stacked and launched.

Where there is a responsibility, mundane or highly critical, BSI is involved. At Edwards AFB, where *Columbia* has landed after orbiting Earth, BSI is primarily responsible for the life support systems used by the orbiter servicing crew. This includes outfitting technicians exposed to hazardous environments. These outfits are self-contained atmosphere-protective ensembles, better known by their typically colorful anacronym as SCAPE suits. They are designed to protect the technicians from toxic chemicals. BSI suits 27 people for duty when *Columbia* or one of its successors touches down. In addition to the 27, two teams of five each provide stand-by service for eight hours in case of hazardous propellant leaks or other emergency situations. Those white suits seen on television after a Shuttle landing are SCAPE suits. If the Shuttle is forced to land at another base because of weather or some kind of emergency such as it had at White Sands, New Mexico, a BSI life-support group, already pre-positioned at Edwards, will begin preparing all systems for shipment.

After landing at Edwards detailed inspections are made of the spacecraft and a mate/demate device is used to lift the Orbiter atop the specially fitted Boeing 747 for transport back to Kennedy Space Center. There are two mate/demate devices, one at Edwards, the other at Kennedy. BSI has total operations and maintenance responsibility for the equipment. Should the Orbiter land on an alternate site overseas, everything needed to ship the space ship back to the US is sent by C-5 cargo planes. It is a big operation, requiring up to 20 aircraft. BSI's Deployed Operation Team is trained and ready to help bring Orbiter back from any location in the world.

Compass Cope (Boeing Model 901) is the largest airplane designed as a remotely piloted vehicle (RPV). Two of the 40 foot long, 90 foot wingspan planes demonstrated the feasibility of performing surveillance and reconnaissance missions from a high-altitude, long-endurance airplane. The Boeing Aerospace Compass Cope, designated YQM-94A by the Air Force, was primarily of fiberglass, the wings having a fiberglass honeycomb core and aluminum skin. The airplane weighed 13,000 pounds and was powered by a single General Electric J-97 turbojet engine.

The initial flight of the first vehicle was in July 1973, from Edwards AFB in California. It was a successful flight, but the craft was destroyed in a landing accident on the second flight. The number two plane completed the entire flight test program, during which it remained aloft for 17 hours.

Compass Cope was operated from a ground station, equipped with standard airplane instruments and controls. The plane and station were connected by digital radio communications, and the pilot saw through a television display relayed from a camera in the vehicle's nose.

Though satisfactory in performance, Boeing was asked to extend the program in 1976. This effort would make Compass Cope fully automatic from takeoff to landing. There would be a station pilot following the airplane's course in case it needed a human hand. However, the Air Force cancelled its contract the following year, and the second series was never finished. A Compass Cope is on display at the Air Force Museum near Dayton, Ohio for those wishing a closer look at this unique airplane.

The Boeing Aerospace Company has become involved in such projects as the 'Thin Film Solar Cell Development.' Under contract to the Department of Energy's Solar Energy Research Institute, Boeing research scientists have been working on low-cost, high efficiency thin-film solar cells. These would be capable of meeting the DOE's goal of an energy conversion efficiency of 10 percent. This means that one-tenth of all available sunlight hitting the cells could be directly converted into energy. For an age threatened with an energy crisis, this is important work.

In November 1975 the Boeing Aerospace Company's Space Division was selected to design, fabricate and test two Applications Explorer Missions (AEM) base modules. The purpose of the AEM, designated AEM-1, and AEM-2, was to study the Earth and its atmosphere. AEM-1, a heat capacity mapping mission, was launched from the Western Test Range, California, under the auspices of NASA, on 26 April 1978. Equipped with a radiometer with which it sensed the Earth's surface temperatures at the hottest and coolest times of the day, AEM-1 provided data which allowed the determination of thermal inertia, or heat capacity, of various segments of the surface. Accurate mapping of these temperatures can lead to: discrimination of rock types and mineral resource locations; measurements of plant canopy temperatures to determine the transpiration of water, which is an early indicator of plant stress; mapping of thermal effluents, both natural and man-made; and the prediction of water runoff from snowfields. Placed into a 373 mile circular sun-synchronous orbit, AEM-1 remained operational until 30 September 1980.

AEM-2 was launched from Wallops Island, Virginia, and its purpose was to establish baseline data on aerosol propellant and ozone concentrations; to understand better the effect of transient phenomena on these concentrations; gain insights concerning the effects of stratospheric aerosol and ozone on the global climate and the implications of this in terms of the availability of solar energy on the Earth's surface. Once again, important work. It was during this period that the aerosol scare began. People were using too many cans of things under aerosol pressure, and too much was escaping into the upper atmosphere. The predicted results were dire. AEM-2 studied what was really happening. Aerosols are still in use.

In addition to all of this, the Boeing Aerospace Company has become involved with developing a space telescope structure. It will hold a telescope out in space, which will enable man to see deeply into the universe. Boeing developed a new material from graphite fibers and epoxy which will keep the telescope structure from feeling the influence of either extreme heat or extreme cold. It will neither contract nor expand, thus providing a stable platform for the extremely sensitive telescope and prevent distortion.

Our knowledge of Space is just beginning, though science fiction has long been with us. But science fiction escapism and space technology are drawing closer together. A 'Space Operations Center' is being studied by BAC, for which a future space shuttle would bring supplies. There would be living quarters in the space operations center as well as food warehouses, service areas, spacecraft hangars and solar panels to provide power. In order to expand the Center and make it more efficient, there would be an area for construction materials.

Some Boeing engineers feel that a space colony would live in an Earth-like atmosphere, have forests and fields – in fact an entire man-made 'outdoors.' Picture windows would give colonists a view of Earth and the stars, and solar collectors would supply energy needs.

The way the Boeing Company and its subsidiaries have been progressing in the past, nothing seems too far-fetched.

A NEW ERA

A new era for Boeing dawned on 4 August 1981 when the prototype of the first new Boeing aircraft design since the 747 rolled out of the world's largest building in Everett, Washington. The world of commercial aviation that the 767 and its sister ship the 757 (which was to make its debut on 13 January 1982) looked out on in the early 1980s was much changed in the dozen years since the 747 first took to the air.

In the world of the early 70s there were six major firms engaged in the commercial jetliner business, five American and one British. Three of these firms, Boeing, McDonnell Douglas and Lockheed were manufacturers of airframes, and the other three, Pratt & Whitney, Rolls-Royce and General Electric were in the business of building the engines for them.

By the end of the decade, Boeing had emerged in the dominant position among the airframe manufacturers, after McDonnell Douglas and Lockheed had neutralized one another through the costly war fought between their rival DC-10 and L-1011. It had been the most vicious fight that anyone in the industry could remember. Among the engine manufacturers, both Pratt & Whitney and General Electric (both being part of larger corporations, United Technologies in the case of P&W, and the larger General Electric Corporation in the case of the GE engine division) remained strong. Meanwhile, Rolls-Royce, fighting its way back from the brink of bankruptcy, was running a poor third.

In the early 80s, the lineup of engine makers, though it has seen some convulsions, was the same as it had been a decade earlier. With the airframe builders, however, the lineup had changed. Boeing was the acknowledged industry leader, running a strong

number one with nearly 4000 planes in the air. Lockheed was out, having announced the closing of the L-1011 assembly line, and McDonnell-Douglas was on the ropes in the commercial field. Both had been eclipsed by a newcomer – Airbus Industrie, a European consortium based in Toulouse, France.

The 70s were a bad decade for the Douglas Division of McDonnell-Douglas. For decades Douglas had been one of the premier builders of airliners. Even with the advent of the 707 and Boeing's ascendancy in the jetliner field, Douglas ran a strong second with its DC-8. Then came the 70s, and with them near-bankruptcy and a shotgun marriage to McDonnell. Douglas had seen a strong market for a short range 100-seat aircraft, and introduced its DC-9. Boeing had seen the same market and rushed in with the 737 (which derived many systems from the 727). Because Boeing could build and deliver planes much faster than Douglas, it was able to grab a large market share even though the DC-9 had been there first. The DC-8 fell victim to McDonnel Douglas's desire to produce too many versions, thus driving up unit cost. Finally there was the trouble-plagued DC-10 with some horrible crashes and the costly war with the L-1011.

Enter Airbus Industrie. There had been European jetliners from the start, indeed the British Comet was first, but none had ever been a real commercial success. The Anglo-French Concorde is a good example of such a commercial failure. As late as 1978, it looked as though the big white Airbus A-300 was just another white elephant of the same sort.

Airbus was turning out to be a well-managed company. Beyond that, the A-300 was gradually taking the lead in the worldwide market for a jetliner in the over 250-seat category.

Above: The **757s** for Eastern Airlines are detailed with the same style '757' tail marking as Boeing's 757 prototype.

The territory over which the battle that had ruined the commercial viability of the DC-10 and L-1011 had been fought was slowly being captured by the A-300. The point was made painfully clear to Boeing when Eastern Airlines abandoned American manufacturers to buy A-300s from Airbus.

In the late 70s, the short range market (around 100 seats) was divided between the 737, the DC-9 and, to a lesser degree, planes such as the British Aerospace BAC-111 and the Fokker (Holland) F-28. On the high end of the scale in the over 350-seat long-range category, the 747 was the only contender for a market that it had created. Below the 747, the next rung down (250+) was crowded with the L-1011, DC-10 and A-300. Between this rung and the 100 seat/short range aircraft are two rungs which are generally referred to in the industry as medium range. On the lower of these two (150+) rests the most successful jetliner of all time (over 1800 sold), Boeing's 727. It might be pointed out that the 727 is successful not only because it is an excellent airplane, but also because it is designed to serve the most densely traveled routes in the world. There was no aircraft serving on the other (200+) medium range rung.

If the glamor of wide bodies attracted airframe builders in the 70s, then the pragmatic approach of tailoring aircraft to the most heavily traveled routes with strict attention to fuel efficiency and seat cost per mile marked their thinking in the 80s. The worldwide oil crisis and airline deregulation in the United States and elsewhere were changing the thinking of both the airlines and the airplane makers.

Enter three aircraft builders with an eye on that empty rung. McDonnell Douglas was the first to drop out. They had made extensive engineering studies for what they called their Advanced Technology Medium Range (ATMR) aircraft which had been designated DC-11. The DC-11 was much sought after by the airlines, but recognition of the condition of McDonnell-Douglas caused the airlines to gravitate elsewhere. Airbus was coming along with its contender, the A-310, a double-aisle wide-body like their larger A-300. Boeing followed with not one but *three* new aircraft.

The 767 (another double-aisle wide-body) was designed for the 200+ market, while the 757, originally designed for the 150+ market (it was to have been the 727's successor) gradually grew on the drawing board to close to (and in some seating arrangements beyond 200.) The 777 was a derivative of the 767 idea with about the same seating capacity but with a longer, intercontinental range. It was to have been a tri-jet, with the third engine mounted in the tail in a fashion similar to the DC-10 or L-1011. Marketing studies indicated that the market for the 777 was weaker than for the 757 and 767, so the project was shelved. When the Model 777 designation does appear, and it will, it will probably be attached to a very different sort of plane.

Above: A **757** wind-tunnel model.

Below: The first prototype **767** in Boeing markings during its first flight in September 1981.

The 757 is a short to medium range jetliner which combines the single-aisle/six across seating typical of the 707, 727 and 737 with a new technology wing and engines. The 757 is capable of carrying about 186 passengers in a typical first class/tourist configuration, and up to 220 in an all-tourist configuration. Boeing offers the 757 in either a 3-door or 4-door model. It is the 3-door model (both have two additional mid-fuselage emergency exits that permits the higher passenger density.

Fuel efficiency was an important goal for the 757, and the goal was met. On a 500-mile flight it burns up to 42 percent less fuel per seat than the aircraft it was designed to replace. A 10-plane fleet of 757s, replacing 727-100s, is estimated to be able to save up to $25 million per year in fuel costs as well as additional labor cost savings due to higher productivity.

The new wing, fitted with double-slotted trailing-edge flaps and full-span leading-edge slats, makes possible takeoffs with a full passenger load using about 1250 feet less runway than an Advanced 727 taking off on an equal 1200-mile flight. With its new wing and high-thrust engines, the 757 will be able to cruise 6000 feet higher than the advanced 727-200, thus contributing to fuel efficiency, as well as allowing the aircraft to use higher flight lanes. The four-wheel main landing gear units will allow operations from runways previously unusable by commercial aircraft of equivalent size. Its pavement loading, in fact, will be about the same as the much smaller 737.

Eastern Airlines and British Airways were the first customers for the 757, ordering 40 airplanes between them on 31 August 1978. The formal contract, calling for Rolls-Royce engines, was signed on 23 March 1979 and production began. One year less two days later, Boeing announced that it intended to certify the 757 for two-crew operation, and revealed the new 757/767 flight deck.

Orders were rolling in, with Transbrasil, Air Florida and Monarch all buying 757s, when Tex Boullioun went down to Atlanta to see Delta. E H 'Tex' Boullioun was then the parent Boeing Company's Senior Vice President for Commercial Airplanes and a member of the seven-member executive council that includes the President and the Chairman of the Board of Directors. Boullioun was also the most successful commercial aircraft salesman in the world. On 11 November 1980, Boeing's 'super salesman' closed what was then the biggest commercial airplane deal in history, selling sixty 757s to Delta Airlines for $3 billion. A month later, Delta announced that it wanted its 757s equipped with Pratt & Whitney PW 2037 turbofans, giving the new jet two engine options.

The first wing was complete on 29 May 1981 and attached to the fuselage on 25 August. The first Rolls-Royce engine was mounted on 28 October. Rollout came on 13 January 1982, followed by the first flight on 19 February from Boeing's Renton field.

The Boeing 767, like the 757, is an entirely new commercial jetliner designed to make use of the latest technology to provide maximum

Below: The Rolls-Royce powered **757 first prototype** during its maiden flight. Eastern Airlines and British Airways, the two 757 launch customers, both requested the Rolls-Royce engines.

Specifications: Boeing Model 757

Span	124 ft 6 in
Length	155 ft 3 in
Wing Area	1951 sq ft
Tail Height	44 ft 6 in
Gross Weight	220,000 pounds
Cruising Speed	600 mph
Service Ceiling	38,400-48,000 ft
Range	2867 miles
Powerplant	two 37,400 pound thrust Rolls Royce RB211-535C or two 40,100 pound thrust Rolls Royce RB211-535E4 or two 38,200 pound thrust Pratt & Whitney PW2037 Turbofans
Capacity	178-224 passengers

efficiency in the face of rising costs, while extending twin-aisle passenger cabin convenience to routes never before served by wide-body airliners. Production of the 767 began with an order for 30 announced by United Airlines on 14 July 1978. The first 767 (destined to be a Boeing-owned test aircraft) was completed and rolled out of the big 747/767 plant at Everett on 4 August 1981 and made its first flight on 26 September. Flight testing and certification were complete in the fall of 1982, and the first 767s went into service in September of that year.

The development of the 767 was an intensive effort aimed at refining the design to give maximum fuel performance, operational flexibility, low noise levels, advanced aircraft systems (including digital electronics) in the most advanced airliner flight deck and finally, growth potential. New structural materials included an improved aluminum alloy, a graphite composite material and a hybrid Kevlar/graphite composite.

The 767's two-aisle passenger cabin follows the tradition Boeing established in the 747 which was the original wide-body jetliner. Extensive passenger research showed the seven-abreast seating concept to be preferred by the great majority of those surveyed. It allows for six out of seven people in every row to have either an aisle or window seat.

The 767 cabin is more than four feet wider than the six-abreast Boeing jetliners and seats about 211 passengers in a typical mixed-class configuration (six-abreast in first class, seven-abreast in tourist). Many other arrangements are possible, with passenger capacity increasing to 290 in an eight-abreast charter configuration option.

With its advanced-design wing, the 767 will require a 5900-foot runway for take-off at a maximum gross weight of 282,000 pounds, 6700 feet at 300,000 and 7200 feet at 310,000 pounds. The wing, a Boeing advanced technology airfoil, is, like the 757 wing, thicker, longer and less swept than the wings of earlier Boeing jetliners.

In August 1978, one month after the 767 went into production, Boeing and Aeritalia, Italy's largest aircraft firm, signed a contract under which Aeritalia became a risk-sharing major participant in the 767 development and production program. It was this deal, some believe, that kept Italy from opting to join the Airbus consortium. On 22 September Civil Transport Development Corporation of Japan became a second risk-sharing participant in the 767 Program. CTDC is a consortium of Japanese aircraft manufacturers and component suppliers that includes Mitsubishi, Kawasaki and Fuji Heavy Industries.

Under these contracts, Aeritalia is responsible for all the vertical tail surfaces and all the horizontal tail surfaces except the horizontal stabilizer which is produced by LTV. Aeritalia also produces the wing flaps and the wing leading edge, while Japan's CTDC is responsible principally for fuselage sections.

The 757 and 767 share more than just having made their first flights a few months apart. They also have many features in common. Having features in common is an important selling point for airlines that must stock parts for their fleets. Interchangeable parts mean easier and less costly maintenance. 'Commonality' is an important factor in Boeing's

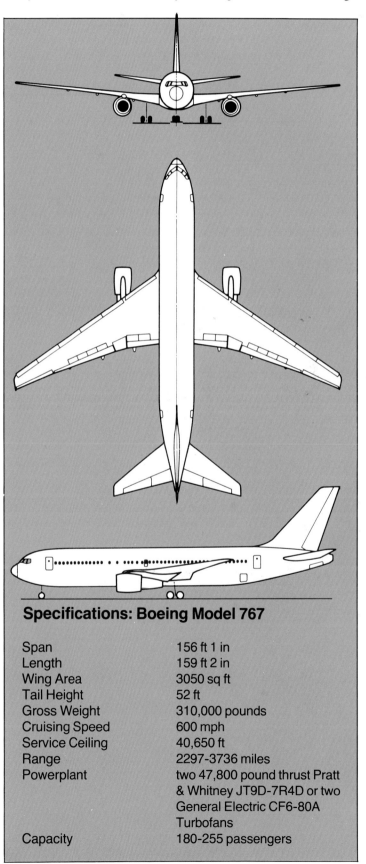

Specifications: Boeing Model 767

Span	156 ft 1 in
Length	159 ft 2 in
Wing Area	3050 sq ft
Tail Height	52 ft
Gross Weight	310,000 pounds
Cruising Speed	600 mph
Service Ceiling	40,650 ft
Range	2297-3736 miles
Powerplant	two 47,800 pound thrust Pratt & Whitney JT9D-7R4D or two General Electric CF6-80A Turbofans
Capacity	180-255 passengers

success in keeping customers. A customer who owns 727s has a least one good reason to come back for 737s. As noted earlier the 707, 727 and 737 have considerable commonality, especially in their fuselages.

The 757 and 767 were designed with commonality in mind, not only to streamline future maintenance, but production as well. While they are all-new by comparison to earlier Boeing jetliners, Boeing figures that the 767 is 42.8 percent *identical* to the 757, and 19.7 percent 'similar'.

The most important feature that the two aircraft have in common is the flight deck. The new two-crewmember flight deck–which is also used on the 747-400–is highly automated so that the pilot and co-pilot can perform all of their own functions plus those that the flight engineer would have performed in the old three-crewmember flight deck. Commonality provides that crew members trained and qualified on the 757 can potentially work on the 767 and vice versa. This provides the airline with training benefits and improved crew productivity.

The new flight deck features digital electronics including an Engine Indicating and Crew Alerting System (EICAS). By graphics and alphanumerics displayed on the center instrument panel (on color cathode-ray tubes),the EICAS provides engine operating parameters, caution and warning alerts and systems status information before takeoff, and for ground personnel, a readout of electronic systems discrepancies to indicate maintenance requirements. The system centralizes all engine displays for two-crew operation, replacing electromechanical instruments with high-technology digital electronic equipment and providing automatic monitoring of engine operation.

The flight deck is based on concepts developed over many years by Boeing and leading electronics firms. Input from major airlines and airline pilots was taken into account in its design. Calling on the experience gained from operations of the two-crewmember 737, of which more than 1600 are operated by over 100 airlines worldwide, the new flight deck has all systems within reach of either pilot. Human engineering studies helped designers determine optimum design and positioning of all controls and instruments.

The flight decks include an inertial reference system making use of laser gyroscopes which are rigidly fixed to the airliner structure, rather than gyros mounted in gimbals as in earlier airliners. This key system also provides information to other flight deck systems, such as the vertical speed indicator and the fuel quantity indicators.

Below: Delivered in 1982, this **United Air Lines 767** was the first of its kind to enter service. *Facing page*: This high-tech **two-crew flight deck** is common to both the 757 and 767. Compare it to those of the 747-300 and 747-400 on pages 202-203.

A flight management computer system integrates navigation, guidance and performance data functions. When coupled with the automatic flight control system ('automatic pilot'), the flight management system provides accurate engine thrust settings and flight path guidance during all phases of flight from immediately after takeoff to final approach and landing. The system can predict the speeds and altitudes that will result in the best fuel economy, and direct the aircraft to follow the most fuel-efficient, or the 'least time' flight path. Depending on the computer programs included, flight planning, ground procedures and airline route information can be stored for use as required.

The first of the production series 767 (designated 767-200) was delivered to United Air Lines on 19 August 1982 and it carried its first load of paying passengers on 8 September. The first production series 757 (designated 757-200) was delivered to Eastern Airlines on 22 December 1982, and made its first revenue passenger flight on New Year's Day 1983.

At the end of 1983, there had been 27 757s and 75 767s delivered to customers. Annual deliveries for the next four years averaged 32 for the 757 and 30 for the 767, but in 1988, 48 new 757s and 53 new 767s entered service.

In the meantime, two additional 767 variations were introduced. These were the 767-200ER (extended range) which first flew on 6 March 1984 and entered service with El Al on 27 March; and the 767-300 which first flew on 30 January 1986 and which was delivered to Japan Airlines on 25 September. The 300 series subsequently succeeded the 200 series as the 'standard' 767.

Two variations on the 757 were the 757-200 freighter which first flew on 13 August 1987 and which entered service with the United Parcel Service on 28 September; and the 757 combi which first flew on 15 July 1988 and joined the Royal Nepal fleet on 15 September.

In February 1989, Boeing began discussing with its customers, a preliminary proposal for an enlarged version of the 767. Given the temporary designation 767-X, the new aircraft would be 196-feet, 2-inches long, representing a stretch in fuselage length of 20 feet over that of the 767-300. The wingspan would in turn be extended by 13-feet, 11-inches with the addition of winglets like those then in use on Boeing's 747-400 and the McDonnell Douglas MD-11.

It was in fact competition from the DC-10-derived MD-11, as well as

Below: The **767-300** made its first flight from Boeing's manufacturing and test facility at Everett, north of Seattle on a rainy day in January 1986. *Facing page*: The Boeing **757** and **767** prototypes in formation flight.

the Airbus Industrie A340, that prompted Boeing to undertake the 767-X project. In its passenger cabin, the 767-X would reportedly be two inches wider than the MD-11, 17 inches wider than the A340 and 41 inches wider than the 767-300. The new 767 would have a 436,000-pound takeoff weight, and be designed to accommodate 300 dual-class passengers on a 4600-mile flight or 250 three-class passengers on a 6300-mile flight. The former scenario is characteristic of North American transcontinental, intra-Asia or Europe-Middle East routes, while the latter is characteristic of the lucrative trans-Atlantic market.

The overall plan of the longer, winglet-configured 767-X — which would probably enter service in 1994 as the 767-400 — would be to provide airlines with a greater passenger load, better range and fuel efficiency–as well as with a member of the Boeing family that could compete with anything else in the large jetliner size and weight class. (The Boeing 747 series must be considered in a 'very large' size and weight class of its own.)

At the time when the first edition of this book was being prepared in 1982, Boeing was the world's largest commercial aircraft builder. Of the two other American jetliner manufacturers, McDonnell Douglas was in decline and Lockheed had announced in December 1981 that it would close its L-1011 production line and abandon the commercial market. Boeing's only major competition appeared to be Airbus Industrie, the European consortium based in Toulouse, France. To meet this competition, Boeing was discussing the possibility of joining with a consortium of Japanese firms to build a new jetliner which was known variously as the 7X7 or 7J7.

In the succeeding years the notoriously-cyclical commercial aircraft industry entered its deepest decline since the early 1970s. The years from 1981 to 1984 saw an industry-wide and worldwide decline in new orders. The industry improved somewhat in mid-decade, but by 1987, the industry sales figures had barely crawled back to their 1981 level. Projections for the early 1990s, however, were quite good with forecasts of a three-fold increase from the 1988 levels by 1992, as airlines began the massive task of replacing their aging jetliner fleets.

By 1989, when this book was revised, the situation was much changed from 1982. Boeing was still the world's largest builder of

Right and below: Boeing's **first 767** photographed during an early test flight. Since these pictures were taken in 1981, more than 350 of these reliable twin-jets have been sold to customers around the world,some of whose logos are seen on this aircraft. Washington state's **Mt Rainier**, seen here under a blanket of new snow is one of the state's most prominent features. A few minutes flying time from Seattle, it has always been a favorite backdrop for Boeing's photographers.

jetliners — with a 56 percent market share — but by now, the competition from Airbus Industrie had largely leveled out and the position of McDonnell Douglas was much improved with expanding orders for its DC-9 series 80 (now called MD-80) and the much improved DC-10 variant designated MD-11.

As Boeing entered the 1990s, its market share was not only the greatest globally, it continued to fill all the niches. The advanced 400 and 500 series 737s continued to hold a dominant position in the small airliner market, while the 747— now represented by the 400 series — was the only player in the very large jetliner market. In the mid-range, the 757 was being accepted by the world's airlines as a worthy successor to the venerable 727, while the 767 was holding its own in competition among the large jetliners such as the A340.

Boeing's firm backlog of orders was increasing substantially: from $21.5 billion in 1984, to $33.2 billion at the end of 1987, to $53.6 billion a year later. This was extrapolated as a need for Boeing to increase its output to 34 jetliners monthly by 1992.

While commercial programs took center stage for Boeing, military programs continued to have a role. It had been more than a quarter century since Boeing had been prime contractor for a major warplane, but non-combat military aircraft programs such as the E-3 AWACS and E-6 naval communications derivatives of the 707 airframe were on the floor at Renton and the VC-25 Air Force One aircraft being built at Everett were certainly highly visible military programs.

Meanwhile Boeing had served since the early 1980s as the premier subcontractor on the super secret Northrop B-2 Spirit stealth bomber which first flew in July 1989 and entered service in 1993. Boeing Aerospace was itself the primary contractor for the US Navy's Sea Lance anti-submarine missile which was first tested in January 1989. Finally there was the V-22 Osprey VTOL military `vertical-lifter' that Boeing was developing in cooperation with Bell Aerospace for the US Marine Corps, US Air Force and US Navy and which made its first flight on 19 March 1989.

The Airborne Warning and Control System (AWACS) was traditionally associated with the militarized Boeing 707 airframe, specifically with the E-3A Sentry which was delivered to the US Air Force, NATO and others during the 1980s. However, the company ceased production of the 707 airframe in 1991, and following extensive studies later that year, the Boeing 767 was picked as the platform of choice for large military aircraft applications, such as AWACS.

The launch customer for the 767 AWACS was Japan's Air Self Defense Force. The first take-off of this aircraft took place at Boe-

Above: Boeing was the principal subcontractor to Northrop on the **B-2 Spirit** stealth bomber project. When the first B-2 rolled out in November 1988, Boeing's participation was evidenced by the landing gear—which were nearly identical to those of the 757 and 767 jetliners.
Right: Boeing's first-ever **747-100** in low level formation flight with the first prototype **747-400** over Seattle in 1988. This 747-100 first flew in 1969 and has been owned and operated by Boeing itself ever since.
Top: The first flight of the **767 AWACS** took place in August 1996.

ing Field in Seattle on 9 August 1996. This was the first time the 767 AWACS would fly outfitted with a 30-foot rotodome mounted atop its fuselage, and the aircraft was the first of four 767 AWACS aircraft that would be delivered to Japan beginning in early 1998.

Boeing's first all-new aircraft in more than a decade was conceived during the late 1980s and announced in October 1990. The Model 777 was to be a twin-engine aircraft similar in configuration to the 767, but half again larger. The initial model, the 777-200, would carry 375 passengers 4630 nautical miles in a two-class configuration. An increased gross weight model would carry 305 passengers 7230 nautical miles in the three-class configuration preferred for long, intercontinental routes. Other members of the family were envisioned that will carry up to 550 passengers or fly farther than Boeing's 747-400. These would be different airplanes, but designed from the beginning as a family. Because the family shared common features, the pilots, flight attendants, and maintenance personnel that were trained on one 777 would, in effect, be trained on all 777s. This would mean savings in training and other expenses for the airlines. All models would draw from the same body of spares, reducing airline investment and operating costs as fleets grow and markets change.

Between 1990 and the first flight, on 12 June 1994, there were 16 airlines that became 777 customers. The first 777 was delivered to

United Air Lines on 17 May 1995. Roughly half of the 777s in service with United Air Lines, British Airways and other customers would be Extended Twin Operations (ETOPS) routes that would fly routinely, 180 minutes from airports.

In its first three months of revenue service, United's 777 fleet, all powered by Pratt & Whitney engines, had experienced a cumulative schedule reliability of 97.7 percent. Schedule reliability is the industry measure for the percentage of time an airplane is free of mechanical delays and able to leave a boarding gate within 15 minutes of scheduled departure. The 777's performance was a dramatic improvement over the introductions of the 767 and the 747, which had achieved this level at 18 months and 38 months respectively.

An in-service experience report by United Air Lines' fleet captain Lew Kosich noted that 'The 777 has shown itself magnificently during its first four months of service. Personally, I'm certified to fly 20 heavy jets, and my background has been in flight test. I've never seen a program go like this. There have been some technical problems, but they've been minimal compared to other programs.'

By early 1996, to meet United's aggressive delivery schedule, United's 777 flight training simulators were running 24 hours a day. United was the largest 777 customer, accounting for 34 of the 187 orders placed though the first year of service. All Nippon Airlines, the second largest 777 customer, took delivery of its first 777 in October 1995. The 777 captured 79 percent of orders for jetliners of its class of airplane, outselling the Airbus A330 and A340 combined.

As Boeing entered the final decade of the twentieth century, it entered its fourth decade as the world leader in commercial aircraft production with an increasing market share and order backlog, making it one of America's biggest industrial exporters. No all-new jetliners were on the drawing boards for the remainder of the century, but the continued evolution of the new derivatives of the existing 'family members' assured that the Seattle company would remain in the 1990s as it had been in the 1960s, planemaker to the world.

Specifications: Boeing Model 777-200

Span	199 ft 11 in
Length	209 ft 1 in
Tail Height	60 ft 9 in
Minimum Take-off Weight	506,000 to 535,000 lb
Range	3780-4630 naut miles
Cruising Speed	Mach .84
Powerplant	two 77,000 lb thrust Pratt & Whitney PW4084 turbofans
Capacity	375 passengers

During 1996 Boeing ensured its place as the world's foremost aerospace firm through the acquisition of two of the largest planemakers in the United States: The North American component of Rockwell International and McDonnell Douglas Corporation. On 1 August, it was announced that the Boeing Company would acquire the Rockwell aerospace and defense businesses. The crown jewel among these was the unit that had been North American Aviation, which was acquired by Rockwell in 1970.

North American Aviation had a distinguished history as the biggest producer of military aircraft in American history. During World War II, North American Aviation produced the AT-6 Texan trainer, the B-25 Mitchell medium bomber and the P-51 Mustang, the greatest Allied fighter of the war. After the war, North American Aviation built numerous aircraft for the US Air Force and US Navy, notably the F-86 Sabre Jet, the top fighter of the Korean War, and the F-100 Super Sabre. North American Aviation built the XB-70 Valkyrie, the only bomber ever built in the West that could cruise at three times the speed of sound. North American Aviation also pro-

Above: The first operational **Boeing 777** began service with **United Air Lines** in May of 1995.
Below, left: The dramatic 1994 roll-out of the 777 prototype at Boeing's Everett, Washington facility.

duced the X-15 research aircraft, the fastest and highest-flying aircraft in history. After becoming part of Rockwell, the company had created the B-1 Lancer and the Space Shuttle Orbiter fleet for NASA.

The major product groups of the acquired divisions included ICBM systems; tactical missiles; sensors; the B-1B Lancer bomber; commercial aerostructures; aircraft and helicopter modifications; Space Station electric power; airborne laser and electro-optics; Space Shuttle integration, logistics and operations; the Global Positioning System (GPS) satellites; space defense and rocket propulsion including the Space Shuttle main engine. The new name of the acquired units would be 'Boeing North American, Inc, a wholly owned subsidiary of The Boeing Company.' The former Rockwell units employed approximately 21,000 people, while the Boeing Defense & Space Group into which they'd be integrated, had approximately 30,000 employees.

Boeing North American would be headed by John McLuckey, who was then the president and chief operating officer of Rockwell's aerospace and defense businesses. He would report to Jerry King, president of the Boeing Defense & Space Group.

Phil Condit, Boeing president and chief executive officer, said, 'The assets and capabilities we are acquiring are an extremely good strategic fit with our long-term objective of creating shareholder value. This merger accelerates us on our way to achieving our 20-year vision, which calls for Boeing to be a fully integrated aerospace company designing, producing and supporting commercial airplanes, defense systems, and defense and civil space systems.'

'My desire,' Condit said, 'is to absorb any necessary employment adjustments through normal attrition and by retraining employees to take advantage of new business or career opportunities within Boeing. Both of our organizations have records of strong performance and we expect to learn new best practices that will bring increased product value to our customers.'

Donald R Beall, Rockwell's chairman and chief executive officer, said, 'This is an historic step in the continuing transformation of Rockwell, which has been shifting strategic focus to higher growth commercial and international businesses, with a particular focus on electronics. The new Rockwell will be essentially debt free and well positioned for significant investments in our strong franchises in

automation, semiconductor systems, avionics, communications and automotive components systems businesses, including internal development and both large and small acquisitions.'

On December 15, 1996, Phil Condit of Boeing and Harry Stonecipher, president and chief executive officer of the McDonnell Douglas Corporation, jointly announced that the companies had signed a definitive agreement whereby McDonnell Douglas would be acquired by Boeing in a stock-for-stock transaction. Based on the closing price of Boeing stock on December 13, 1996, the deal was estimated to be worth approximately $13.3 billion.

At the time of the merger, McDonnell Douglas was the largest producer of combat aircraft in the world, and second largest producer of commercial aircraft in the United States, and possibly in the world. Military programs then in progress, primarily in St Louis, included the AV-8B Harrier, the F-15 Eagle, the T-45 Goshawk, the F/A-18 Hornet and the Harpoon cruise missile. At the Douglas component in Southern California, the firm was producing the C-17 Globemaster military transport, as well as such commercial aircraft as the MD-11, the MD-80, the MD-90, and the MD-95. Space systems programs then in progress included the Delta II Launch Vehicle, the Delta III Launch Vehicle, and the Titan IV Payload Fairing. Helicopter programs then in progress, primarily in Mesa, Arizona, included the AH-64 Apache attack helicopter, and the commercial MD-500, MD-600 and the MD-Explorer helicopter.

The combined company would have about 200,000 employees, including those who worked for the Rockwell aerospace and defense units being merged into Boeing North American. It would operate in 27 states with estimated 1997 revenues in excess of $48 billion, making it the largest integrated aerospace company in the world. The company would operate in three major locations: the Puget Sound area of Washington State; St Louis, Missouri; and Southern California. The Boeing Company headquarters would remain in Seattle.

Condit noted the rich history of both companies and said, 'Today's announcement brings together two strong aerospace companies with complementary capabilities. The merger enhances our position as the number one aerospace company in the world and truly among the world's premier industrial firms. The merger strengthens our competitive position for the Joint Strike Fighter, it improves our position in space transportation, and it enhances our ability to provide the best products and services to our airline customers. This is great news for the airline industry, for our nation's defense programs, and for space programs worldwide.'

INDEX